STRANGE TALES
FROM STRANGEWAYS

AND OTHER EXTRAORDINARY PRISON CASES

by Sara Lee

True Crime Library
A Forum Press Book
by the Paperback Division of
Forum Design,
P.O. Box 157, London SE20 7QA

An Imprint of True Crime Library
© 1995 Forum Design
© 1995 Sara Lee
All rights resvered
Reprinted 1998

Editorial team:
Tristan Ashman & Anna Bennett
12 Flitcroft Street, London WC2

Typeset by Techniset,
1 Back Cross Lane, Newton-le-Willows,
Merseyside, WA12 9YE.
Printed and bound in Great Britain by
Cox & Wyman Ltd, Reading, Berkshire.

ISBN 1 874358 09 5

SARA LEE

Sara Lee is a crime writer and researcher who was born and brought up in Manchester and has written widely about the history of crime in the area. She is a regular contributor to True Detective magazine in which many of these extraordinary stories were first published. Strange Tales from Strangeways is her first book.

The complete
TRUE CRIME LIBRARY

CONTENTS

1

THE MURDERED BRIDE

*John and Annie were about to be married. But the
priest knew nothing about it, nor did the
registrar*

John Aspinall Simpson met Annie Ratcliffe across the bar
of her father's pub, the Blue Bell Inn in Church Street,
Preston, in 1879. He was 19 and she just 14. But though
Annie was little more than a child, Simpson was so taken
with her that he began calling at the Blue Bell every day just
to see her.

Annie's father, Alfred Ratcliffe, considered his daughter
far too young to be courting. Besides, he neither liked nor
trusted Simpson. Though well educated and considered by
some to be a gentleman, Simpson rarely did any work.
Instead, he lived on what money he was able to make from
gambling at the racecourse or could scrounge from his
widowed mother. He was, said Mr Ratcliffe, "a lazy fool
who'd never come to any good." He forbade his daughter
to see him and banned Simpson from the pub.

But young love cannot be tamed. Forbidden to see each
other in person, they continued their courtship by letter.
But it was hard on them, as one letter from Annie to
Simpson made clear:

Dear Jack,
*I think you had better come down either tonight or in the morning
and ask my father what he has against you and I speaking. If I
had not to speak to you any more I have made up my mind to
make away with myself as I cannot live without seeing or*

speaking to you. I am nearly heartbroken. Goodbye for the present.

A million kisses from your darling wife.

A. Simpson

Excuse bad writing and spelling. Written in haste. Tell him that you really love me and if he will only serve you, you will wait a few years for me.

Simpson took the girl's advice and spoke to her father. But Alfred Ratcliffe wasn't about to change his mind. He had no time for the young man's entreaties and, after telling Simpson exactly what he thought of him, he showed the lad the door and warned him once again to stay away from his daughter.

Ratcliffe's uncompromising attitude did him no good, however. If anything it only inflamed the young couple more. Soon afterwards they began to arrange clandestine meetings. At first these took place only occasionally, but soon they became much more frequent. It was at about this time that Annie's mother died, so there was no one to stop the girl doing as she liked, and this was exactly what she did.

Over the next two years Annie and Simpson met as often as three times a day and enjoyed many passionate embraces in alleys and barns. It was always in secret and away from Annie's father. Simpson still did not have a proper job – he worked part-time as a clerk in the registry office – and Mr Ratcliffe still refused to let him be served in the pub. But now Ratcliffe's wishes didn't make any difference. They saw each other all the same. And then the inevitable happened. Annie found herself pregnant.

At first she was in a terrible panic. Thoughts of suicide crossed her mind as did ideas of abortion. But soon enough those initial fears gave way to feelings of elation. Annie suddenly realised that her father would now have to acknowledge Simpson and let her marry him. Dreams of their future happiness filled the young girl's waking hours.

Unfortunately, in her excitement, Annie didn't notice her sweetheart's lack of enthusiasm for wedding bells.

Simpson was positively morose as he promised his future bride that he would get the necessary written consent form from her father. But his fiancée didn't notice it at all.

Initially, Alfred Ratcliffe refused to sign the form, but when Annie's pregnancy began to show, he realised that there would be no peace until she got what she wanted. Thus, on July 7th, 1881, he took the document and reluctantly penned his signature. He refused to attend the wedding, however, and still would not allow his future son-in-law in his pub.

Saddened though she was by his attitude, Annie was too happy at the prospect of being married to be miserable. She and Simpson set the date for the wedding – Monday, August 1st, 1881.

At 7.00 a.m. on their wedding day, Annie, wearing her finest clothes, met her bridegroom outside the Queen's Arms in Preston. As she kissed him in greeting she noticed that he looked drawn, but assumed it was pre-wedding nerves. However, once he'd ushered her into the pub she realised that the reason for his sadness was much more serious. Tears welled up in her eyes as he sadly broke the news.

They could not be married that morning, he said. The registrar had called at his house very early that day to inform him that owing to unforeseen circumstances he would be unable to conduct their wedding. At first Annie stifled her sobs but then burst into tears of disappointment and rage. Simpson put his arm out to comfort her. He assured her that the wedding would go ahead on Wednesday morning instead. Annie took a handkerchief from her pocket and dried her tears before going home alone.

On the morning of Wednesday, August 3rd, Annie again decked herself out in her best clothes, said goodbye to her father, then kept her 8.30 a.m. appointment with her husband-to-be. This time she met him outside the Sir Walter Scott Inn in North Road, Preston. Inside the couple ordered two small lemonades and sat in the otherwise empty private bar.

Seventeen-year-old Mary Ann Quigley, the landlady's daughter, served them. She was so struck by how silent they were that she peeped into the private bar a few minutes later to see if they were still there. The couple stood staring out of the window. Miss Quigley withdrew. She supposed that the two wanted to be alone with their thoughts.

Ten minutes later, however, the sound of a breaking glass drew Miss Quigley back to the bar. Annie pushed past her, desperately clutching at her throat. Blood was pouring through her frantic fingers.

Miss Quigley's screams brought her mother running downstairs just in time to see Annie wheel round, then collapse between two tables.

Simpson remained seated at the window, looking out. He seemed utterly oblivious to the mayhem going on around him.

"Who has done this?" demanded Mrs Quigley in an imperious screech.

"I don't know," Simpson answered, as if offended by the question.

William Bradshaw happened to be walking by when he heard the commotion and popped his head around the saloon door to see what was going on.

Little suspecting that a murder had just occurred, he was astonished to see Mrs Quigley with her mouth opening and closing like a goldfish. Her daughter, in an attitude of terror, had backed up against the bar, jabbing wildly at the air. Bradshaw's eyes followed the direction of their horrified gazes until his own eyes came to rest on the lifeless form of the young woman on the floor. Then he glanced around and saw Simpson sitting absolutely still at the window table. There was a closed and bloody razor before him.

"Did you do this?" asked Bradshaw. Simpson nodded. "Yes, it is me," he mumbled.

As the news of the murder spread, crowds of people swarmed into the Sir Walter Scott to stare. More police had to be drafted in just to keep them out.

As poor Annie's heavily pregnant body was being taken

to the mortuary, neighbouring barber Samuel Weights noticed that one of his razors was missing. He informed the police that Simpson, one of his regular customers, had come to his shop to be shaved the previous Saturday morning. At that time Weights had had a number of razors on a shelf, and three of them were similar to the one Simpson was in possession of in the pub. They had the words "John Heiffer, 3 Paradise Square, Sheffield" engraved on the handle. He later identified the razor found at the scene of the crime as the one missing from his shop.

Simpson was charged with Annie Ratcliffe's murder but he made no statement and seemed unnaturally calm about the whole matter.

The police began their investigations at Simpson's house. It was a bizarre scene. The prisoner's two sisters were still waiting for somebody to come and escort them to the church. They were surprised to be greeted instead by two burly policemen.

"No," the men explained, "there will be no wedding." They then told the Simpson girls that their brother had just murdered his bride-to-be.

The case became more curious still when it was discovered that no wedding had even been arranged. George Dickson, Superintendent Registrar for the Preston district, told the police that Simpson had never spoken to him about a marriage between himself and Annie Ratcliffe. The consent form for the marriage of a minor had never been handed in nor had any other documents been submitted. Roger Kenyon, verger of St Paul's Church, Preston, where the supposed marriage was to have taken place, supported his story. He told the police that he had never received any notice of the intended ceremony.

It seemed clear that Simpson had been planning the killing of his girlfriend for some time. Why else had he told her the wedding was arranged? Why had he carried the razor with him that morning? The newspapers where quick to stress the likelihood of premeditation. "The probability is that the man contemplated this atrocious deed for some time," declared one, adding that the Sir Walter Scott, a particularly quiet pub, "was a well selected spot for the murder."

One of Simpson's many friends, however, was keen to dispel this notion. He had visited the accused in prison and had asked him what made him do it. "I don't know. I had no idea that I should do it five minutes before," Simpson declared. This friend also revealed that John Simpson habitually carried a razor in his pocket. "Just as an ordinary bloke carries a penknife."

Preston came to a standstill when Simpson was taken under guard from the prison to the magistrate's court. Despite huge displays of public hostility towards him, he showed no sign of discomfort as, with his hands in the pockets of his still bloodstained trousers, he swaggered into court. His indifference did not falter even when the magistrates ordered him to stand trial for murder at the following Manchester Assizes.

Simpson was taken straight from the court to Preston railway station where a crowd of several hundred people had gathered to watch his departure on the 3.15 train. Many were shouting and hooting their disapproval as he boarded.

One newspaper reporter noted disapprovingly that Simpson behaved in an unbelievably callous and shameless manner. "He shouted out to friends he spotted in the crowd. He held up his manacled hands and confidently assured them he would soon be back again." There were also reports that he made coarse replies to ladies in the crowd who called for the reintroduction of gibbeting.

Simpson's trial began at Manchester Assizes on Monday, November 7th, 1881, before Mr Justice Kay. Mr Henry Shee was the prosecutor.

Simpson, defended by Mr Foard, pleaded not guilty and sat in the dock exhibiting the same air of bravado he had shown before the magistrates.

Surgeon Charles Green described to the court the scene of carnage that had awaited him at the Sir Walter Scott.

Annie Ratcliffe was already dead. Her neck was horribly mutilated as a result of an incised wound about two inches deep and four inches long, and all the soft tissues including the carotid artery and jugular veins were divided. The spinal column had been laid bare to the extent that he had been able to see two or three of the vertebrae. In his opinion, death from shock and loss of blood must have been almost instantaneous. He also confirmed that the young woman was heavily pregnant.

Edith Ratcliffe, Annie's sister, who was allowed to sit to give evidence, told the court that she had met Simpson and her sister at 8 o'clock on the Monday morning that they were originally to have been married and had asked them if they were now wed. Simpson had said that they were not, explaining that it hadn't been convenient for the registrar to attend the wedding that morning. He'd added that they were going to be married that coming Wednesday instead. Edith said that both Annie and Simpson appeared to have been crying.

The following day, all three of them had taken a pleasure boat out on to the River Ribble. Shortly after the murder a newspaper reported that someone had seen Simpson deliberately trying to overturn the boat. However, Edith Ratcliffe now told the surprised jury that in fact nothing unusual had taken place that day on the river. Simpson, she averred, had certainly not tried to overturn the boat. She added that although her sister's fiancé was a little wild at times, she thought he had been trying to better himself of late. He had more than once assured her that he was looking for a proper job, and she was certain she had never seen anything between her sister and Mr Simpson which led her to suspect that they were anything but fond and loving to one another.

Thomas Taylor Jackson, whose bakery was in an alley leading from Grimshaw Street to Water Street, told the court that Simpson and Annie Ratcliffe had been meeting in the passageway two or three times a day for many months. He then recounted one particular occasion which cast a new light on the entire trial.

It was about six weeks before the murder that he was walking through the passageway on his way to the pub, and overheard the two lovers in conversation. "Have you got me any more money?" Simpson had asked Annie. She had answered: "No, I can't always be robbing my father for you."

Mr Jackson said that he did not hear anything more that was said between them, but under cross-examination he told the court that the couple usually met for about 30 minutes at a time and were always affectionate.

Emily Richardson, one of Simpson's former girl friends, told the court that one winter Saturday, months before the murder, she had a surprising encounter with Simpson in Market Square. He had spoken first, asking her, "Why don't you get married?" She had tersely informed him that she didn't wish to, and then turned the question back to him. "Why don't you? You've courted long enough."

"To hell with getting married," he'd answered with an ugly sneer. "I am only after the cash bags there."

This testimony caused such a sensation in the courtroom that the judge had to call for order several times before the shocked reactions died down.

Mr Shee claimed that after Annie Ratcliffe discovered that she was pregnant she had pestered Simpson to marry her. He had consented to do so, the prosecution claimed, only on the condition that she robbed her father for him. However, when the marriage had been agreed Annie refused to steal any more from her father's pub. Simpson then decided he would rather murder her than marry her.

In his closing speech for the defence Mr Foard told the jury that, assuming Simpson had committed the crime, was he responsible for his actions or was he mad? He argued that no one could have made Simpson marry Annie against his will. A sane man, he declared, would have just given her the slip and perhaps taken the first ship to America. He certainly did not have to resort to murder and all that that entails merely to free himself from his responsibilities.

Mr Foard asked the jury to discount the part of Thomas Jackson's evidence in which he had supposedly overheard Simpson asking Miss Ratcliffe for money. He argued that it was monstrous to suggest that Simpson was in the habit of receiving money from Miss Ratcliffe. There was neither the proof nor the prior suggestion that Simpson had ever received a farthing from her. Mr Foard also questioned how it was that Jackson had only heard these words and no others in all that time. He reminded the jury that Jackson had said Simpson and Miss Ratcliffe met up to three times a day and were always affectionate towards one another. Could Simpson have taken the trouble to go and see her so often unless he really loved her?

"And who," he went on, trying to discredit Emily Richardson, Simpson's former sweetheart, "is more jealous, venomous, or savage than a woman who has been jilted? Or did Simpson say those terrible things to Emily Richardson about Miss Ratcliffe simply because he thought they were what Miss Richardson wanted to hear?"

Foard then asked the jury to consider the possibility that the girl might have committed suicide and reminded them of Annie's letter in which she had threatened to do away with herself. Perhaps, argued Foard, she might have despaired over her father's attitude towards Simpson and her impending marriage to him.

Foard also argued valiantly that when Simpson said, "It's me," to William Bradshaw, he'd really meant to say, "I am the cause of it. She killed herself because of me."

Mr Justice Kay summed up pointing out that the absence of motive did not mean that Simpson was insane. "To infer a man was insane merely from the act he committed would make society altogether unsafe. For then in every case of crime, the jury might be at liberty to infer from the crime itself that the man was insane."

He reminded the jury that the defence counsel had not called any doctors to vouch for the state of Simpson's mind and dismissed the possibility that the girl might have committed suicide. He pointed out that Annie Ratcliffe was a frail young lady, and the medical evidence had clearly stated that a very deep cut, requiring great strength, had killed her. "Then again there was no proof that she had a razor with her," he told the jury. "How had she acquired it, and was she likely to have taken such a thing with her to her wedding?" he asked.

The jury took just 20 minutes to reach a verdict. When asked what decision they had come to the foreman announced, "I am sorry to say, guilty." Simpson was then sentenced to death.

Having had a jaunty air throughout the trial, Simpson looked shocked at the outcome as he was taken down to the cells.

At Strangeways Prison, Simpson was visited by his sister Lizzie. He told her he did not want to live and said he hoped he would meet Annie in Heaven. He kept her photograph beside his bed and said he wished to have it buried with him. He also expressed the wish to see Annie's father.

At first Alfred Ratcliffe said he would not stand in the young man's way if he wanted to ease his conscience, but he later changed his mind. He sent a message, via Lizzie, expressing regret that he had brought himself to his present position, and that far from bearing ill-will towards the Simpsons, he hoped a friendship would now exist between them.

John Aspinall Simpson was executed inside Strangeways Prison, Manchester at 8.00 a.m. on Monday, November 28th, 1881, by Marwood. Although downcast, Simpson didn't make a confession or acknowledge his guilt in any way. He died instantly.

2

THE WOMAN CALLED BILL

*Margaret "Bill" Allen was an unusual woman.
But her peculiarities were no excuse for murder.
She was found guilty and sentenced to hang.*

For the first time in thirteen years, Margaret Allen was wearing a dress. It was quite a novelty. Usually she wore dark blue trousers, a check shirt and a brightly striped tie and looked every inch a man, but today was different. It was a special occasion. Alas, however, it was not a happy occasion. The dress she was wearing was not a party frock, it was the striped prison attire of Strangeways Jail. Forty-two-year-old Margaret Allen was on her way to the scaffold.

Margaret Allen was no normal woman. Even her crime was odd, committed without apparent motive. It was a vicious and brutal assault, and yet she carried it out with no malice or real anger. "I was in one of my funny moods," she said. This, however, was considered to be no excuse by the court.

For four years until shortly after the Second World War, Margaret had worked as a bus conductress for the Rawtenstall Corporation Motors in Lancashire's Rossendale Valley. She no longer worked there, but it was from a Rawtenstall bus that her crime was first discovered.

Buses are not normally to be seen driving from Rawtenstall to Bacup at four o'clock on a Sunday morning, but it was at 4 a.m. that one set out on that route from Rawtenstall on Sunday, August 29th, 1948. It was taking bus drivers and conductors home from a union meeting which had begun at midnight and hadn't concluded until 3.30 a.m.

As the bus approached the junction of Fallbarn Close and Bacup Road, its lights fell on a bundle in the middle of the road. It appeared to be a long sack, and it was obstructing the entire highway. The driver stopped, got out of his cab and walked over to move it.

As he approached the bundle, however, he realised it was not a sack at all. It was the body of an elderly woman. She was wearing a grey coat and lying face down on the tarmac. Her hair was matted with congealed blood. She was obviously dead. Assuming her to be the victim of a hit-and-run motorist, the bus driver called the police who arrived at the scene just as dawn was breaking.

The corpse was identified as that of an eccentric, penny-pinching widow, 68-year-old Mrs Nancy Ellen Chadwick. And it was when a doctor examined her that it became clear she was no victim of a traffic accident. Mrs Chadwick had been dead for at least 10 hours.

Nobody could remember when Rawtenstall had last had a murder, but there was one to investigate now.

Scotland Yard was informed, and Detective Chief Inspector Stevens and Detective Sergeant Campbell were soon on their way from London.

Meanwhile, the local police began making their own inquiries. Had anyone heard or seen anything? When was the last time Mrs Chadwick had been seen healthy and well? Did anyone have a grudge against her?

One of the first doors at which Detective Sergeant Thompson knocked was that of Margaret Allen. She lived in a tiny two-roomed house at 137 Bacup Road. The body had been found a few feet from her home.

Still in her pyjamas when the detective called at 8.30 that Sunday morning, she said she had neither heard nor seen anything unusual during the night. She had slept soundly and not been disturbed once. The sergeant took her at her word and, soon after, he departed. In fact, he was rather glad to go.

Margaret wasn't a dangerous woman nor a likely suspect in the case. But she was a strange individual. Preferring to be known as 'Bill', she was Rawtenstall's resident lesbian, and would walk about town dressed as a man and with her hair cropped short. It was innocent enough, but for a man like Thompson, a straitlaced individual with a wife and two children, she was very disconcerting. He preferred to avoid her. Still, he would soon see her again.

That afternoon, in her usual shirt and trousers, Margaret joined the crowd of people watching PC Thompson and other officers as they began searching the River Irwell nearby. The officers were wading by the weir at Fallbarn railway crossing, about 80 yards from where the body had been found, when Margaret shouted to them from the bank.

"There's a bag in the water," she yelled. "Look, it's down there!"

Directed by her pointing finger, an officer retrieved a string shopping bag. Inside it, detectives found the murdered woman's imitation leather handbag, a pack of playing cards – Mrs Chadwick had told fortunes – some sewing materials and three pairs of scissors. The victim's purse was still missing.

Robbery had already been considered as the most likely motive for the murder, and now the police were sure. Although Mrs Chadwick had dressed poorly and was not above begging for cups of tea to passers-by in the town, she was known to be a wealthy woman. She had inherited four houses from which she collected rents, and she was believed to carry large sums of money. When she had been attacked and robbed two years earlier, £25 had been stolen. It was a small fortune.

For the next couple of days the police continued with their investigation, but they were not getting very far. No suspicious strangers had been seen in the vicinity and none of the locals seemed like likely killers. By Wednesday they decided to begin their efforts anew, and started to revisit all those they had spoken to before.

Detective Chief Inspector Stevens went to Margaret Allen's home, accompanied by the chief of Lancashire

Constabulary's CID, Detective Chief Superintendent Woodmansey. As Woodmansey asked her to tell him again about the events of Sunday night, Stevens walked around the property and inspected the garden. Suddenly he noticed what appeared to be bloodstains on the back of the front door. There was some stains on the wall too.

Stevens then began a full search of the house. He looked in a cupboard and was intrigued by the contents of a shopping bag. It contained some ashes from a fire grate, and three rags – one wet, and two dry.

Holding up the rags, he asked Margaret: "What are these?"

She didn't reply.

Indicating the ashes, he asked where they were from.

"From the grate upstairs," said Margaret. "I've had them there some time."

Returning to the rags, Stevens held up the wet one and asked Margaret what she used it for.

"It's a floor swab," she said.

"When did you use it?"

Margaret had had enough. "Come on," she said, picking up her mackintosh. "I'll tell you all about it. Let's get out of here." Then, indicating the coal cellar, she told the detectives. "That's where I put her. I didn't actually do it for money. I was in one of my funny moods."

Taken to Rawtenstall Police Station and charged with Mrs Chadwick's murder, she replied simply "I did it."

In a statement Margaret Allen made later in the day, she explained all the events of that fateful Sunday:

"I was coming out of the house on Saturday morning about 9.20 and Mrs Chadwick came round the corner. She asked me if this was where I lived and could she come in? I told her I was going out. I was in a nervy mood and she just seemed to get on my nerves although she had not said anything.

"I told her to go and she could see me some time else. But she seemed to insist on coming in. I happened to look round and saw a hammer in the kitchen. At this time we were talking just inside the kitchen with the front door shut.

"On the spur of the moment, I hit her with the hammer. She gave a shout and that seemed to start me off more. I hit her a few times, but I don't know how many. I pulled the body into my coal house."

It was a chilling, insensitive description of the killing, the sort of account to be expected from a man rather than from a woman. But then, Margaret Allen had long considered herself to be a man trapped in a woman's body.

Born in 1906, she was the twentieth of her mother's 22 children. Like most other girls in the Rossendale Valley, she had gone to work in the mill on leaving school. But there the resemblance with her contemporaries stopped. Whilst her friends fell in love and married, Margaret stayed single, remaining at home until she was 37, devoted to her mother who died in 1943, and whose photograph was one of the few possessions Margaret took with her to Strangeways Jail.

Told in the condemned cell that she was not to be reprieved, she asked for that photograph of her mother to be sent to her sole friend, Annie Cook.

Although Annie was unable to return "Bill" Allen's physical, lesbian affections, she was one of the few people who tried to understand her. The two had taken a Blackpool holiday together and although Annie had declined to share her friend's bed, she and her mother had continued to give Margaret Allen what support they could, trying to help her cope with her deteriorating health and impoverished circumstances.

Short but stocky "Bill," who had once been proud to boast that she did a man's work as a labourer, had since been afflicted by vertigo and listlessness. Ill health finally forced her to give up her job on the buses and then things went from bad to worse. She was shattered by the menopause and beset by money worries. She no longer fed herself properly and did little or no housework – not that she had ever had much time for such a feminine occupation. She could cobble, repairing her own shoes, but she couldn't sew, and darning socks was beyond her. She received 11 shillings a week public assistance, a further 22 shillings a week in National Health benefit, and that was that. Most of it seemed to go on drink and cigarettes.

It was at about this time that Annie came into her life. The two met a couple of years before the murder, and Margaret at last fell in love. Annie was petite, feminine and vivacious, and she showed Margaret kindness, affection and generosity. She was a mill-worker in her early thirties, and most nights they would meet for a drink and a smoke in a pub. Margaret could ill afford it. Recently she had been so hard up she had sold her stove. But she wouldn't change her ways. The nine pounds she got for the stove wasn't used to pay off any debts. She spent that also on beer and cigarettes.

Margaret and Annie often visited each other at home. Annie would later recall: "Often she arrived at our house just as we were going to sit down to dinner. Many's the time I've seen my mother put her own dinner in front of 'Bill' and make do with a sandwich herself."

Annie's return calls to her friend's home cannot have been as pleasurable. The place was filthy. As Annie put it, Margaret had "completely let herself go." Deeply in debt since she had been unable to work, and facing the possibility of eviction due to rent arrears spanning nearly a year, she was in dire straits. To cap it all, she also had to contend with the problem of her menopause. This is something that can trigger irrational behaviour even in women who are well-balanced; for someone who was already ill, lonely, depressed and a social misfit, the likelihood of trauma was considerably greater.

Advised by Annie not to sit around moping but to get up and have some proper food, Margaret lost her temper even with the one she loved. Accusing Annie of trying to ruin their friendship, she rushed to the gas jet, put the tube in her mouth and turned on the tap. Annie promptly wrested the tube away from her. "Don't be so daft," she said.

"I was her only friend," Annie later commented.

Margaret Allen did, however, have other acquaintances.

Mrs Chadwick was one. Some time before her fatal visit to 137 Bacup Road, she had met Margaret at the home of a Mrs Haworth. Seeing her later in the street, Mrs Chadwick had asked Margaret if she could spare any sugar – then still rationed and in short supply. Margaret had said that if she could get some, she would bring it over to the old lady's home. She subsequently paid Mrs Chadwick several visits, renewing her promise each time, but the sugar never materialised.

Had she borrowed money from Mrs Chadwick against the promise of supplying sugar? And was it an angry Mrs Chadwick who had called on her to demand the return of her money when the sugar wasn't supplied? This theory was put forward in court in an effort to explain the motive behind the killing. However, it was not pursued. Tragically, the one person who could have shed light on the matter was not available to give evidence.

Eighty-two-year-old Paddy Whittaker lived on the Hall Carr estate about five minutes' walk from Margaret Allen's home. He had kept house for Mrs Chadwick for the best part of ten years and it was said that he knew all her secrets. But he was a man with an extremely nervous disposition. When he was informed by the police that he would be required as a prosecution witness in court Paddy found it all too much. "I can't face it," he told a neighbour. "I'm going for a walk and I don't think I shall come back." That walk took him to Holme Farm, where three hours later his drowned body was found in a pond.

The prosecution continued with its case by settling on the more mundane motive of simple robbery. It was supposed that Mrs Chadwick must have had a few pounds in her bag and it was well known that Margaret Allen was hard up. It was therefore suggested that she killed the old woman to get her hands on her money.

Reasonable though this sounded, to the people who knew Miss Allen, it seemed implausible. She had admitted to killing the old lady so they had to agree that she had done so. But they were certain that Allen's actions had not been premeditated or motivated by greed. She wasn't that sort of woman. Much more likely, they thought, was that Margaret had killed the old lady in a fit of madness and, if she then stole her money, it was only because the money was there and she might as well have it. This notion was put forward valiantly by Margaret's defence counsel, who was clearly trying to establish the justification of insanity.

That it was insanity that led her to murder was also supported by her extraordinary behaviour after the crime. It was as if nothing had happened. Within an hour of the murder, she met Annie Cook, went into town with her, accompanied her while she did some shopping and had a drink with her at the Ashworth Arms.

At 12.15 p.m. the pair parted company and Margaret went to see her sister in Bacup, returning to Rawtenstall at about 9.15 p.m.. She had a couple of drinks at the Ashworth Arms and then went home to bed. For a while, she slept soundly.

But, "when I awoke, the thought of what was downstairs kept me awake," she later said. "I went downstairs... there were no lights in the road and I could not hear any footsteps."

She had intended to dispose of Mrs Chadwick in the river (although it was only two feet deep) but found her too heavy. Having thrown the hammer-head and Mrs Chadwick's shopping bag into the water, she hauled the body from her cellar, dragged it into the road outside her house, and went back to bed.

She was still awake when she heard the bus stop suddenly. On looking out of her window she saw a group of people outside in the road, and knew the body had been discovered.

Were these the actions of a callous killer, or was this the behaviour of somebody mentally disturbed, someone out of touch with reality?

The problem for Margaret Allen, however, was that her statement to the police had been so lucid, and her subsequent behaviour so normal, that she could not be considered insane. Odd, yes. Eccentric even. But not mad.

Furthermore, her statement read out at her trial at Manchester Assizes did nothing to encourage the jury to make a recommendation for mercy: it was too cold, too dispassionate, too matter-of-fact. Too honest, perhaps, by half.

Then there was Margaret's lesbianism. There was a much greater prejudice against homosexuality in the 1940s than there is today. As she stood there in the dock, dressed in her shirt and tie and giving every impression of being a man, Margaret Allen was condemned almost before the case had begun.

In vain, Mr William Gorman KC defending, did his best to persuade the jury to commiserate rather than to condemn; to have some sympathy for an unstable abnormal woman tragically affected by the change of life, a stage during which "the most extraordinary things can happen." But the jury were not swayed.

It took them only 15 minutes to find Margaret Allen guilty of murder. Moments later the black cap was donned and the sentence declared.

On January 12th, 1949 Margaret "Bill" Allen was hanged by the neck until she was dead.

3

THE MURDER OF LITTLE NORMAN PINCHEN

Murder is always a terrible crime, but when the victim is a child the terror is much greater. Never more than in the case of little Norman Pinchen.

Five-year-old Norman Widdowson Pinchen was a lovely little boy. With his copper-coloured curls, cherubic face and friendly, outgoing personality he was often likened to the American child-actor Jackie Coogan, who in 1920 had scored such a hit in Charlie Chaplin's film *The Kid*. In fact around his hometown of Pendleton, near Salford, he was proudly known as "Pendleton's own Jackie Coogan."

Norman often played in Peel Park close to where he lived at 9 Crescent View. Eric Wilson was usually with him. He was Norman's best friend, though no one could quite work out why. Three years his elder, Eric was a scrawny little boy, shy and introverted. The complete opposite to Norman. Neither was he particularly healthy. He always seemed to have a runny nose and wore thick spectacles, without which he was almost blind. Still, the two boys seemed to like each other well enough and revelled in each other's company.

It was June 10th, 1924, and all the schools in Pembleton were closed for the day. Norman and Eric had spent that morning in the back yard of Norman's house playing with Billy, the Pinchen family dog, but by midday they had grown bored. They were itching to do something else.

Eric suggested going to the "Summer Shed" – a little house in the middle of Peel Park which was a favourite place for children to play. Norman enthusiastically agreed. So, after Mrs Pinchen had given them a bite of lunch, they set off. It was approximately 2.30 p.m.

The boys had just started skipping down the road when Norman had an idea. "Dad, give us a penny!" he shouted, running back to the house. His father, Harold, who was just getting ready to go to work, wearily searched his pockets.

"I've only got a half-penny," he said, "you'll have to make do with that."

"Come on, Eric," said Norman, taking his friend by the hand. "We've got a half-penny again."

The pair then hurried off to a nearby sweet shop to spend it before going to play in Peel Park.

They had been in the Summer Shed for a while when a man came in. He chatted with the two boys for a couple of minutes and then said he wanted to show them something interesting. He asked if they would like to go with him. Both the boys had been warned about speaking to strangers, but in the excitement of the moment those warnings were quickly forgotten. Within a few minutes all three were walking hand-in-hand towards the park gates.

Just as they were about to leave the park, the man turned to Eric and, handing him four pennies, told him to go and buy two twopenny wafers – one for himself and the other for Norman. Then, looking down at Norman, he said: "Let's go to the canal and look at the water." The Bolton, Bury and Manchester canal was close by.

Eric, who was by now feeling uneasy, tried to stop his friend from going. "No, come on!" he said and tried to pull Norman away. But the man held firmly on to his hand and refused to let him go. Norman, who was looking forward to his wafer, treated it like a game, and just giggled. Eric pulled him again, but Norman yanked his arm away.

"Wouldn't you like to see the water?" asked the stranger coaxingly. The boy nodded in excitement.

Eric knew when he was beaten. He let his friend go and hurried off to buy the wafers. The shop was quite close by and, in next to no time, he was heading back to the park, guzzling his wafer as he walked. He could see Norman walking down Crescent View with the strange man. They had passed Norman's house and were going towards Hall Street, which was near the canal.

Eric was going to chase after them, but it had started to rain heavily and he didn't fancy getting wet. He hesitated for a moment as he watched them go, then he turned tail and headed back in the direction of his home. As he ran along the road Eric licked first one wafer and then the other. Soon his little pal was forgotten.

At 3.50 p.m. Harry Barnes, who worked for J. H. Ashton Ltd, timber merchants, was sitting on the wall of the works yard which overlooked the canal. He was waiting for the paper-boy to pass so that he could check the racing results. As he waited he noticed a man and a little boy come through the Wallness Road gateway, which led directly from Wallness Road on to the canal bank.

The man and the child then walked along the towpath towards Windsor Bridge. Barnes assumed they were father and son.

He had a clear view of the canal for several hundred yards, but when the man and boy passed beneath the bridge they disappeared from sight. Still, Barnes continued to gaze idly in their direction. The paper-boy still hadn't arrived.

Ten minutes later the man reappeared, making his way back towards the Wallness Road gateway. Barnes was horrified to see that he was carrying the limp body of the little boy who minutes earlier had been walking obediently by his side. The man was holding the child face downwards by his clothes. Barnes then saw him kneel down by the edge of the canal and throw the boy into the water.

Dumbstruck, Harry Barnes looked on in horror as the boy struggled helplessly in the water. He was surely going to drown. The man who was with him did not so much as reach out a hand to help.

Recovering from the initial shock of what he had witnessed, Barnes dropped back into the timber yard.

"I've just seen a man throw a boy into the canal!" he yelled to his astonished foreman as he raced out of the yard, through the Wallness Road gateway and on to the canal towpath. As he hurried towards Windsor Bridge he passed the boy's killer, who was now sauntering back the way he had come. Barnes couldn't see his face. But he recognised his coat. What should he do? Should he confront him, grab hold of him and take him to the police? Surely he should try and apprehend him?

Perhaps he was afraid – although he later denied this – or maybe he hoped to be in time to save the child. In any case Barnes made no attempt to stop or even talk to the villain. He just carried on running down the path.

At last Harry Barnes reached the spot near Windsor Bridge, where he had seen the lad being thrown. But now he could find no trace of the boy. As he stared at the black water, its surface broken only by the rain which now fell steadily, he feared the child had drowned.

Realising he mustn't let the murderer escape, Barnes turned back and ran after him. He didn't have to go far. The man was still walking at a slow, untroubled pace and Barnes caught up with him as he approached the Crescent, opposite Peel Park. By good fortune it was there that Barnes spotted two policemen. He ran to them and excitedly pointed out the man whom he swore he had just seen throw a child into the canal.

One of the policemen, Constable Smith, hurried after the man and waylaid him as he passed Peel Park gates. The constable struck up a conversation with the stranger who seemed somewhat distracted and in a world of his own.

"We're having some awful weather, aren't we?" observed the policeman.

"Yes, we are," the man agreed.

"Where are you going?" asked Smith.

"Salford Royal Hospital," the man replied, slurring his words and moving his arms from side to side.

"Oh, what are you going there for?" enquired Smith.

The man said he was going to meet his girl friend who worked at the hospital. He then turned around, and stumbled over the pavement.

"What, like that?" challenged the policeman, holding the man by the arm. "Are you drunk?"

"Get away!" shouted the man, trying to walk on. But by this time Smith's colleague, Constable Lawrenson, had joined them. Together the two policemen told the man that a member of the public – they turned and indicated Barnes – had just accused him of throwing a little boy into the canal.

"Well, he's just a bloody madman then, isn't he?"

The stranger denied all knowledge of the episode and said he had only been out for a brief stroll. The policemen refused to accept his denial.

They took him back to the spot near Windsor Bridge where Barnes claimed the incident had taken place. The policeman gazed into the water and prodded at the bushes nearby, but they found no sign of a body nor evidence of a struggle.

"Did you throw a boy into the canal?" Smith asked the man again.

"Nothing of the kind!" the man roared in reply, lunging at Barnes. But the policemen now snapped handcuffs on him and took him to Pendleton police station.

Whilst the stranger was being interrogated and persistently denying any wrong-doing, the police made arrangements for the canal to be dragged and the surrounding area to be thoroughly examined. Half an hour later the body of a small boy was pulled from the water. After unsuccessful efforts to resuscitate him, he was rushed to Salford Royal Hospital, where he was declared dead on arrival.

The child was fully clothed except for his short trousers, which were recovered from the water the next day. A description of the boy was immediately circulated around the district, and it wasn't long before the name of Norman Widdowson Pinchen was suggested. The police went to the Midland Hotel in Manchester, where Norman's father worked as a waiter. He was taken to Pendleton Town Hall mortuary where, with tears streaming down his face, he identified the drowned boy as his youngest child.

Meanwhile, the man who had been arrested on suspicion

of the murder had also been identified. He was 23-year-old John Charles Horner of Lissadel Street, Pendleton. He worked as a carter, but was also a known thief and had a criminal record. He had recently been released from Strangeways Prison after serving six months' hard labour. An identity parade of nine men, including Horner, was held at Salford Town Hall. Short-sighted though he was, Eric Wilson immediately picked him out as the man who had spoken to Norman and himself in the Summer Shed in Peel Park, and who had later enticed Norman away to the canal on the pretext of looking at the water. Fourteen-year-old Norman Thomas, who knew Norman Pinchen well, also identified Horner as the man he had seen walking hand-in-hand with Norman on the afternoon of the murder, going in the direction of the canal.

News of the terrible murder had quickly spread through the town and, three days later when the inquest was held, the crowd outside Pendleton Town Hall was so large that it seemed as if everyone in Salford was there.

A newspaper reporter noted: "In the corridor outside the courtroom, supported on a seat, was the boy's mother, pale and haggard, with a strained, pain-racked face, evidently barely conscious of her surroundings. Beside her was the boy's father staring blankly before him..."

As Mr Pinchen entered the court – his wife was too distressed and had chosen to remain outside – Horner was being led in by another door. Harold Pinchen glared at him with hatred in his eyes. Then he lost control. "You bastard!" he shouted. "If I could only get hold of you!" Pinchen lunged across the courtroom and tried to grab hold of the suspect. Before he could get to him, however, two burly policeman grabbed the distraught father's arms and escorted him to his seat.

Horner seemed unmoved by the outburst. Smartly dressed in a black suit and light-blue serge overcoat, he calmly took the chair offered him, placing his trilby hat beneath it.

Mr Pinchen burst into tears before giving evidence, and

throughout the proceedings he glared angrily in Horner's direction.

Dr Stanley Hodgson, who had conducted the post-mortem examination, told the court he had found the boy's lungs free of water which strongly indicated that he was already dead when he was thrown into the canal. It seemed, therefore, that Barnes must have been mistaken when he said he saw the boy struggling in the water. But Harry Barnes still stood by his story.

The doctor added that, in his opinion, death had been caused by shock. The boy had been violently raped and viciously assaulted. He then detailed the injuries he had found on the boy's body. These were confined to the child's lower parts, and were not described in the press as they were considered too shocking.

The inquest heard both Harry Barnes and Eric Wilson give their evidence. Eric identified Horner as the man who had spoken to Norman and himself in the Summer Shed in Peel Park and had then led Norman off to the canal. Barnes gave his account of what had happened.

After deliberating for four minutes the jury had little trouble in concluding that the child had been murdered and his killer was before them. They returned the appropriate verdict. Before disbanding they also complimented Barnes on the way he had followed and then helped to apprehend Horner.

As Horner was being led from the courtroom, Norman's mother made a dash at him, but her friends stopped her from striking him. She screamed abuse at her son's killer and the tears streamed down her face. Then she fainted.

Mrs Pinchen's fury was echoed by the crowd that were waiting outside to hear the news. Fury erupted when Horner emerged from the building. "Lynch him!" screamed a woman in the crowd, and there was a surge towards him. Horner now lost his previous calm and turned deathly pale, but the police succeeded in parting the crowd and then shoved him unceremoniously into a prison van.

So many people attended Norman Pinchen's funeral the

following day that Christ Church, Salford, was soon filled. Hundreds of people were forced to wait outside. As the funeral cortège set off the entire route to Peel Green Cemetery was an almost unbroken line of mourners, and when it reached the cemetery many of the onlookers fainted.

During the burial service Mrs Pinchen became so distressed that her voice could be clearly heard above that of the rector as she called out her dead son's name again and again. When the coffin was lowered into the ground she was in such a state of collapse that her husband practically had to carry her from the grave side.

"Everyone knew Norman," Mr Pinchen told a reporter. "He was a red-hot favourite. He had never been scolded in his life. His mother made a god of him."

On July 11th the crowds gathered once more. Now they queued outside the court for Horner's trial at Manchester Assizes. The courtroom was soon filled to capacity and many hundreds had to be turned away disappointed.

Under new legislation that had only just come into force, young Eric Wilson was allowed into the court to give evidence. Though only eight years old, he behaved with all the solemnity and seriousness that the occasion deserved.

"You know you have to speak the truth, Eric," Mr Justice Talbot reminded him.

"Yes," the child replied.

Eric then gave his full account of his friend's last day on earth. He told the court of the games they had played in the morning and then of their walk to Peel Park and their encounter with the stranger. In addition to the testimony he had given earlier, Eric now said that the man who later took Norman away had also made an indecent suggestion to him whilst they were together in the Summer Shed.

"Do you see that man here?" asked William Madden KC, prosecuting.

"Yes," replied the boy without hesitation.

"Where?" asked Madden.

"There!" said the child, pointing to Horner.

Cross-examined by Mr J. McKeever for the defence, Eric agreed that he was very short-sighted, but he insisted that he nevertheless recognised the prisoner.

Dr Hodgson again described Norman Pinchen's injuries to the lower part of his body. He was asked by the judge if the alleged improper suggestion made to Eric Wilson in Peel Park might have any relation to Norman's injuries.

Hodgson replied: "The injuries found are consistent with such a suggestion having been put into operation."

Unable to bear any more, Harold Pinchen suddenly got up, weeping. His face white and his jaw moving convulsively, he pointed a threatening finger towards Horner.

Fearing trouble, several policemen rushed at him and after a few words managed to get him to sit down. But only for a second. He then jumped up again and almost ran out of the court, followed by the policemen.

Fourteen-year-old Norman Thomas told the court how he had seen Norman Pinchen walking hand-in-hand with Horner, whom he had later picked out of an identity parade and had now identified again in court. They had been going in the direction of the canal, he said. But Thomas disagreed with Eric Wilson on the route the pair had taken. While Eric Wilson said they went down Crescent View towards Hall Street, Norman Thomas swore he saw them going along Park View near Wallness Road.

Harry Barnes told how he had seen a man throw Norman into the canal. He could not swear that that man was Horner because he had not seen his face, but Horner was certainly the man he had passed on the towpath making his way from Windsor Bridge.

McKeever asked Barnes why, when he saw the man throw the child into the canal, he did not jump down on to the towpath and keep the murderer in view all the time. Instead he had dropped back into the timber yard and asked the foreman's permission to leave before rushing through the gateway on to the towpath – thus completely losing sight of the murderer.

"Well, I used my discretion," said Barnes, claiming that he was very nimble and had only lost sight of the man for about a minute. Asked by McKeever why he did not speak to Horner as he passed him on the towpath, Barnes simply replied: "I didn't."

"And you didn't," McKeever suggested, "Because you did not think at that moment that he was the man who threw the child into the canal?"

"There was no one else in sight," replied Barnes.

"No," pursued McKeever, "there was no one else in sight at the time and so you thought that it was Horner. The murderer might easily have gone in the direction of Bolton Road. He could have gone off in the opposite direction to the Wallness Road gateway."

"But I saw the coat he was wearing," protested Barnes.

"I suggest," challenged McKeever, "that if you were certain that Horner was the man who dropped the child into the canal, you would have collared him and said: 'Come along with me.'"

"I didn't, sir," was all Barnes replied.

"I suggest you didn't," McKeever continued, "because you didn't think at that moment that he was the man. If you had done so you would not have passed him."

"Yes, I would have passed him," insisted Barnes.

"I should have thought," said McKeever, "that you would sooner have pushed him into the canal and told him to wait there until you came back."

"What if he had drowned?" retorted Barnes. "Then I might have been in his place."

John Charles Horner, tall, well-built, fair-haired and considered by many to be handsome, belied both in looks and manner the crime of which he was accused. Pleading not guilty, he looked composed, although his face was very pale.

He told the court he had been "keeping company" with a girl named Sarah Verity who worked as a ward maid at Salford Royal Hospital. They had known each other for seven years and saw each other quite regularly. On June

10th Horner had a day off work and had arranged to meet her at their usual meeting place, Old Trafford railway station, at 3 p.m. He had arrived at the station at 2.55 p.m., but Sarah did not turn up.

It had been arranged that should it rain he was to see her at the hospital instead, but even though it had been raining that day, Horner still waited for her at the station until 3.05 p.m. When she still didn't arrive he had gone by tram to her rooms at the hospital.

"I looked up to the windows where I generally see my lady waiting for me," he told the court, "but I did not see her. I expected to see her later. I thought she might come out during her tea-hour, which began at 4.30 p.m."

As it was then only 3.25 p.m. Horner, in spite of the rain, decided to while away the time by walking down Oldfield Road to the canal. He and his girlfriend often strolled by the canal, he told the court. He had walked down the canal as far as the Wallness Road gateway, passing under Windsor Bridge as he did. He remembered passing Barnes.

He then went through the gateway and up Wallness Road in the direction of Peel Park and the Crescent. He had just reached Peel Park gates when a policeman came up to him and spoke first about the weather, then accused him of being drunk and finally to his astonishment informed him he had been accused of having thrown a little boy into the canal.

Horner swore he had never before seen the two boys - Eric Wilson and Norman Thomas – who had picked him out in an identity parade. He knew of the Summer Shed in Peel Park, but denied being in the park that afternoon.

The next witness to be called was Sarah Verity. A plump but attractive woman, she appeared to be in something of a trance. When the name "Miss Verity" was called out in court she was so overwhelmed by the occasion that she did not move for several seconds. It was not until Horner pointed her out that she finally responded. In the witness box she confirmed her boyfriend's account of their arrangement to meet on the afternoon of June 10th.

Mr McKeever, summing up for the defence, told the jury that the evidence against Horner was all a matter of identification. Barnes had admitted that as he ran from the timber yard to the canal he had lost sight of the man who had thrown the child into the water. How then could he be certain it was Horner? He had been unable to swear that it was him. And wasn't it remarkable that Barnes had passed Horner – whom he alleged had committed a dreadful murder – without saying a single word?

Barnes had also testified that when he passed him Horner was "sauntering" along the canal towpath. Surely, argued McKeever, if he had just committed a murder he would have been hurrying away from the scene as quickly as possible?

Then there was the question of time. Horner had testified that at 3 p.m. he was at Old Trafford station waiting for his girlfriend. He had then travelled by two tramcars to Salford Royal Hospital where his girlfriend worked before walking along the canal towpath. He had passed Barnes at about 3.50 p.m. He could not therefore have been in Peel Park at the time Norman Pinchen was taken away.

McKeever maintained that Horner was an innocent victim of circumstance. He had simply been in the wrong place at the wrong time. While Barnes was busily having him arrested the real murderer had slipped off in another direction.

The prosecution made short shrift of McKeever's claims. The circumstantial evidence was overwhelming and, though Horner did have a convenient alibi to account for his movements that afternoon, it had to be noted that not one single witness could be produced to substantiate his claims.

In his summing up Mr Justice Talbot explained to the jury that although the boy was dead when thrown into the canal this did not make the crime anything less than murder. The actual cause of death made little difference, he said. "The man, whoever he was, threw the child into the water with no more compunction than if the body had been that of a cat or dog."

The jury was absent for 65 minutes before returning with a verdict of guilty. Horner went pale when he heard their judgement but his face betrayed no emotion.

Describing the murder as "a most atrocious crime," Mr Justice Talbot sentenced John Horner to hang.

An appeal against the sentence was lodged immediately but, on July 28th, it was rejected.

Two days later the prisoner's father, Mr Richard Horner, a Pendleton shopkeeper, visited his son in prison. Describing this meeting, Mr Horner said: "This is the first time in the interviews I have had with him that my son has broken down. Burying his head in his hands, he murmured, 'I would not have cared what they did to me had I done it, but I did not do it.'"

Richard Horner had had a lot of trouble with his son and had no illusions about his bad ways. Only six months earlier he had actually stood up in court himself and given evidence against John on a charge of stealing money and jewellery. But there is a world of difference between theft and the ghastly crime for which his son now stood condemned. Mr Horner was adamant that on this charge his son was entirely innocent.

Mrs Horner also, though she had suffered from John's thieving, believed in his innocence. So too did all the members of the Horner family. They stood by him throughout the ordeal, despite the abuse and condemnation they suffered from the local community. Never did they concede that it was even possible that John had been the killer.

On the morning of August 13th, 1924, John Horner was hanged at Strangeways Prison. Willis was the executioner, having come up from London where the previous day he had hanged the French poisoner Jean Pierre Vaquier in Wandsworth Prison.

There was a wild cheer from the crowds gathered outside as the execution was confirmed.

Dr Shannon, the prison doctor who was in attendance during the execution, told the subsequent inquest that the hanging had been without incident and that death was instantaneous.

"As far as I can make out," the coroner, Mr Stuart Rodgers, observed, "it is a case of a moral pervert gaining lust through cruelty. Is that not so?"

Dr Shannon agreed.

"And had he escaped," the coroner continued, "he would probably have tried again."

Dr Shannon nodded his head.

Mr and Mrs Horner walked away from Strangeways Prison with their eyes downcast. Nothing could persuade them that justice had been done. They persisted in claiming that their son was free from blame.

They hoped to raise a petition, to claim a pardon and clear John's name. But no one outside their family would agree to help. Eventually they gave up.

Six months after the execution Mr Horner sold up his shop and the family moved away from Pendleton. They were not heard of again.

Whether their son was truly guilty of the crime for which he was hanged is still open to question. Certainly under modern rules of justice it is unlikely that John Horner would have been convicted. But in that summer of 1924 there were few people with any doubts that the right man had been punished.

4

THE KILLING OF
CATHERINE TYRER

*Catherine Tyrer was a sweet little old lady.
She was found one evening with her head
reduced to a bloody mess.*

One Saturday evening in October 1893, William Denson, a 25-year-old carter, was sitting with his wife in the scullery of their London Street home in Salford when their peace was disturbed by a loud thud from next door. They didn't know what it might be, but they feared the worst, especially when it was followed by the sound of loud moaning.

Their neighbour was an elderly lady by the name of Catherine Tyrer. A widow, she lived all alone in the house next door and had suffered nasty falls in the past. But this sounded worse. Maybe she had tumbled down the stairs they thought as they dashed round to her front door and gave it a rap.

The Densons were soon joined by another neighbour, Mrs Rose Atkins, who had also heard the commotion. She too knocked on the door and joined in the chorus of shouts. But they got no reply.

Mrs Atkins suggested that Denson might try to knock the door down. He was a burly chap and probably could have easily managed it. However, just as he was bracing himself, a shout came from inside the house. To their surprise it was the gruff voice of a man.

"What do you want, knocking at my door?" he called out.

Mrs Atkins explained they had heard noises and wondered if there had been an accident.

"There's nothing to worry about," the man shouted.

Denson then asked if they could see Mrs Tyrer just to make sure she was well. To this the man did not respond and the door remained closed.

The three neighbours were now very suspicious. Going round to the back of the house to see if he could gain entrance that way, William Denson saw a young, slightly-built man emerge from Mrs Tyrer's yard door.

"Hey, do you live here?" Denson called out.

"Yes, yes, I do," he replied. "It's all right."

"Oh, no it's not," said Denson. "What's going on?"

The man gave him a fixed stare, then turned and fled. Denson set off in hot pursuit.

After chasing him through several streets, Denson cornered the man in Pritchard's Yard and closed in on him. Finding himself trapped, the stranger produced a pen-knife.

"Can you fight?" he snarled, lunging at the carter with the knife.

Denson glared at him. He was not at all daunted by the puny blade. He knocked it from the man's hand and it fell to the floor. Then he grabbed hold of the stranger and pushed him up against the wall. The man tried to resist, but he was no match for Denson. The carter could have thrashed him and probably would have had done so had the police not arrived in time. Fortunately, however, summoned by Mrs Denson, they got there just before the carter delivered his first blow. They pulled the two men apart and took them both to Trafford Road police station for questioning.

Meanwhile, back in London Street, Mrs Atkins had entered her neighbour's house by the back door, which the intruder had left ajar. Everything was in darkness, but on lighting a candle she saw Mrs Tyrer, her clothes pulled up over her face, lying on her back in a thick pool of blood. Pulling the clothes away from her face, Mrs Atkins was horrified to find the old lady's head had been beaten to a pulp. For a while Mrs Atkins was sure that she was dead. But then she saw her lips move. Rose Atkins breathed a sigh of relief. The woman had been horribly injured, but at least she was still alive.

With the help of two other neighbours, she lifted Mrs Tyrer off the scullery floor – now slippery with her blood – and placed her on the sofa. They were in the middle of settling her down when Detective Peter Milne arrived at the house.

Seeing the injured woman, he immediately sent for a cab to take her to Salford Royal Hospital. He then began to examine the scene of the crime and work out what had happened.

In Trafford Road police station, the man caught running from Mrs Tyrer's house was being questioned. But he was not being very cooperative. He refused to tell the police anything. He would not even give them his name. Only when he was searched and a club card found in his pocket bearing the name Victor Emmanuel Hamer was his identity established. Further enquiries revealed that he was 25 years old and had recently been employed by a firm of painters who had just completed work on the exterior of a number of houses in London Street, including Mrs Tyrer's.

"I will tell you nothing," Hamer told Milne defiantly when he was charged with causing Mrs Tyrer grievous bodily harm. "You can charge me with what you like. It will have to be proved yet."

Milne had little doubt that proof would be found. It seemed inconceivable that Hamer was not the culprit. What was more, he even knew how he had done it. Milne had already found the lump of coal near Mrs Tyrer's grate. It was covered in blood and hair. This had been the villain's weapon.

Victor Hamer was thus charged with the assault. The following Monday morning he was also charged with murder. Mrs Tyrer had died.

As news of the murder leaked out, the whole community was enraged. It was a brutal attack on an elderly widow who had been barely five feet tall and was of bird-like proportions. So great was the local feeling about the outrage that when Hamer appeared at Salford police court on November 8th, angry crowds packed the streets. Those who couldn't get into the court building banged on the doors, demanding that Hamer be strung up there and then.

Hamer's appearance inside the court was itself causing a minor sensation: few had expected such a slender and delicate-looking man to have been responsible for battering in the head of a frail old widow. Few were left in any doubt, however, that he was indeed the killer.

At his trial at Manchester Assizes, Hammer confessed to the crime but he blamed his plight on drink. He said he had consumed about eight pints on the day of the murder and had no idea what he was doing. He pleaded that he was not responsible for his actions. Drunkenness, however, proved to be no defence for such a barbaric assault. He was duly found guilty and sentenced to death. He was removed from the court and taken to Strangeways Prison to await execution.

On the Saturday afternoon prior to his execution Hamer's mother and stepfather visited their son for the last time. Hamer had just heard that the last avenue of hope had been denied – the Home Secretary had refused to grant a reprieve – and he was so overcome he was unable to speak. All hope was extinguished in his sunken eyes and he could barely stand. Mrs Hamer's cries were pitiful as she strained to try and touch her favourite son through the bars that cruelly separated them. Eventually, she broke down completely and had to be led away. No words had passed between them during this painful, heart-rending visit. The last, anguished goodbye was a look of pain. Hamer's last sight of his mother was as she was half-dragged, half-carried, whimpering from the visitors' chamber. Neither she nor his step-father saw the look imploring their forgiveness in his eyes.

Hamer's brother, a soldier, was permitted to see him on Monday. Both young men put a brave face on it, and Emmanuel beseeched his brother to tell the family he craved their forgiveness, and tell them not to dwell in grief for him. And Victor Hamer did indeed plead for forgiveness, firstly in a confession to the superintendent of the Sunday School he had attended as a child and then in a letter to his sweetheart:

Dear Agnes,
I received your very kind letter and was very pleased to see by it that you had not altogether forgotten me . . . I hope you will not think wrong of me for being where I am, for all the fault of drink that I can blame it on. I know that if I had only done to you what was right and kept off the drink, I should not have been in the terrible position that I am placed in today; but it is done now and can't be undone, and I only ask you for one thing, and that is that you will forgive me for any wrong that I have done to you; and I wish you would promise me one thing, and that, my dear, is to keep away from the accursed drink, for you see what it has done for me.
So hoping you will lead a sober and religious life, I would now close with the fondest love from your most loving but miserable and heart-broken lover,

Emmanuel Hamer

Victor Emmanuel Hamer was executed inside Strangeways Prison on Tuesday, November 28th, exactly one month after the murder of Mrs Tyrer. Just as the white cap was pulled over his head, Hamer turned and in a voice trembling with emotion, said: "I hope you will all forgive me."

Later, in his cell, the warden of Strangeways found a poem that the killer had composed. Entitled *A Murderer's Grave*, it described Hamer's feelings as his execution approached. It was poor verse, but perhaps the exercise was therapeutic... and no one could deny it was written from the heart:

A wretched man I lie in this dreary prison cell,
Waiting day by day to meet my fate;
No-one can judge my feelings and my thoughts they cannot tell

Repenting, when, alas! it is too late.
To be tried for murder is a shocking thing,
And that is why I am placed here (I am told)
For a cruel, wicked deed committed whilst mad in drink,
For taking the life of that poor dame!

Now, all young men take warning, and don't be led astray to
     drink,
For the past I am sure you never can recall;
While young your life enjoy, take a lesson from poor Hamer,
Let his fate be a warning to you all.

What strange things overcome me as I sit here all alone,
My childhood days I fancy I can see;
All things were bright and cheerful in my peaceful, happy
     home,
When I prattled round my dear old mother's knee.

If I had heeded what she told me it would have been very well,
Or took the kind advice she gave,
I should not have been brought to this dreary prison cell,
And laid low in a common felon's grave!

On the scaffold I have to die forever now goodbye,
Dear brothers, for your brother you will weep;
When we played in childish sport, years ago, I little thought
That in a murderer's grave I e'er should sleep!'

5

THE CARR'S WOOD MURDER

*Few murders had caused such public outcry as
the killing of fourteen-year-old Percy
Sharpe in Carr's Wood. But would the police
ever catch the killer?*

Sitting in a wooden box all day, waiting for trains, can be
a tedious business. Jim Edwards, a signalman at Northenden
Junction, near Manchester, often found it so. Any diver-
sion, however trivial, was a welcome distraction. On that
particular afternoon, Tuesday, September 4th, 1923, he
noticed a child walking towards the signalbox along a
footpath which ran beside Carr's Wood.

At first Edwards thought it was a little girl in a red dress.
Then, as the figure drew close, he realised that it was a boy
wearing red trousers. As there happened to be a school
nearby where the boys wore a red uniform, he assumed the
lad must be from there.

Meanwhile, the signalman had work to do. It was
2.30 p.m., and the Hull to Manchester express was due.
After it had whistled past, Edwards again looked for
the child. The boy had left the footpath and climbed the steps
on to Northenden Bridge, close by the signalbox, where he
slumped to the ground. Edwards, who now had a clear view
of him, was horrified to see that it wasn't red trousers that
covered the lower part of his body. It was blood!

At that moment the boy, who was now clutching
his chest and screaming in agony, caught sight of Edwards.
Waving his arm desperately, the child shouted: "Come
quick, I am dying! A man has stabbed me yonder."

Then, grasping his chest again, he began to scream and
moan. As Edwards scrambled down from the signalbox,

James Hetherington, a platelayer who had been working further up the line and had also heard the boy's screams, arrived at the scene.

The boy, who was wearing only a shirt, collar, tie, underwear and shoes, gasped that his name was Percy Sharpe. He said that he was from South Street in Ardwick, Manchester. He had been stabbed by a man in Carr's Wood. He was just fourteen years old.

"Did you know who did it?" asked Hetherington.

"No," replied the boy, but he managed to describe his attacker. He was middle-aged, clean-shaven and wearing a check cap and mackintosh. Hetherington had seen such a man just a few minutes earlier, hurrying away from the woods.

The platelayer lifted the boy's shirt to see what injury had been inflicted. He was shocked by the sight. There was a gaping hole just under the lad's heart, and it was "bubbling blood."

"My God, Jim, get some help from the station," said Hetherington. Northenden Station was close by.

As Edwards hurried off, Hetherington picked up the boy and ran with him to the nearby Rose Hill Ophthalmic Children's Hospital. There, he handed Percy to Nurse Eastman saying: "Quick, nurse, the boy has been stabbed!"

"Let me go into a soft bed," the boy pleaded weakly, "for I am dying."

Carrying him into the treatment room, the nurse first attended to the haemorrhage, and then treated him for shock by wrapping him in blankets, to which she added hot-water bottles. While he was still conscious she asked him what happened. He repeated his story about the man in Carr's Wood and gave her the same description of him.

"Where did you meet him?" asked the nurse.

"In Oxford Road," he said, "where I was looking for work. We then went by tram to Alexandra Park in Whalley Range."

By this time two policemen, Sergeant Furness and PC Bramhall, had arrived at the hospital. Seating himself by the boy's bed, Furness began gently questioning him. In a faltering, barely audible voice, Percy gave him more details. But the lad's strength was ebbing away and the policeman could only make out snatches of his story. "Come from Manchester with me... Oxford Road.. promising me work... he did it with a knife... he wiped it on the grass and put it in his pocket."

Percy later added more to the statement, though it was again in the same faltering, breathless tones. "By tramcar to Alexandra Park. Come by bus about dinner-time to Northendon. He bought me a ginger beer. We walked to the woods. I didn't know the man."

At this point Sergeant Furness left Percy for a few minutes to go to the telephone, but on his return he again asked the boy several times if he knew the man who had attacked him. Each time he replied: "I didn't know the man."

On the third time of asking, the boy, by now exhausted and on the point of lapsing into unconsciousness, angrily told the sergeant to "shut up!"

Dr Hardman had now arrived. Having dressed the boy's wounds, he drove him at once to Stockport Royal Infirmary in his car. But Percy was by now in such a weakened state that the doctor doubted that he would survive the journey. Before setting out, he had offered the boy a glass of brandy, but the lad pushed it away saying, "No more of that – I am a teetotaller."

On his arrival at Stockport Infirmary, Percy underwent an immediate emergency operation, but though he survived the surgery, he never regained consciousness. He died at 5 a.m. the following day, with his parents at his bedside.

Percy Sharpe's description of his attacker was now circulated to the press: *About 45 years of age; 5ft 9ins tall; clean-shaven; going grey; full face; stoutish build; dark, prominent, glaring eyes, wearing a check cap, light-coloured mackintosh and strong black boots.*

Local newspapers published this description, together with a description of Percy Sharpe, in case anyone should recall seeing the boy that day. It appeared in the Thursday editions.

Meanwhile, the police had already made a thorough search of the area around Carr's Wood. Police Constable Samuel Jones had gone to the scene of the crime at 2.45 p.m. on the day of the murder. He had searched for the spot where the boy had been attacked. On entering a clump of willow trees approximately 100 yards from Northenden Station he found some boy's clothing, consisting of an overcoat, jacket, waistcoat and cap. He noted that the sleeves of the jacket were inside the overcoat, as if they had been taken off or pulled off together. But there was no sign of the boy's trousers and braces. About 18 inches away from the clothing, Jones found three patches of blood, about nine inches apart.

The area was cordoned off, and detectives armed with revolvers scoured the wood and surrounding countryside for the boy's attacker. About 100 officers working shoulder to shoulder had to cut through thick brushwood with scythes before a systematic search could be carried out. Streams in the wood were also dragged, but neither the murder weapon nor the boy's trousers and braces were discovered.

The houses nearest to the murder scene were on Northenden Road, Gatley. The police questioned residents, many of whom remembered hearing screams, but no one had seen anything. It now seemed that Percy Sharpe had first met his murderer at the Labour Exchange in Albert Square, Manchester, which he visited twice a week in his search for work.

Three boys who regularly went to the Exchange remembered seeing him and a man who resembled the description given, in conversation on several occasions. Sharpe had presumably met the man again in Oxford Road on the morning of the murder, and when the man promised to find him work, the boy had gladly gone with him.

Percy had been desperate to find employment, his father having been laid off due to rheumatic fever. Young Percy had the same illness, which had changed his appearance from that of a fine, well-built boy to a skinny youth.

"There is no doubt," a neighbour told the police, "that the kid regarded the financial position of the family as being in some way down to himself. He was the eldest child of four children and he took his responsibilities very seriously indeed."

Before leaving home on the day of the murder, Percy had paid special attention to his appearance and had taken his Labour Exchange Card with him. This, together with his diary, was now missing. Although he had said nothing to his parents, Sharpe had told a neighbour that at last he was going to get some work, but he did not say how or where.

The inquest into Percy Sharpe's violent death was held on September 7th. A pathologist said that he had found a clean-cut wound on the left side of the boy's body, just below the heart. The cut was 1½ inches in length and 1 inch deep, and it had pierced the diaphragm and the upper lobe of the liver. Death had resulted from the subsequent shock and loss of blood. The wound had probably been caused by a sharp, long-bladed knife, possibly a jack-knife and had not been self-inflicted.

Dr Roland Nightingale added that the boy's shirt and vest had been raised at the time the wound was made, because neither garment had a puncture mark. Bruises and abrasions found on the boy's arm and wrists would have occurred during a violent struggle, possibly an attempt at sexual assault. But the pathologist found no evidence of sodomy.

Because no main artery had been severed, which would have caused a spurt of blood, the murderer would probably have had few bloodstains on his clothing. But he would have had blood on his hands and sleeves.

On the following day the police issued a new description of the suspect after a fruit seller, Mrs Isabella Pearson, came forward to say that at about 11.30 a.m. on September 4th, she had seen a man with a boy answering Sharpe's description in Gatley Road. She said the lad had wanted some fruit from her cart, but the man had refused to buy him any – Percy had left home that morning without any money.

Taken to the mortuary, she identified Sharpe as the boy. She told the police that the man she had seen with him was about 50, of stout build, full-faced, with rather red cheekbones, clean-shaven and with a "laughing, grinning expression."

This amended description of the suspect was circulated to the press and duly published. Thereafter the investigation proceeded rapidly.

On September 9th, a boy out for a walk with his brother at Chorlton discovered a jack-knife hidden in a heap of sand. It was a large horn-handled weapon with a badly stained blade curved at the point. He took it home to show his mother. Having heard about the murder and the type of weapon thought to have been used, she took it at once to the police.

Detectives investigating the case included Detective Inspector Kingman. On September 12th, Kingman was on his way to Barnes Convalescent Home at Cheadle to make more enquiries. In a lane near the home, he noticed a man who seemed to fit the new description of the killer. The man was talking to a group of boys. Kingman approached him.

On speaking to the man the detective learnt that his name was David Colthorpe, 45, and, for a while, he had been a patient at the home. Since leaving, he had revisited it frequently, and was at times employed there to wheel patients around the grounds.

Struck by how closely the man fitted Mrs Pearson's description of the suspect, Kingman took him into custody. Colthorpe denied murdering Sharpe and loudly protested his innocence, claiming he had been at the home at the time the boy was attacked. Unfortunately for him, however, his story could not be backed up. Although staff there recalled seeing him that afternoon, none could give him an alibi for the crucial time of 2.30 p.m.

Colthorpe had lodgings in Canal Street, Stockport, and Kingman immediately arranged for these to be searched. There the police found a pair of trousers and a jacket with what appeared to be bloodstains on them. The jack-knife discovered three days earlier was then shown to several people who knew Colthorpe. Many swore it was the one they had often seen in his possession. Colthorpe denied it was his.

But Colthorpe had been incriminated in other ways. For example, the police heard that, moments after reading about the murder in a newspaper, he had told two acquaintances, "I've done nothing to any children round here. Go and ask them." That, to the investigators, sounded very much like the voice of a guilty conscience.

Further inquiries revealed that Colthorpe liked the company of young boys and would often give them presents and take them on walks. On being questioned, however, none of the children reported any "irregularities" in his behaviour towards them.

Colthorpe was then put on an identity parade with 15 others. To his horror, Mrs Pearson, the fruit-seller, immediately identified him as the man she had seen with Percy Sharpe on the morning of the murder. Other witnesses who had also seen the pair were less certain but it made no difference. Already Kingman had enough to make an arrest and Colthorpe was taken to Withington police station where he was charged with Percy Sharpe's murder. He was then transported to Strangeways Prison to await trial.

If the police were certain that they now had their man, however, they were soon disappointed. As the investigation continued evidence began to pile up that Colthorpe was, in fact, completely innocent. Though initially he had been unable to corroborate his story of his movements on that fateful Tuesday, it wasn't long before a number of witnesses were found who were able to confirm it. Most significantly, at the time when it was assumed Percy Sharpe had been picked up by his killer in Oxford Road, it was shown beyond question that Colthorpe was miles away at the Stockport Labour Exchange. Besides this, a Home Office analyst, who had examined Colthorpe's blood-stained clothing and the jack-knife, reported that although he had found a little blood which might be human, what there was was very old and certainly pre-dated the murder.

Colthorpe's boots also played an important part in demolishing the case against him. All the witnesses, including Percy Sharpe himself, had said the killer was wearing "strong black boots." But Colthorpe had only one pair of boots, and these were falling apart.

Clearly Colthorpe was not the murderer and, in due course, he was released from jail.

With the real killer still at large, rumours abounded that he might have escaped from a local lunatic asylum or that he had committed suicide. On September 15th, a man was found dead on the railway line near Northenden. A forty-seven year old Manchester fire surveyor by the name of Stethill Lonsdale Mattinson, he had apparently committed suicide.

Suspicion fell on him, not only because he had chosen to kill himself close to where Percy Sharpe had been murdered, but also because of discrepancies in his diary entries for September 4th. According to these entries he had been in Oldham all that day, but when police checked the addresses given, they quickly discovered he had not kept one appointment.

The police took two people to the mortuary where Mattinson's body lay, and both identified him as the man they had seen with Percy Sharpe in the vicinity of Carr's Wood on the day of the murder. But other witnesses also came forward to testify that Mattinson could not have been there. They said he had been in Chadderton, near Oldham, on that day. A heavy drinker, he apparently had pressing personal financial worries. It was this, rather than remorse for the killing, that accounted for him lying down on the railway line.

As the months passed, the trail inevitably went cold and it seemed that the Carr's Wood murder would remain unsolved. Then, on January 4th, 1924, PC Lawrence arrested Francis Wilson Booker, an unemployed warehouseman.

For some time, complaints had been made by a number of small boys in the Alexandra Road district of Whalley Range, concerning a man whom they claimed had been terrorising them by taking them into a field at the rear of the Alexandra Park Aerodrome. There he had made them stand in a corner whilst he inflicted "punishments," either by striking them with his hands or beating them with a small leather strap.

Constable Lawrence kept watch and finally spotted a man chasing little boys down Alexandra Road towards the park. Booker, who looked much older than his 28 years, explained that he was a sort of "public chastiser" of lads he claimed were guilty of such "crimes" as smoking and riding bicycles on the footpath.

When he was searched, a toy pistol and a small leather strap were found on him. There were also five notebooks which he had used as diaries and which gave detailed accounts of the "punishments" he had given young boys over the months. After his arrest Booker was formally identified by five boys and charged with common assault against four of them. He did not contest the charge. "I admit it," he said. Booker was thus remanded in custody pending a hearing.

On January 8th, PC Lawrence searched Booker's lodgings in Carter Street, Greenheys, Manchester. Booker slept in the front bedroom of the house, a room he shared with two other male lodgers. On a shelf over his bed, behind a black portmanteau, Lawrence found three pairs of boys' short trousers. He also found a black box in which he discovered a small diary and a Labour Exchange Card bearing the name and address of Percy Sharpe. The constable didn't have to think twice to realise the significance of his find.

Before returning to the station, however, he also searched through the rest of the house. On going down into the cellar, which Booker had been using as an upholstery workshop, Lawrence found a zinc bath filled up with wireless sets, a quantity of flock (apparently from the sofa) and finally, at the very bottom, wrapped in a piece of brown paper, another pair of boy's short trousers. They were badly worn and looked as if they had been well washed. Could these have been the pair missing from the murder scene at Carr's Wood?

Lawrence also discovered that Booker owned a check cap, a light-coloured mackintosh and a pair of strong black boots.

The next day, police searched Booker's allotment on Princess Road. This allotment was in a field adjoining Alexandra Park, where Percy Sharpe had alleged his killer took him prior to their journey to Carr's Wood. In a locked greenhouse on Booker's plot, a pair of boy's braces were found. They were stained with blood.

The trousers and braces were taken to the home of Mr and Mrs Sharpe in Ardwick for identification. Mrs Sharpe wept as she examined the torn trousers. She confirmed the investigator's suspicions. They were indeed the trousers belonging to her son. She knew them by the stitching she had done on them. Both she and her husband were certain their son had been wearing the trousers and braces when he left home on the morning of the murder. The trousers had since been washed, they said.

On January 11th, Booker was shown the murdered boy's trousers, braces, diary and Labour Exchange Card.

Police Superintendent Tongue was later to say of the interview: "I never noticed any change in his appearance until I produced the pocket book and Labour Card. Then his lips began to tremble. Then I showed him the braces and I may say that he appeared to be distressed, as though he was repressing excitement."

Booker claimed the boy's possessions had been in a parcel he had found on a road outside Northenden a day or so after the murder. He said he did not take them to the police because he was frightened. Superintendent Tongue did not believe him, and Booker was charged with Percy Sharpe's murder.

Francis Booker's trial at Manchester Assizes before Mr Justice Greer began on February 26th, 1924. Smartly dressed and apparently cool and self-possessed, he pleaded not guilty. Mr Wingate-Saul KC led for the prosecution, and Mr Kenneth Burke KC defended.

Mr and Mrs Sharpe had both identified the short trousers and braces found at Booker's lodgings and allotment, and to make certain they could not have been mistaken, the prosecution called two independent witnesses. Edith Tatley identified the braces as those she had made for Mrs Sharpe. She said she was certain, because she had never made another pair exactly like them. Then Fred W. Borwick, a textile expert, told the court that the jacket and waistcoat found at Carr's Wood were of the same material as the short trousers found in the bath at Booker's lodgings. However, under cross-examination, he admitted that the clothing was of a mass-produced variety.

Witnesses testified that Booker, who had always been clean-shaven, had changed his appearance soon after the day of the murder by growing a moustache and beard, though he later shaved off the beard. They also claimed that he had stopped wearing his usual cloth cap and mac and begun wearing a trilby and overcoat.

Norman Bellis, a 13-year-old schoolboy, recalled that he had been to Northenden with Booker on several occasions and admitted that the man had often suggested indecent acts to him. John Meyerscouch, also 13, said he had been to Northenden and Carr's Wood with Booker many times, and Booker seemed to know the district very well.

In a statement to the police Booker had claimed he had spent the entire time of the murder on his allotment, and said he had spoken to another allotment-holder named Davies on that day. Mr Davies was thus summoned to the court and took the witness stand. He refused to confirm Booker's story. In fact, he said, he had spent September 4th fishing in Sale.

Booker then took the witness stand himself. A reporter noted that he seemed so eager to go into the box that he walked from the dock "at a very rapid rate." In taking the oath, he kissed the Bible "fervently."

Explaining how Sharpe's personal possessions had come to be found in his lodgings he said, "It may have been the next day, after I heard of the crime, or the day after that. I do not know the name of the road. I had been riding my bike and had got off it to pump the wheel up. There was a slow puncture in the tyre.

"There was a kind of recess in the roadway where courting couples would go, and I mended my puncture there. It was in this place that I found a parcel. I then took it to my lodgings. I did not open it until the middle of November."

Booker claimed that without opening the parcel, he had put it on the shelf over his bed, and had only found it again when clearing out some rubbish. On opening it he discovered it contained a pair of boy's short trousers, braces and a diary. He said he hadn't noticed the Labour Exchange Card with Sharpe's name and address on it.

He could not explain why the trousers had been found at the bottom of the zinc bath and not with the other three pairs of boy's trousers on the shelf in his room. He could not remember putting them there. He said he had put the diary and the Labour Card, without looking at either, in the black box where they were found.

In his original statement Booker claimed he had found the parcel "just outside Northenden." Now, however, he claimed that it was a considerable distance away, near Halebarns. The prosecution accused him of changing his statement because he had learnt that the police had carefully searched all the roads around Northenden immediately after the murder and would have found the parcel if it had been there.

Booker was asked why he had not opened the parcel to see if a name and address were inside. The accused said he did not know, but he did not think the parcel contained "anything serious". He claimed that the first time he had realised the property contained in the parcel belonged to Percy Sharpe was when he was told by Superintendent Tongue that they were the boy's things.

Mr Saul now reminded Booker that when shown the clothing he had told Tongue: "I was frightened and did not take them to the police station." Booker said he could not recall saying that.

He admitted that the letters "N. B. K." and "G. K." written in his diaries stood for "navy blue knickers," and "Grey knickers," to describe the colour of short trousers a particular boy he had met was wearing.

Mr Saul pointed out that one diary had several pages missing which would have contained entries, had there been any, relating to September 4th, 1923. Booker said that he could not explain why the pages were missing.

He claimed that the three pairs of short trousers found at his lodgings were his. He said he had stolen one pair off a washing line, another pair he had picked off a rag-and-bone cart and the third from a refuse tip.

Mr Saul suggested that given Booker's fetish for collecting boys' trousers it was pertinent to note that the only items of clothing missing from the murder scene were the boy's trousers and braces.

Addressing the jury on behalf of Booker, Mr Burke submitted that there was so much doubt as to who had actually committed the crime that Booker was entitled to be acquitted. Mrs Pearson, who had seen Sharpe in Gatley Road with a man on the morning of the murder, had failed to identify Booker as that man. Indeed, her description of the man did not in the least resemble Booker.

Similarly Sharpe's own description of his killer did not tally with Booker's appearance. Booker did not have a full face, was not stout and he certainly did not have "dark, prominent, glaring eyes."

The prosecution had accused Booker of keeping Sharpe's clothing in order to gloat over his crime, but surely, argued Burke, if he were guilty he would have burnt these incriminating articles either at his lodgings or on his allotment.

Burke was clutching at straws and the jury knew it. After an absence of just 25 minutes they returned to find Booker guilty of Percy Sharpe's murder. When sentence of death was passed, Booker wheeled about, his hands still in his pockets. Looking totally unmoved, he walked quietly from the dock towards the cells.

Subsequently, his appeal rejected, Booker passed his time playing cards with his warders and usually winning. His only visitor was his aged father, who had travelled from his home in Horncastle, Lincolnshire.

Francis William Booker was executed at 8.00 a.m. on April 8th, 1924, at Strangeways Prison.

With the proposed Bill to abolish hanging being hotly debated in the newspapers, emotions were running high. On the morning of the execution several hundred men, women and children gathered outside the prison entrance. Some of the women wept.

Furious at the pity shown to Booker, the coroner, Mr Stuart Rodger, later told the jury at Booker's inquest, "I sometimes wonder how the relatives of a murdered person regard the sentimentalists who appear to lavish more compassion on the perpetrator of an atrocious crime than on the innocent victim. Reprieve signatures are sent in their thousands and the victim is all but forgotten."

Though questioned by the press, the Governor of Strangeways, Major H. E. Fitzclarence, refused to say whether or not Booker had made a confession before he was hanged.

Those who attended Booker's trial included David Colthorpe, the man earlier imprisoned as a suspect. Later, Colthorpe tried to obtain compensation for wrongful arrest, but his claim was rejected.

6

THE MANCHESTER SETTEE MURDER

*An old woman was bludgeoned to death as she
lay dozing on her settee. Was the man who
hanged for the crime her killer or did he sign his
life away for a glass of whisky?*

All was quiet at Claremont, a large semi-detached house
on Cheetham Hill Road in the Cheetham district of Manchester, on that hot July afternoon in 1933. In her tiny, first-
floor bedroom the 17-year-old maid, Freda Phillips, sat
sewing at her open window. In the front room downstairs
her employer, 61-year-old Mrs Fanny Levine, was taking
her usual afternoon nap on the settee.

The rest of the family – Mrs Levine's bachelor brothers,
Lewis and Michael Davies, and her two daughters, Clara
and Esther, who all lived with her – were out.

As there was nothing more to be done in the house until
tea-time, Freda was catching up on her sewing. There
wasn't much of a view from her window, which looked
directly down on to the passageway between Mrs Levine's
house and that of her neighbour, Dr Lees. But Freda could
see the doctor's garage, in front of which Sam Woodcock,
his chauffeur, was working on the car.

Sam and Freda often chatted together when they had a
moment, and Freda now leaned out of her window, calling
down to him. They exchanged a few words. Then, at four
o'clock Woodcock, needing something for the car, said
goodbye and cycled off to a nearby garage.

Shortly afterwards Freda glanced out of the window
again and was surprised to see a middle-aged, stockily built
man wearing a trilby and a brown coat walking along by the
side of the house towards the trellis-gate which opened on

to the drive. He appeared to have come from the back of the house, and she wondered who he could be. Then she remembered that a few days earlier a man had called enquiring about some hens which Mrs Levine kept. Perhaps it was he, but Freda could not be certain as it was impossible to see his face.

A few minutes later Woodcock returned to the car and Freda went downstairs to prepare tea. On going into the kitchen, she was startled to see the heavy bar used for lifting the cover of the grate lying across the hearth rug. Puzzled, she went towards it, and saw that its square end was dripping with blood. And that wasn't all. A white cricket shirt she had earlier put on the clothes-rack above the fire to air had been knocked down and was now lying crumpled on the kitchen table. This also had blood on it.

Running to the side of the house, Freda shouted to Woodcock to come over.

The chauffeur rushed in. Freda pointed a trembling finger at the bar.

"God, what's been going on?" cried Woodcock. "Are you alone in the house?"

"No," said the maid. "Mrs Levine is in the front room."

When he received no reply to his tentative knock, Woodcock gently opened the door of the front room and peeped inside. Blood was splattered everywhere – across the walls, the carpet and the settee where Mrs Levine lay sprawled, blood pouring from her face and shoulders. Woodcock hurried across to her.

"What's happened?" he asked, taking hold of her hand. She opened her eyes and moved her head to look at him. Woodcock shuddered. The old lady was unrecognisable. There were bruises and cuts all over her face. Her eyes and lips were horribly swollen.

Woodcock could see that she was struggling to tell him something, and for a moment he thought that she would say who had attacked her, but the effort proved to be too much. She closed her eyes and although she opened them once or twice afterwards and appeared to be conscious, she did not speak.

Woodcock ran from the house, dragging Freda after him. He raced down the road to a telephone box and called the police and an ambulance. In his panic he appeared to have forgotten his employer, Dr Lees, was at home that afternoon and could have attended the old lady immediately.

Within minutes PC James Turner arrived. Mrs Levine was still conscious, but she was unable to reply to any of the policeman's questions. Part of her skull had been shattered, leaving her brain exposed, and her wrists had been cut, probably when she raised her hands to try and protect herself.

The constable wondered if the attack had happened during a robbery, but nothing seemed to have been disturbed in the room, which was filled with expensive antiques. An empty purse lay open, however, at the victim's side.

An ambulance soon arrived and Mrs Levine was rushed to the Jewish Hospital. But her skull had been so badly fractured that nothing could be done for her. Four hours later she died.

Detective Inspector Page and Detective Sergeant Blenkharn interviewed Woodcock and Freda Phillips, and then Mrs Levine's family. Not surprisingly her two daughters, Clara and Esther, were in a very distressed state. So too was her brother Michael. He had been so shocked by the news that he had passed out. Nevertheless, they did their best to help the detectives who were soon able to piece together the events that preceded the attack.

The officers learned that Mrs Levine had had lunch as usual that day with her brother Michael and her daughters. Then, for some unknown reason, she had counted the money in her purse which Clara, who had been watching, estimated had amounted to about nine shillings. Mrs Levine had then replaced the purse in her handbag which she always kept at her side.

At 12.45 p.m. her daughters left the house and from then

until 2.15 p.m. Mrs Levine sat chatting with Michael. When he left she sent for the maid, who brought in books and magazines from another room for her to read. Freda then left Mrs Levine sitting with her feet up on the settee reading a book and returned to the kitchen, where she stayed until 3.30 p.m. when she had gone upstairs to her room.

Freda confessed that, because of the extreme heat, she had left the back door wide open. The detectives did not reprimand her for this. It was, after all, the middle of the afternoon in a respectable, residential district. Who could have seen the harm in it? Everyone knew, however, that if the door had been closed the tragedy might have been averted.

Woodcock hadn't seen anyone near the house that afternoon, so the police had only the description of the man Freda had seen: "About 45-50 years old, of large build, 5ft 8in tall, dressed in a brown jacket, brown trilby hat, dark trousers and of working-class appearance."

Detectives believed that the murderer would not have had time to get out of Manchester and must still be in the city, so a close watch was put on railway stations and trams. They also thought that there would be blood on the man's clothing.

But if the murderer had blood on him, how had he managed to get away from the house without being seen? Cheetham Hill Road was a busy thoroughfare and rarely empty, especially in the afternoon. As the maid had not seen the man leave by the front, the police wondered if he had retraced his steps and gone round to the back of the house again. But this did not solve the riddle because the garden at the rear was surrounded by a high wall and the only exit, a small door, led directly on to Cheetham Cricket Ground.

Had the man climbed over the wall which was in full view of many houses, or had he gone through the door on to the cricket ground? There had been a match that afternoon which had lasted from 2.30 until 5 p.m., and the assistant groundsman – who had been there all the time – was certain he had seen no stranger.

Both Page and Blenkharn were struck by the fact that although Mrs Levine, whose family dealt in antiques, had good pieces of furniture and china in every room, nothing had been taken except the meagre contents of her purse. This indicated an opportunist thief, probably a vagrant, who simply walked through the open back door into the house.

With this in mind the detectives organised a general round-up of hawkers, tramps and "sleepers out," while common lodging houses and cheap hostels throughout Manchester and Salford were raided and men answering the description of the wanted man detained. But the suspects all had alibis and, one by one, they were all released.

The police also had to consider the possibility that they were dealing with a homicidal maniac who had attacked Mrs Levine simply for pleasure and had taken the money as an afterthought, or to make the murder look like a robbery gone wrong. If this were the case, the man could kill again...

Mrs Levine's funeral was held on July 21st at the Jewish Cemetery, Crumpsall. Her husband – from whom she had been separated for 37 years – was a wealthy landowner, living in Inchicore, Dublin. Ill health prevented him from attending the ceremony. But the rest of the Levine family were there.

When the cortège left the house a policeman directed it to the off-side of the road so that the Jewish funeral custom of passing as close as possible to synagogues on the route could be observed. Four times the slowly moving procession halted. First it stopped for a few seconds outside the Great Synagogue, where Mrs Levine and her family had worshipped. Next was the United Synagogue, then the Spanish and Portuguese Synagogue and finally the Home for Jewish Incurables. All along the route people came out of their houses to pay their respects and voice their horror at the crime that had shocked the entire neighbourhood.

Meanwhile, the police carried out a reconstruction of the murder. Due to the extreme heat of that July afternoon the front window of the house – which looked directly out on to Cheetham Hill Road – had been left open about six inches. Mrs Levine had been lying on the settee beneath the window, with her handbag close by. Opposite the window was a sideboard with a large mirror over it.

Detectives speculated that the killer had been passing the house, and on seeing the open window, he had nipped up the drive, put his hand through the window, drawn back the net curtain and peered into the room.

Spying the dozing figure of Mrs Levine reflected in the mirror and, more importantly, her handbag, he had gone round to the back door and, finding it wide open, had simply walked in.

Once in the kitchen he had picked up the iron bar kept by the fire and had gone quietly through to the front room. Since Mrs Levine was a semi-invalid she would have been unable to offer much resistance even if she had woken up and seen the intruder.

After bludgeoning his victim, detectives theorised, the killer must have quietly left the room, carefully closing the door behind him.

In order not to leave any fingerprints he had wiped the handle of the iron bar on the cricket shirt pulled down from the rack above the fireplace. He had then strolled from the house along the asphalt path and fled. Scotland Yard fingerprint experts confirmed that there were no prints on the iron bar. They did, however, find a well-defined imprint on the handbag.

On July 27th, a week after the murder, a 47-year-old unemployed seaman, William Burtoft, was arrested in Hyde, eight miles from Manchester, on a charge of drunkenness. With only one eye, the heavily built, red-faced seaman had found it hard to find work and was drifting from one lodging house to the next, consoling himself with what drink he could afford. At the time of his arrest this was methylated spirits.

The Hyde police at once suspected him of the Cheetham murder. Not only did he fit the general description of the man seen leaving the house, but he had left Manchester only a few days before and admitted that he had been in Cheetham Hill Road at about the time of the murder. They contacted the Manchester police and Inspectors Page and Willis drove over to interview the suspect.

The two detectives questioned Burtoft for a short while at Hyde station and then took him back to Manchester, where he was interrogated further. What happened next would become the subject of much dispute.

Three policemen were present during the interview – Page, Willis and Blenkharn. Inspector Page always maintained that he was the only one to question Burtoft – the others apparently just listened and took notes.

First, Page asked Burtoft to give an account of his movements over the past week. The suspect did so, detailing everything he had done on July 18th, 20th, 21st and 22nd. When Page pointed out that he had omitted to say what he had been doing on the 19th, the day of the murder, Burtoft broke down. According to the police he admitted everything. "Go on," he said, "I will tell you everything. Write it down. I admit being the murderer of Mrs Levine owing to drinking methylated spirits and also to the maid being where she was.

"I was cool, calm and collected. Of course, when I got to the front room the old lady got up and asked who was this and I went back and took the poker off the fire range and struck her repeatedly. When I left the house she was not dead, but owing to the state of my nerves I thought everyone was looking at me.

"I went down to Angel Meadow [a slum district near Manchester city centre], went to Cain's lodging house, washed my hands and threw the handkerchief [on which he said he had wiped his bloodstained hands] down the lavatory and pulled the chain. I walked calmly into Sawn Street and had a bit of tea and jumped on to a tram for Oldham. I was only three minutes or so in the house. I had no intention of doing it, but well, I did it. I was sorry when I thought about it after. After I did it I took the poker back into the kitchen and wiped it on a shirt to remove any fingerprints."

The police next sought out and questioned those who had seen Burtoft on the afternoon of the murder in order to confirm as many of the facts contained in the confession as possible. They knew that, in court, there was always the possibility that the suspect would retract everything he had said and they would need evidence to prove their case.

Prior to the murder, Burtoft had been at a lodging house in Elizabeth Street, which was about 15 minutes' walk from Mrs Levine's home. A woman who had been in Elizabeth Street that afternoon said Burtoft had asked her for a cigarette, telling her he had no money, but hinting that he might have some that night. She supposed he meant to obtain this by begging from door to door.

A short while later, at about 3.15 p.m., she saw him going off in the direction of Cheetham Hill Road. She was certain he was wearing a light brown trilby hat, a brown coat and dark trousers.

At 5.20 p.m. a man named James Hughes – who had known the suspect since the First World War – was in Cain's lodging house when Burtoft entered hurriedly. Hughes called out to him, but to his surprise Burtoft didn't reply. He just rushed straight past his friend and into the kitchen where he washed his hands. This had struck Hughes as most unusual.

The following Saturday Hughes met Burtoft in the street and asked why his old friend had walked past him at the lodging house.

"Oh. I don't know you," Burtoft said, staring hard at him. "Who are you?"

"I'm Sailor Hughes," replied the man, hurt and annoyed that Burtoft should have forgotten him. At that Burtoft seemed to remember, and the two went for a drink together. At the pub, said Hughes, Burtoft asked him if the police had visited Cain's lodging house in connection with

Mrs Levine's murder. Hughes told him that officers had been coming to the house "in droves," so frequently that he and his fellow-lodgers had no peace. When he heard this Burtoft rose and swigged back his beer. "I'll beat it," he said, and hurried from the pub.

Burtoft's recollection of having a meal in the late afternoon of the murder was confirmed by the wife of a Swan Street café proprietor. She had served him with a meat pie and a cup of tea, costing fivepence.

With such witnesses and Burtoft's confession, the police felt that their case against the seaman was unassailable. But their confidence began to fade when, at an identity parade, Freda Phillips failed to pick out their suspect.

It had not been a normal identity parade. Instead of viewing a number of men walking past her, she was asked to observe them from about the same height (26 ft) as her bedroom window at Mrs Levine's house.

A second parade was held. This time, perhaps feeling under pressure to pick someone, Miss Phillips did make an identification. But it was another man, not Burtoft.

There was another person who had seen a man in a trilby hat near Mrs Levine's house on the afternoon of the murder. He had been visiting Dr Lees at 4 p.m. and had seen a man wearing a light brown trilby, which was rather dirty, standing in the passageway at the side of Mrs Levine's house. He was also summoned to the identity parade. Alas, he too failed to identify Burtoft.

The police had no better luck with the forensic evidence. The fingerprint on Mrs Levine's handbag may or may not have been that of the killer. But it certainly wasn't that of William Burtoft.

Another blow for the investigation came when Mr Harry Heap, the Manchester city analyst, reported that he had failed to find blood on any of Burtoft's clothes. There was little doubt that due to the frenzied nature of the attack the murderer would have had blood on his clothing. The police also knew that as a vagrant William Burtoft would have had no other clothes to change into, and little opportunity of acquiring fresh ones. The absence of bloodstains could thus not be explained.

Nevertheless, the police still felt that they had enough evidence to charge Burtoft with Mrs Levine's murder and this they duly did. "I have nothing to say," was the seaman's only comment.

Having withdrawn his confession, William Burtoft pleaded not guilty when his trial began on November 13th, 1933 at Manchester Assizes before Mr Justice Atkinson.

For the defence Mr B. S. Wingate-Saul questioned Freda Phillips about a change she had made to her initial description of the man she had seen. First she had said he was wearing a dark brown trilby, but on the following day she had said it was light brown. Mr Wingate-Saul suggested that this was because she had read in the newspapers that the other person who had seen the man in the passage had said he had been wearing a light brown hat.

"You never saw the man's face?" said Mr Wingate-Saul.

"No," she replied.

"Then how could you tell how old he was?"

"I saw his chin," said Freda.

Under further questioning she admitted not only that she had failed to pick Burtoft out in two identity parades, but also that even now, face to face with him in court, she still did not recognise him as the man she had seen leaving the house just before her employer was found beaten.

There then arose the question of whether Burtoft's confession was admissible as evidence. The police claimed it had been made voluntarily, but Burtoft said it had been forced from him, and as he wasn't sober at the time he had been unaware of what he was saying.

Having considered both sides the judge ruled in favour of the prosecution. He declared the confession was admissible and could thus be read out in court before the jury.

Mr Wingate-Saul then challenged Inspector Page's claim that he was the only one to question Burtoft, suggesting that in reality questions from all three officers had been fired at

Burtoft until, wearied and browbeaten, he had finally said something to the effect of: "Go on, I will admit it. Anything for peace."

Page denied this, and further refuted the allegation that whisky was offered to the alcoholic Burtoft as an inducement to make a statement. But he agreed that the facts contained in the alleged confession could easily have been obtained from reading the newspapers.

Sir Walter Greaves-Lord KC, MP, summing up for the prosecution, told the jury that apart from his confession there was other strong evidence pointing to Burtoft's guilt. The seaman did not deny being in the area of Cheetham Hill Road at the time of the murder. And just before the crime he had no money, but a short time afterwards he was in a café ordering a meal.

Concluding for the defence, Mr Wingate-Saul pointed out that apart from the alleged confession the evidence against his client was highly circumstantial. There had been blood everywhere in Mrs Levine's room – on the window, pictures, walls, cushions and settee – and yet not one spot was found on Burtoft's clothing. This could only be because he wasn't there.

Having been drinking heavily on the day of his arrest, Burtoft had been taken to Manchester barely sober, and then put into a room with the intimidating senior police officers. Here, Mr Wingate-Saul claimed, the defendant was bullied and cajoled with tempting offers of drink until, in the end, he confessed.

"I am not calling the policemen liars," Mr Wingate-Saul told the jury, "but do you think it is right to convict a man on evidence of this sort with no direct evidence against him?"

He then pointed out a major flaw in Burtoft's confession. Burtoft had said that on his entering the front room Mrs Levine had risen from the settee. But Freda Phillips, the last person to see her before the attack, had testified that her employer was lying back on the settee with her feet up – the position in which she was later found after the attack. She had never risen from the settee.

As to the penniless Burtoft having money later that afternoon, Mr Wingate-Saul said that his client had been begging from door to door and that was how he had acquired the fivepence for a meal. Besides, a man supposedly with nine shillings in his pocket would surely have dined out on something more substantial than a meat pie and a cup of tea.

Summing up, the judge drew the jury's attention to the fact that Burtoft had not given evidence in court – surely an innocent man would want to speak up for himself.

The jury took two hours and ten minutes to find William Burtoft guilty, and Mr Justice Atkinson then passed his first death sentence since becoming a judge.

On December 4th Burtoft's appeal was dismissed, and on the morning of December 19th, 1933, he was hanged at Strangeways Prison, not far from Mrs Levine's home.

But was William Burtoft guilty? There was no evidence against him and the questions raised by his disputed confession leave one uneasy.

As we now know, intense police questioning accompanied by threats and inducements can often lead vulnerable but otherwise innocent people to become so undermined that they will admit to anything, even murder. But in 1933 such things were unthinkable. Policemen didn't lie and only guilty men confessed.

To the jury at Burtoft's trial it must have seemed inconceivable that a man would sign his life away for a glass of whisky. As incredible, perhaps, as someone killing an old lady for a mere nine shillings.

7

THE DEATH OF KATIE GARRITY

Jack Griffiths was not a man to take rejection easily. When his sweetheart said she did not want to see him any more, tragedy was bound to follow.

Seventeen-year-old Kate Garrity met Jack Griffiths in Shaw near Oldham, Lancashire, in 1905, when she moved into a house a few doors away from his in Middleton Street. She was very attracted to the 19-year-old former soldier and soon they became sweethearts. But Jack was not an easy man to love. He was a hothead, and would always be scrapping with someone, usually over nothing very much. He would fight with Kate too, shouting, screaming and getting into a terrible temper. Eventually, it all proved too much for the young lass, and after yet another of their frequent quarrels, she told him she didn't want to go out with him again.

Characteristically, Griffiths couldn't accept a decision like that, and he began pestering her. When she finished work at the mill, he would be waiting for her, and he'd follow her all the way to her front door. It annoyed her, but there wasn't any real trouble until the occasion she stopped in the street to speak to her best friend's young man, Will Newall. As they chatted amicably, passing the time of day, Griffiths suddenly appeared out of nowhere and threw the young man to the ground. Will, more lightly built than Jack, was in no mood for a fight. He scrambled to his feet and ran off as fast he could go. Kate was left, angry and dumbfounded, to confront her old boyfriend on her own.

On another occasion, Kate Garrity had stopped in the

street to chat with a neighbour, a Mrs Smith. Griffiths marched up to them, and ignoring Mrs Smith, demanded that Kate should come for a walk with him. When she refused, he lunged at her, grabbed her arm and dragged the protesting girl away. When she struggled he lost his temper completely and punched her hard in the face. Outraged by this disgraceful display, Mrs Smith tried to intervene, whereupon Griffiths, with clenched fist, threatened to punch her too. Luckily, a policeman arrived before things got worse and he held Griffiths back. Then he was arrested.

At the police station, Griffiths vehemently denied having done any real harm to Kate, describing his vicious assault on her as nothing more than a "love tap." The blood dripping from the young girl's mouth, however, told a different story. Griffiths was bound over to keep the peace for three months.

From then on, Jack kept away from Kate. But he didn't leave her in peace. Instead of pestering her himself he now sent a young friend, fourteen-year-old John Bardsley, to carry messages to her. They were not received with pleasure.

Whenever she saw the lad, Kate's heart sank. She did her best to avoid the boy, but he was persistent. Coming out of the corner shop one cold December morning, Kate was annoyed yet again to find John Bardsley standing outside, waiting for her. "Kate! Kate Garrity!" he called. Kate was determined to ignore him and walked on. However, Griffiths had promised the lad sixpence to deliver his message, so deliver his message he would.

"Jack says he wants thee to meet him down by the back of Dawn Mill," said the lad as he breathlessly caught up with her.

"I'll meet him nowhere!" shouted Kate angrily.

"But he says thee's got to, or else..." John Bardsley hesitated.

"Or else what?" demanded Kate, so angry now that despite the cold, she let her shawl slip from her head. Bardsley looked a little uneasy, then grinning awkwardly replied quickly: "Or else, or else he says he's going to do for thee before Christmas."

Christmas! That was only eleven days away. Jack Griffiths is nothing but talk, Kate said to herself, but it was more than just the cold that was making her shiver.

On the morning of December 20th, Kate's father, Robert Garrity, who hadn't slept a wink all night, was still worried. Kate had gone out at ten past eight the previous evening to fetch beer from the Blue Bell, and she still hadn't come back. Knowing about the threats Jack Griffiths had been making, Garrity felt certain something dreadful had happened to her. Time and again he had gone up and down the street following her usual route to the pub and back, but look where he might, he could find neither hide nor hair of her. As soon as dawn came, he put on his coat again, and went back outside. He stopped people on their way to the mill to inquire if they had seen his Kate. None of them had.

Then, as he was crossing some waste ground close to Greenfield Mill, Garrity spotted the beer jug Kate had taken with her when she went out. Excitedly, he picked it up, feeling certain that at last he was close to finding his daughter. There were some sacks piled up against a factory wall close by, and almost without thinking, he went across and lifted one up. Staring at him was Katie's face, stark and lifeless.

Garrity stood there for some time, rooted to the spot. Then he let out a piercing scream. A passer-by ran to him to find out what had happened and he too saw the sickening sight of the young woman's corpse. Her eyes were bulging and her tongue was lolling out of her mouth. She was covered in blood and bruises.

The stranger raced to fetch the police who made good time getting to the Mill. Shortly afterwards the body of Kate Garrity was removed to the morgue.

Dr Forbes Kinnear performed an immediate post-mortem examination of the dead girl and found numerous marks of violence, but the main cause of death had been strangulation: a piece of cord or string had been pulled tight around her neck.

Inspector Hyde, who was leading the investigation, observed that there were clog prints near the body. He and other investigators traced the prints as far as the Temperance Hall, and as Jack Griffiths was already the prime suspect, questions were asked about him there.

William Ward and Fred Sutcliffe volunteered the information that they had seen Jack come into the Temperance Hall at about 9.20 the previous evening. He had entered, washed his hands and gone straight into the billiard room.

Hyde was already aware that two women, Mrs Morris and Mrs Leech, had seen Griffiths with a girl at around 8.30, but they hadn't known who the girl was because she had been wearing a thick shawl over her head.

Mark Sanders, another witness, said he had seen a couple on the corner of Moss Hey Street and Greenfield Lane at about 8.45. They were engaged in a heated argument and his attention had been held when he saw the man take hold of the woman's shoulder and heard her cry out in protest. Then the two of them had walked purposefully off in the direction in which Kate's body was later found.

On being questioned at his home, Griffiths at first denied his meeting with Kate, but when they told him about the three witnesses he said he'd bumped into her when he was on his way to the Temperance Hall. According to his account, they had exchanged a few words, then parted on friendly terms. He had gone on cheerfully to the Hall, although he could not adequately explain how it had taken him nearly an hour to get there.

Griffiths was taken to Shaw police station for further questioning, and there his clogs were examined to see if they fitted the prints found near the body. They were indeed similar. Not only was the metal stud on the first clog broken just as in the prints, but adhering to the stud were traces of ultramarine, some of which had been found on the prints.

Examining his clothes, police discovered bloodstains on

both his shirt and the cuffs of his coat.

From Griffiths's pockets, investigators fished a small bundle of love letters sent by the dead girl. There was also a photograph of her and a wire brooch forming the name Kate. The police also found a long piece of string. Could it have been the murder weapon? They were certain that it was.

Griffiths was arrested and formally charged with the murder of Kate Garrity. He was remanded in jail to await trial.

Meanwhile, in Middleton Street, the Garrity household was deep in mourning. Robert Garrity seemed unable to get the image of his dead daughter out of his mind and woke up constantly with terrible nightmares. His wife was equally disturbed. She and Kate had always been very close and the idea that her daughter was now dead took some time to sink in. It was at the funeral that Mrs Garrity began sobbing. She had been inconsolable ever since.

She had no doubts that Jack Griffiths was her daughter's killer, but she was unable to take comfort in his arrest. That same morning a letter had arrived on her doorstep. Sent from someone in Ashford, Kent, it cruelly suggested that the police had got the wrong man. The writer expressed regret that "my old pal, Jack Griffiths" was being charged with a crime of which he was innocent and then went into detail as to what had actually occurred. The mystery writer claimed that he had committed the murder after quarrelling with the girl. It was signed S.H.B., though Mrs Griffiths had no idea who that might be.

Understandably, this letter caused Mrs Griffiths considerable distress. Friends and relatives rallied round and told the distraught woman to dismiss it as nothing more than an evil prank. Mrs Griffiths tried to do so and to a certain extent she succeeded. But, at the back of her mind the seeds of doubt had been planted.

Jack Griffiths's trial began on February 6th, 1906, at Manchester Assizes, before Mr Justice Grantham. Griffiths maintained his innocence and pleaded not guilty.

Catherine Garrity, Kate's mother, in a state of near-collapse, told the court that her daughter had been bright, lively and healthy, and that she had left the house on the night of her murder perfectly well and happy. In fact she had been singing. Mrs Garrity then went on to tell about the extraordinary letter she had received on the day of the prisoner's arrest. There was a hushed silence as the missive was read out.

Under different circumstances that letter might have saved Griffiths's neck. It certainly made the jurors think twice about the young man who stood in the dock. But as they listened to more witnesses and the weight of all the other evidence and testimonies began to mount, its impact became negligible.

William Turner, a man who worked with the accused at Lyon Mill, told the court that he had asked him about Kate on the morning after the murder. Griffiths, he said, had slumped over a machine and began sobbing.

"He said that he'd better go home but I advised him against it as everyone would be staring at him and following him about."

Young John Bardsley told the court about the many messages he had been paid to deliver to Kate from Griffiths and particularly about the one threatening to "do for her before Christmas."

Deborah Blackley, who had worked alongside Kate at the mill, said she well remembered Griffiths hanging around the workplace a few days before Kate's murder, and hearing him threaten Kate that he would "do for her."

Many other witnesses also testified to the stormy nature of Kate's relationship with Jack Griffiths and of Griffiths' readiness to use violence.

Although much of the evidence was only circumstantial, it was enough to convince the jury, who took only five minutes to find Griffiths guilty of murder. As the death sentence was passed, he stoically remarked, "I have but once to die." Other than those words, he betrayed no emotion before being led away.

A campaign for Griffiths's reprieve was started immediately by J. H. Butterworth, the Manchester solicitor who represented the defence. Butterworth made much of the anonymous letter to Kate's mother, particularly the passage which read: "I did not know what to do with the body so I covered it up with sacks."

Butterworth inferred from this that the murderer probably intended to hide the body in Nalls's factory, the building adjoining the place where Kate's body had been found. He had probably tried to force open the door, but had been unable to do so owing to a big bar behind it. Instead, therefore, he had covered the corpse with sacks.

Butterworth also thought, quite rightly, that the strange letter raised an element of doubt, and one which he felt should be resolved. It never was, however, and the identity of the sender remains a mystery to this day.

Meanwhile, Griffiths was in Strangeways Prison, Manchester, and there, during a visit by his parents, and in the presence of the Governor, he swore again that he had not committed the murder.

"I am innocent, as innocent as can be," he told them. However, on February 15th, he wrote to his mother:

"My dear Mother,
I am sorry to tell you it was me that murdered my dear Katie. I hope that you will keep that photo of Katie's for my sake, and you will go and see Mrs Garrity and tell her from me how sorry I am for what I have done. Whatever got into me to do it, I cannot say."

Despite his confession, sympathy for Griffiths was still very great and encouraged by this, the Reverend Pinniger, Vicar of Shaw, and Mr Morris, the Secretary of the Shaw Temperance Society, began a public petition to reprieve him on the grounds of his youth, and also, "our belief that owing to bad home influences and degrading surroundings he had not as good a chance as ourselves."

Ten thousand signatures were obtained.

Meanwhile, Butterworth still continued to do what he could to save Griffiths's neck, and claimed that his client had told him that he had not used string to strangle Kate. The new version was that during a violent quarrel, Kate had turned to go, so, in a moment's temper, Griffiths grabbed the neckband of her dress and dragged her to where her body was eventually found. A medical expert agreed with Butterworth that this action could have caused strangulation. Under these circumstances, Butterworth argued, Griffiths would be guilty only of manslaughter.

Because Griffiths had now confessed to strangling Kate, however, the Home Secretary refused to allow the new evidence.

Butterworth doggedly refused to be beaten, and asked the Bishop of Manchester to intervene. The Bishop agreed, and wrote to the Home Secretary pointing out that the murder had not been premeditated and that according to the medical evidence, it had not taken more than 32 seconds to produce death. But the Home Office stood firm, stating: "There is no change in the decision."

Jack Griffiths was hanged on February 27th, 1906, in the morning. Pierrepoint was the executioner. The newspapers reported that although it rained continuously, this did not deter the crowd of several hundred strong from gathering outside the prison gates.

While in prison, Griffiths wrote a last letter to his mother, gravely urging her to send his brothers and sisters to Sunday School so that they would not end up like him. He assured her that he was cheerful, even going as far as to describe his stay in prison as "the happiest I have ever been in all my life."

Griffiths almost seemed to welcome his approaching death, writing: "I hope that we shall meet in the next world, and I hope that when I leave this world for the next I shall meet my loving Katie. I will ask her to forgive me, and I hope that she will."

8

MANCHESTER'S ONE-EYED MONSTER

A prowler was about. Riding a bicycle, he was making lewd suggestions to young children. When Constance Inman was found dead it was naturally assumed that the cyclist was to blame.

In the early evening of September 22nd, 1931, ten-year-old Olga Roberts was playing alone in front of her home at 73 Victoria Road in the Victoria Park district of Manchester. At 6.30 she saw her friend, nine-year-old Constance Inman, who lived just opposite at number 56. She came running out of the entry at the back of her house.

Constance was crying and seemed very distressed. But it probably wasn't as serious as it seemed. Being a slight and delicate child, Connie was prone to "upsets" and tears were not unusual. Olga shouted across to her and asked what was the matter, but all Connie would say as she ran off towards nearby Dickenson Road was that she was going to play with some other children and couldn't stop.

Lonely though she was playing by herself, Olga did not follow her friend. She was under strict orders to stay in her front garden. There had been talk of a prowler in the neighbourhood, a man on a bicycle who had been accosting children. He had spoken to two little girls in Raincliff Avenue, and because of what he had said to them they had become hysterical.

Fearing what might happen if he found a child alone, most parents were not allowing their children to wander too far from home. Olga knew Connie would "cop it" when her mother found out she had run off somewhere. And it didn't take long for that to happen.

A short while later Mrs Lillian Inman came to her front

door and called for her daughter. Connie was nowhere to be seen. Looking worried, Mrs Inman approached Olga, who was still playing in front of her house, and asked her if she knew where Connie had gone. The child told her she had last seen Connie running in the direction of Dickenson Road.

Mrs Inman then asked her if she knew anything about a man who had promised Connie some cigarette cards. Another friend of her daughter's had mentioned something about a man who had said he would give her some cards if she met him that evening. But Olga knew nothing about it.

Mrs Inman stayed outside for a little while, looking anxiously up and down the road. But Connie was nowhere in sight. By 7 o'clock she had still not returned and her father, Mr Christopher Inman, began searching the streets for her.

At 7.15 Mrs Eva Radford, an elderly widow lady who occupied a ground floor flat in a large Victorian house at 97 Dickenson Road in the neighbouring district of Rusholme, heard a knock on her door. Opening it, she found Mr Price outside. Thin, balding and in his early thirties, he rented the attic room in the house.

After apologising for disturbing her, he asked if she would tell the caretakers, Mr and Mrs Broadhurst – who also had a flat on the ground floor – to leave the back door unbolted for him as he intended to be late in that night. "I am going to the second house at the Ardwick Empire," he explained.

"Why do you ask that?" said Mrs Radford in surprise. It had been the arrangement since Price first took the attic room the previous December that the back door would always be left for him to bolt when he came in.

"Well," said Price, "they might lock it tonight."

Mrs Radford couldn't think why tonight should be any different to any other, but she didn't argue. "All right, I'll tell them," she promised.

Mrs Radford put Price's confusion down to his being rather simple-minded. As she watched him go out she wondered why he didn't have any girlfriends. Why was he always on his own? It wasn't natural for a man of his age. True, he had lost an eye in an accident, but he was not altogether unattractive.

At 8.55 p.m., having searched everywhere for his daughter, Mr Inman went to Claremont Road police station to report her missing. The police immediately issued a description of the girl to all the patrolling officers in the area. He hoped that the child was only playing a prank and would soon turn up.

"Children are always running off for one reason or another, but we soon find them," the desk-sergeant told the anxious father. Mr Inman, however, was not reassured. Tired though he was, he would not go home and leave the search for his daughter to the police. Together with his brother and some neighbours, he continued to tramp the streets, peering into every garden, shed and outhouse – anywhere a child might hide.

At 11.15 p.m. Mrs Anna Broadhurst, the wife of the caretaker at 97 Dickenson Road, was sitting with her servant, Miss Rose Powell, in the kitchen of their ground-floor flat. Suddenly they were disturbed by a noise at the bottom of the stairs which led from the back door to Price's attic room. It sounded as if someone had stumbled. As they listened they then heard a light thud, followed by the sound of something being dragged along the passage towards the back door.

The two women were convinced it was a burglar. Being alone in the house – Mr Broadhurst was at the pub – they were too afraid to go out into the passage to see what was going on.

But when the noises ceased, they crept into a bedroom which overlooked the road and stared out of the window, knowing that if there were a burglar he would have to go down the passage which ran along the side of the house in order to get into Dickenson Road. And when he did they would see him. The women watched for several minutes, but nobody emerged.

Then they heard the back door being bolted, followed by the sound of steps on the stairs leading to Price's attic room. They supposed that the burglar, or whoever it was, had run off on hearing Price returning from his evening out. Oddly, however, neither woman had heard Price go down the passage at the side of the house – which was the only way to reach the back door.

At 7.15 the next morning Mrs Radford went to the front door as usual to collect her mail. She was startled to see Price in the passage with a broom, vigorously sweeping. As he was unemployed, he rarely got up before noon, and often he wasn't seen until three o'clock in the afternoon. Although cleaning the passage and the stairs leading to it was his responsibility, his day for this chore was Saturday, and this was Wednesday.

Looking up from his task, he remarked casually: "I'm just doing a bit of sweeping down." Later, as Mrs Radford was coming up from the cellar, he told her: "It was a very good show at the Empire last night."

At 8.20 a.m. Jane Birkett, a maid at 42 Park Range, was opening the study window which overlooked the disused and largely overgrown garden of 97 Dickenson Road when she saw what she at first took to be a large doll lying at the bottom of the garden. Then she realised that it was a young girl. Leaning out of the window as far as she could, she called out: "Little girl, are you hurt?"

Receiving no reply, she hurried downstairs, screaming as she went. "There's a girl's body outside!" she cried to her employer Mrs Warnes.

At first Mrs Warnes thought her maid was simply hysterical and just tried to calm her. But when Jane repeated that she had just seen a child lying unconscious outside the house, her employer told her to investigate.

Jane Birkett rushed into the kitchen, grabbed a step-ladder and climbed over the fence which divided the two gardens.

Kneeling beside the body, she touched the child's hand. It was ice-cold. The maid hurried back to the house and telephoned for the police. They arrived a few minutes later.

They found the little girl, who was dead, lying on her back with her knees half-raised and her head inclined to the right. She was dressed in a jersey and blue blazer and had been wearing a necklace of blue and white glass beads which was now broken. From the position of the body it was assumed at first that she had fallen off the fence while playing. But red marks around her neck and a large ball of froth at her mouth indicated that she had been strangled.

Her knickers had been removed, which suggested a sexual motive for the murder, but none of her other clothing had been disturbed. The police quickly concluded that she had been killed elsewhere. Her body had then been carried to this isolated spot, probably under cover of darkness.

As the description of Constance Inman matched that of the dead child, the police went immediately to tell Mr and Mrs Inman of the discovery. Connie's mother almost collapsed with shock and it was left to her husband to go to Ancoats Hospital, where he confirmed that the body was that of his daughter.

Mrs Critchlow, whose house in Conyngham Road was only a few yards from where Connie had been found, told the police that just after midnight she had heard a cry. "I was having a bath," she said, "when I heard a scream. I thought it was my ten-year-old son who was sleeping in the bedroom next to the bathroom. He often shouts out in his sleep. After my bath I called in his room, but found him all right."

It was also at midnight that several dogs in the district had started barking. One man, who went outside to calm his pet, believed he heard some sort of "commotion" at the spot where Connie's body was later found. But he took no notice of it and went back to bed.

Had Connie become the victim of "the man on the bicycle"? Mrs Brandon, a neighbour of the Inmans, told the police that she had often seen a middle-aged man riding a scruffy bike along Victoria Road. "The man I have in mind," she said, "is middle-aged, he rides a dirty bicycle and is well-clothed."

Mrs Brandon went on to say that the mysterious cycling stranger had recently spoken to her son as he was going out on an errand and had tried to entice him away.

"He said to my son, 'Hello, sonny, where are you going? Come with me.' But the boy told him that I'd break his back if he went with strangers. Then he ran home to tell me. I rushed out into the street, and when the man saw me he jumped on his bicycle and pedalled away furiously. I didn't mention it to the police at the time because I wasn't sure I could identify the man if I saw him again."

Miss Clerk, the headmistress of Birchfields Road School where Connie had been a pupil, remembered her as an intelligent, if somewhat nervous child. She did not think that Connie would go away willingly with a stranger. She told the police that Connie had left the school the previous afternoon with her brother and two sisters. It was during that walk home that she had told a school friend that she was going to meet a man who had promised her some cigarette cards.

The headmistress also spoke of the man on a bicycle. She recalled that one child from the school – who had been accosted by the stranger – had been so upset that arrangements had been made for her parents to come to school each day to take her home.

News of the death and the mysterious cyclist soon spread through the city and, in next to no time, the finger of suspicion was being pointed at all sorts of individuals. The middle-aged man of whom Mrs Brandon spoke was not apprehended but many other bicycle riders were. Anxious parents were quick to detain almost anyone riding a bicycle and quiz them about their movements. Many innocent men were approached that day.

In the meantime, however, the police were following a more carefully reasoned line of inquiry. They carried on questioning everyone who had been in the neighbourhood of 42 Park Range the previous evening. In due course they visited 73 Dickenson Road. This was the home of Mr Broadhurst's parents.

When the police knocked on the door Mr Broadhurst's father was busily discussing the recent murder with his son and daughter-in-law, who had come to see him from number 97. Mr Price, the attic lodger, was also there, and so was Miss Powell.

Even before the police had arrived it was a strange scene. Price had arrived about ten minutes before, at 1.30, and seemed nervous and somewhat confused.

"Have you heard the news?" asked Mrs Broadhurst excitedly as he came in.

"Yes," he said, "I know all about it."

Looking at him suspiciously, Mrs Broadhurst went on: "We" – indicating Miss Powell – "heard something being dragged along the hall to the back door last night."

Price looked scared, as Mrs Broadhurst would later recall.

"Was that before I came in?" he asked.

"Yes, about ten minutes before you came in," Mrs Broadhurst replied.

Price looked down miserably and said: "The police will take me."

The words were hardly out of his mouth when the door was rapped. Inspector Edwards and Sergeant John Blenkharn were outside.

The policemen questioned everyone in the house, but particularly Price. He seemed decidedly uneasy and immediately aroused their suspicions. They became all the more suspicious when the man revealed that his name was actually an alias. His name wasn't Price. It was George Alfred Rice. Originally from Bolton, he had come to Manchester 18 months before and had worked in a hotel until he had lost his job because of the Depression.

So what were his movements yesterday night, the evening of September 22nd?

"I left Dickenson Road at 6.35 p.m.," he said, "and went to the corner of Wilmslow Road and stayed there until seven o'clock. I then went to Adams, the barbers, for cigarettes. I returned to Dickenson Road and told Mrs Radford that I would be late as I was going to the Ardwick Empire, and I asked her to tell Jack Broadhurst to leave the back door open.

"I took a tram to Brunswick Street and then walked to the picture house next to the Empire and asked an attendant when the next show would be on. He told me I would have to wait because it was two houses. I waited and eventually went to the second show. When I came out I walked along Brunswick Street and got up to Upper Brook Street, and then took a tram and went home to bed.

"I did not see anyone round the back of the house. About three o'clock I heard a noise. I did not know what it was."

Rice produced two used tram tickets and a portion of a cinema ticket in an attempt to back up his story. But it was not possible for him to prove that the tram tickets were his. He could easily have picked them up off the street. And the cinema ticket was of no use at all. Far from being for a show on September 22nd it was more than six months old.

Taken to Cavendish Road police station, Rice was put in a police cell, where he almost immediately went to sleep. At 4.30 the next morning he was woken. Yawning, he told Sergeant Blenkharn: "Give me a cup of tea and I will tell you all about it."

George Rice then made the following confession: "I met a little girl in Dickenson Road at about 6.30 p.m. Tuesday night. I took her down the passageway near my house where I live and took her behind the garage. I was cuddling her but did nothing wrong to her. I must have hit her on the head or something. I do not know what happened, but she collapsed at my feet. I spoke to her, but could get no answer, so I left her on the ground and went into my house and told Mrs Radford to tell Jack Broadhurst to keep the back door open for me.

"I then left and went to the second house of the pictures next door to the Ardwick Empire. After the show I returned to Dickenson Road. I went behind the garage where I had left the girl. When I touched her I found she was going cold and appeared to be dead. I picked her up in my arms and carried her to the bottom of the garden and laid her gently where she was found. I then went to bed. I can't tell you any more."

Later he added: "When I first took the girl behind the garage I went dull," probably meaning that his brain had become even more fuddled than usual and he couldn't remember exactly what happened. Then he broke down and wept.

When Sergeant Blenkharn formally charged him with Connie's murder, Rice said, "That means that I did it on purpose?"

"Yes," replied Blenkharn.

"I couldn't have done it," Rice moaned miserably.

At his trial, which opened at Manchester Assizes on December 14th, 1931, George Rice pleaded not guilty.

Although the police had initially assumed that Constance Inman had been strangled, Dr Arnold Renshaw – who had carried out the post-mortem examination – now told the court that he believed Connie's death had not been due to strangulation but to extreme pressure on her chest which had closed her lungs, driving out all the air. She had literally been squeezed to death.

He was certain the red marks around her neck had not been caused by finger-nails – the marks were too small and closely set and were in the wrong position and direction. They had been caused by pressure from the glass beads of the necklace Connie had worn when they were forced against her skin either by her assailant's hand or by being caught on her jersey if it was held at the back. The doctor said that neither the necklace nor a large bruise on Connie's head had in any way contributed to her death.

Although at the inquest Renshaw had stated he could find no definite evidence of sexual assault, he now thought it likely that Connie had been raped, probably while she was dying. The ball of froth seen at her mouth, which was a sign of asphyxia, had been caused by someone having carried her in a doubled-up position.

Mrs Eva Radford told the court about Rice's curious behaviour on the evening of Constance Inman's disappearance. At 5.30 a hawker had called at the house. She had just seen him off and was closing the door when Rice came running down the stairs and asked, "Is that someone for me?" When she told him it wasn't, he seemed disappointed. "I was expecting a man to see me about a job," he'd explained. She thought this peculiar because in the entire ten months that he had lived there he had not once had been known to have a visitor. The prosecution made it clear that they thought the caller he was expecting that afternoon was Connie Inman, coming for her promised cigarette cards.

At 6.30 the following morning Mrs Radford had heard noises coming from Rice's attic room as if he were shifting the furniture about. She had wondered what he was doing, as he was rarely up before noon.

Mrs Broadhurst described the strange noises she and Miss Powell had heard late on the evening of Constance Inman's disappearance, and how scared Rice had looked when she had mentioned this to him the following day. Going into the witness box Rice denied that he had "interfered" with Constance Inman in any way, or that he held her so tightly as to crush her. He claimed that he had seen her standing near the garden and had merely put his hand on her shoulder, when she collapsed. Afterwards, he went to see a film, which he had enjoyed. Finding the child still lying on the ground when he returned home, he became frightened and carried her to the bottom of the garden.

Rice said he had asked Mrs Radford to tell the caretakers to leave the back door unbolted for him because he had been locked out of the house on previous evenings. His explanation for sweeping the stairs and passageway on Wednesday morning was that it had been raining the previous Saturday and he had been asked not to sweep.

He then alleged that he had been woken very early on the morning after his arrest by Sergeant Blenkharn waving a piece of paper in his face, saying: "Come along, wake up, sign this." He claimed the police had prepared the statement beforehand and made him sign it.

Mr E. G. Hemmerde KC, defending, criticised Sergeant Blenkharn for taking a statement from Rice at 4.30 a.m. when he was barely awake. But Blenkharn maintained that Rice had been wide awake and knew exactly what he was saying.

Mr Hemmerde then asked Blenkharn if he thought Rice was of low mentality. "I should not consider him very bright," said the policeman. The defence counsel then observed that it was strange that although Rice did not speak grammatically, the confession he had supposedly made to the police was grammatically correct. Blenkharn insisted that the statement contained Rice's own words. He denied Rice's claim that he had been forced to make a statement which had in fact been prepared by the police.

Mr I. C. Jackson KC, MP, summing up for the prosecution, said that the noises heard by Mrs Broadhurst and Miss Powell during the evening of Constance Inman's disappearance could have been made by Rice taking the dead child from his attic to dispose of her in the garden. If this were so, his sweeping the next morning would be an attempt to get rid of any marks which might have been left on the staircase or in the passageway where he had dragged Connie along.

The prosecutor argued that what Rice had meant when he told the police he was cuddling the girl was that he was raping her. Although Rice might not have meant to kill Connie, Mr Jackson concluded, what he had done to her had led to her death and it was therefore murder

Mr Hemmerde , summing up for the defence, told the jury that they could acquit Rice. They could find him guilty or rape, or of attempted rape, which would mean it was murder. Or they could convict him of the lesser offence of indecent assault, which would entail a verdict of manslaughter. "You may ask why should you concern yourself whether his intentions were to rape the girl or not. The difference is this," Mr Hemmerde continued. "One means death and the other does not."

Arguing that Connie's death had been accidental, and that the proper verdict for the jury to reach was therefore manslaughter, Hemmerde warned the jury: "You want to be particularly careful not to let your horror of this ghastly business, this fearful tragedy, blind you to the fact that even people of the lowest mentality have a right to be dealt with according to the law."

Summing up, Mr Justice Finlay commented on Rice's evidence in the witness box. "You must have been struck by the utter heartlessness of the story," he told the jury. "You may probably think it is a false story, for it does not account for the facts which we know."

After 40 minutes the jury returned to ask if it would be considered murder if Rice had been attempting rape, without completing the act, and the child died. The judge answered "Yes, it would be murder." At this point Rice collapsed and was taken to the cells below. The jury again retired, but after an absence of only five minutes, they returned.

Rice, now back in court with his collar loosened and his face deathly pale, anxiously clutched the rail of the dock. When a verdict of guilty was given he gripped the rail even more tightly, moaning pitifully. By the time the death sentence had been pronounced, he was in a state of complete collapse. He began to sob silently. Unable to move, he had to be carried from the dock to the cells below.

Rice was hanged at Strangeways Prison on February 3rd, 1932. On the night prior to his execution he was visited by his mother, two aunts and an uncle. As they said their final tearful goodbyes, Rice promised them that he would meet his fate like a man. But when Pierrepoint, the executioner, entered his cell, Rice broke down completely and had to be half-carried to the scaffold.

The press had dubbed him the "one-eyed monster" and there was no petition on his behalf for clemency.

But was he justly convicted? Should he instead have

been found guilty of manslaughter?

Dr Renshaw only *thought* Connie had been raped. He wasn't sure. At the trial he stated that the child's death had been due to asphyxia caused by extreme pressure on the chest. He had dismissed the possibility that the necklace which had marked her throat could have been involved in her death.

Writing about asphyxia some years later, however, the noted pathologist Dr Keith Simpson came to the conclusion that it can be caused by many different factors. One is vagal reflex which can occur from light, momentary neck compression, bringing about death within seconds. Such compression was not necessarily applied with deliberate intent by the assailant, and it therefore constituted manslaughter rather than murder.

And the man on the bicycle? The police never found him. And Rice could hardly have been this cyclist who terrorised the children of Victoria Park. He had no bicycle.

9

THE KILLING OF BETTY MARTIN

William Martin always said his daughter would come to a miserable end. In the early hours of a July morning in 1925 his prediction came true.

Pretty and with a lively sense of humour, Beatrice Philomena Martin – or "Betty" as she was widely known – was a very popular young lady. Many men adored her, and she in turn liked them... particularly sailors.

Salford docks was not far from where the 23-year-old lived with her parents in Wingfield Street, Gorse Hill, Stretford, and it was here where Betty was seen most often, flitting in and out of the pubs along the Trafford Road and flirting with every man in sight.

She shouldn't have been there of course. Trafford Road had an awful reputation. Known locally as the Barbary Coast, it was the haunt of all sorts of rogues and criminals. Avoided by all respectable people it was the sort of place where even the policemen walked in pairs. And not without reason. During the day drunken brawls were commonplace and, at night, fights with knives and cudgels, razors and chains were far from rare. And, as if this were not enough, there was also the sleaze.

Trafford Road was famed for its prostitutes. Many bore exotic names and even more offered exotic specialities. Whatever perverse fantasies a visiting sailor might have nurtured, a Trafford Road prostitute could be found to oblige him. And it would not have taken a long search. Afraid of neither the police nor the law, the prostitutes dressed like film stars, in picture hats and fox tails, and sauntered up and down the road with brazen relish. Competition was harsh, however, and they had to work hard at their trade. It was often joked that the Trafford Road prostitutes knew the sailing times of the ships better than many a shipping clerk.

Betty Martin knew the sailing times too, though perhaps her reasons were more innocent. Betty was no prostitute but she loved to meet the new sailors and hear their tales of adventure in faraway places. She was also very fond of the spending money they brought with them. She didn't charge for her favours directly, but whoever spent the evening with Betty would always end up with his wallet considerably lighter.

Both her parents were worried by what they called her "antics". In 1925 a girl needed to look after her reputation if she was to stand any chance of making a good marriage. The way Betty was going, all her chances were slipping away. But she liked her men friends too much to want to change. In any case, Betty reasoned, her reputation was lost a long time ago. Why bother to try and redeem it now? Mr Martin was exasperated by his daughter's behaviour. He constantly battled with her to change her ways and warned her that she would come to a miserable end if she did not. But Betty paid him no heed. She enjoyed the life she led, she said, and had no desire to be reformed.

Betty insisted that it was all just innocent fun and she wasn't doing anyone any harm. But her behaviour did have its costs. Not least, her lifestyle made it impossible for her to hold down a job. Her parents tried to find her a job, but her employment never lasted long. Eventually they gave up and, instead, it was decided that Betty would stay at home to do the housework and mind her five-year-old sister whilst her mother went out to work.

It was an easy life for her, or so it seemed. Most of the neighbours regarded Betty with disdain. She appeared to be nothing but a selfish good-time girl, who cared only for fun and wouldn't think twice about dumping a man when he no longer had money to spend on her. But it wasn't always like that. Betty had also known pain and heartache.

In 1924 she had fallen in love with an American sailor and a special marriage licence had been obtained. Betty Martin prepared herself to become a wife. But alas, just before the wedding was due to take place in Patricroft, her fiancé's ship had sailed from Salford docks and he had sailed with it. Betty never saw him again.

The young woman took this desertion badly and experienced a period of deep depression. For a while nothing could console her. But then she began to return to her old ways. Indeed, now Betty was even more wild than before, drinking, laughing and flirting all through the night and often not returning home until the early hours of the morning. It could be said that it was her American lover that brought Betty to ruin.

In the months that followed, Betty made many new friends. She also reacquainted herself with lovers from her past. One of these was 28-year-old Sam Johnson, who had first met Betty in 1923 in a pub in Trafford Road. Unusually for her, he was not a sailor but a labourer working on the nearby Trafford Park Industrial Estate. But he seemed to have money to spend and was willing to spend it on Betty.

He found her attractive, not only because of her sultry good looks, but also because she was fun to be with. And having just separated from his wife, he needed cheering up. For the past year they were no more than friends but now, with both of them suffering the pains of a failed relationship, their affair deepened. Betty even took the unusual step of inviting Sam back to her parents' home. He was to be the only man out of the many she had known, including her American fiancé, ever to enjoy this privilege.

Sam was outgoing and friendly and Mr and Mrs Martin took to him immediately. They tried to encourage his romance with their daughter and hoped it would lead to better things. They both knew that Sam had a wife, but such was their desperation that they still felt it was better that their wayward daughter should have just one regular boyfriend rather than many casual ones. That he was a

Margaret "Bill" Allen murdered Mrs Nancy Chadwick.
She was, she said, in "one of her funny moods."

WOMAN TO BE HANGED

The Home Secretary announced yesterday that in the cases of Margaret Allen, who was sentenced to death at Manchester on December 8, and George Semini, who was sentenced to death at Stafford on November 30, there are no sufficient grounds to justify him in recommending any interference in the due course of the law.

Margaret Allen, 41, a spinster, of Bacup Road, Rawtenstall, Lancashire, murdered her neighbour, Mrs Nancy Ellen Chadwick, aged

The Woman Called Bill

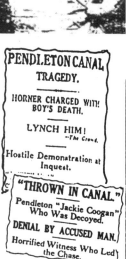

"LYNCH HIM!" CRY BY CROWD AT INQUEST.

RUSH AT PRISONER.

Police Save Man Accused of Killing Boy.

FATHER'S ANGRY OUTBURST

Grief-Stricken Mother Also in Painful Scene.

CROWD'S ANGER.

How Boy Was Lured to His Fate.

Horner has now paid the penalty for a vile crime which aroused the keenest indignation of the public and revived in an acute form the question of the safety of children ...

PENDLETON CANAL TRAGEDY.

HORNER CHARGED WITH BOY'S DEATH.

LYNCH HIM!
—The Crowd.

Hostile Demonstration at Inquest.

"THROWN IN CANAL."

Pendleton "Jackie Coogan" Who Was Decoyed.

DENIAL BY ACCUSED MAN.

Horrified Witness Who Led the Chase.

Richard Horner with his wife and daughter at the door of their shop at 15 Lissadel Street. The date is 1915, nine years before his son murdered five-year-old Norman Pinchen (above).

The Murder of Little Norman Pinchen

BRUTAL MURDER IN SALFORD.

AN OLD WOMAN'S HEAD BATTERED IN.

DESPERATE STRUGGLE WITH THE ALLEGED MURDERER.

On Saturday evening, about seven o'clock, the inhabitants of London-street, Trafford-road, were

Victor Emmanuel Hamer beat elderly Mrs Tyrer's head to a bloody pulp. He blamed it on the drink.

The Killing of Catherine Tyrer

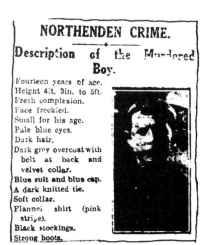

NORTHENDEN CRIME.

Description of the Murdered Boy.

Fourteen years of age.
Height 4ft. 9in. to 5ft.
Fresh complexion.
Face freckled.
Small for his age.
Pale blue eyes.
Dark hair.
Dark grey overcoat with belt at back and velvet collar.
Blue suit and blue cap.
A dark knitted tie.
Soft collar.
Flannel shirt (pink stripe).
Black stockings.
Strong boots.

Fourteen-year-old Percy Sharpe was murdered in the woods near Northenden Station (below). A platelayer saw blood bubbling from the boy's chest as he stumbled along the footpath.

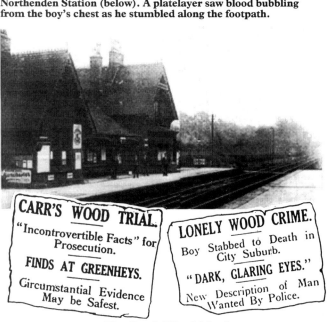

CARR'S WOOD TRIAL.

"Incontrovertible Facts" for Prosecution.

FINDS AT GREENHEYS.

Circumstantial Evidence May be Safest.

LONELY WOOD CRIME.

Boy Stabbed to Death in City Suburb.

"DARK, GLARING EYES."

New Description of Man Wanted By Police.

The Carr's Wood Murder

Despite his eagerness to get into the witness box, Francis Booker (above) was at a loss to explain away any of the evidence against him. Eventually he was found guilty and hanged for the murder of Percy Sharpe.

PRISONER'S BEARD

Said to Have Grown After Murder Discovery.

FINDS IN GREENHOUSE.

Newspapers Referring to the Crime.

TROUSERS HIDDEN IN CELLAR.

Dramatic disclosures were made by the prosecution to-day when Francis Wilson Booker (28), of Greenheys, appeared on remand at Manchester City Police Court charged with murdering the fourteen-year-old

I DID NOT—MURDER PERCY SHARPE!

Booker's Emphatic No to the Accusation.

CONTENTS OF A PARCEL.

Opened It Two Months After the Crime.

Mr. Saul on Coincidences in the Case.

BOOKER'S STORY.

Where He Found Articles Identified as Sharpe's.

OPENED THE PARCEL.
Forgot the Existence of It!

The Carr's Wood Murder

A photograph of 93-97 Dickenson Road, Rusholme, Manchester taken just before demolition in 1955. No. 97 is on the far right. It was here in the attic flat that George Rice lived. The corpse of little Constance Inman (inset) was found in the overgrown back garden of the house.

Manchester's One-Eyed Monster

Two photographs of the overgrown back garden of 97 Dickenson Road, where the body of Constance was found.

The hangman James Berry performed a good number of Strangeways executions. He was often surprised by the calmness of those who were led to the gallows. Walter Wood, in particular, made a remarkable impression on him.

Walter and Emma

married man was something they could learn to live with.

For Betty, however, it was not so easy. A labourer with a wife to support was nowhere near as exciting as a sailor fresh from foreign parts with a wallet full of money. Moreover, though Sam was charming to her parents, in private he was becoming a bore. Being in love had made him a sombre and suspicious companion.

Sam was desperate to keep Betty. He even announced that he would divorce his wife so he could marry her. But it was no use. Betty, unable to be faithful to one man for very long, soon found someone else. In May, 1925 the S.S. *Iceland* had sailed into Salford docks. Betty had given Sam the slip for the evening, and, as was her custom, she had gone down to a pub on Trafford Road. It was there that she met a member of the S.S. *Iceland's* crew: Able-Seaman Jack Hunter. She was immediately smitten with the handsome 26-year-old seaman, who arranged to see her each time his ship was in dock.

It did not take long for Sam Johnson to get wind of the affair. Enraged, he stormed over to Betty's home and accused her of going out with men only for what she could get out of them – he had by now spent a great deal of money on her himself. Sam also warned her that no other man would stand between them. Many angry words were exchanged between the couple that evening and ended only after Sam had threatened to "do her in."

Mr Martin liked Sam, but he wasn't going to stand for threats being made against his daughter. He showed Sam Johnson the door and told him never to come to their house again. Sam, however, could not keep away. He began watching the house and following Betty whenever she went out. Even when he didn't follow her, Betty would often find him waiting on her doorstep when she got back. It was intolerable. Soon she was at breaking point. She wished Sam would just disappear.

On the afternoon of Sunday, July 26th, Sam arrived at the house while the Martins were having tea. Betty caught sight of him from the window and told her mother to say she had gone out. Mrs Martin opened the door and gave Sam the news but, seeing he had brought presents, including a jar of her daughter's favourite face-cream, she decided to ask him in. She took him through to the sitting room.

Betty, who was in the kitchen, was furious. She charged into the room, yelling at him for pestering her and not giving her a moment's peace. Sam, however, ignored her shouting and meekly offered her the presents he had brought. Betty was not impressed. Giving them a disdainful glance, she told him to keep them. She wanted neither them nor him and would be pleased if she never saw his ugly face again. Sam Johnson knew when he was beaten. He turned tail and quietly left the house.

Later that evening Betty set out to see Jack Hunter. They had arranged to meet on Trafford Road Bridge and all the way there Betty kept turning round in case Sam might be following her, but she couldn't see him among the men who now thronged the streets on their way to the pubs. She did see Jack, however. He was waiting at the bridge just as they had planned, and after a brief kiss the couple walked arm-in-arm down Trafford Road.

By now Betty was feeling free and easy, more like her usual self. But then, as the couple walked into a pub, her face fell. There, standing at the bar and glaring at them intently was Sam Johnson.

It was obviously no coincidence. Sam had shadowed them so many times that he could anticipate where they would go. Betty and Jack looked at each other and began to make a move for the door. But then, realising he would only follow them if they left, they decided to brazen it out.

Their hopes of having a quiet drink, however, were soon shattered when Sam began to harangue them from the bar. At first they tried to ignore him but then Betty began shouting back and the landlord warned them all that he would send for the police if so much as a glass got broken. Sam was not deterred. He continued to abuse the couple.

He made it clear that he wanted to fight Jack – and the winner would have Betty. Fearing he would lose his ship if he went to prison for fighting, Jack refused the challenge. He grabbed his cap, and marched outside. Betty, angry that her evening had been ruined, stayed on for a moment to tell Sam what she thought of him. Then she followed Jack outside, and the couple went to a café.

The couple stayed there for the remainder of the evening, with neither sight nor sound of Sam Johnson. But Betty was certain he was still close by and when the café closed she didn't want to go home in case he was waiting for her. Instead she and Jack decided to walk the streets.

Meanwhile, back at Wingfield Street, Mrs Martin had gone to the front door to put a penny in the gas meter when she heard a noise. Looking outside, she saw Sam Johnson standing in the garden. She asked him what he was doing, He said he was expecting Betty home in about five minutes and was waiting in the hope of having a few words with her before she came in.

At 1.45 a.m. Mrs Martin went to the front door again and found he was still waiting. She told him it was no use his staying as Betty would not return while he was there. Sam, however, refused to leave. In exasperation, Mrs Martin locked the front door and went upstairs. But, fearing there might be trouble when Betty eventually got home, she did not try to sleep. Instead, she sat fully clothed on the edge of the bed, but with the light off so as not to disturb her husband.

A little before 2 a.m. Mrs Martin heard an urgent knock on the front door. She hurried downstairs. Opening the door she found Betty shaking in fury and desperately trying to turn the handle. Close behind her stood Sam.

"You're not going to follow me in," she shouted at him angrily as she tried to push her way in.

Sam lunged at her and grabbed her by the arm. A violent struggle began. Betty fought to be free, but Sam would not let her go. Mrs Martin grasped her daughter and tried to pull her inside. But Sam jerked her back. Then something flashed in the moonlight. It was the blade of a knife and it was just inches away from Betty's neck.

"Murder! Police!" screamed the distraught mother as her daughter collapsed with a groan, blood pumping from her body. Jack Hunter was half-way down the street when he heard the screams. He ran back to find Betty sprawled across her doorstep, her mother weeping inconsolably as she cradled the girl's head in her lap. Betty, he quickly realised, was beyond help. Nearby, Sam Johnson, his hands covered in blood, looked on in silence as if what had just happened was as much a shock to him as it was to everyone else.

Jack was not surprised to see him there. Sam Johnson had been in the garden when he brought Betty home. Betty had gone up to him and they had exchanged a few words. Jack was standing too far away to hear what was being said but Betty returned to him later and said everything was alright. He had wanted to wait until Sam had left and Betty was safely in the house, but she'd assured him she would be all right, so he had gone. How bitterly he regretted that now.

"I'll go for the police," he said, glancing with hatred at Sam, who stood outside the house staring vacantly into space.

"No," said Sam, "I'll go for the police. I've done it." The killer then strode off down the road.

Jack hurried after him, suspecting he meant to make a getaway. But on reaching the corner of the street he saw Sam approach a passing policeman.

"I want to give myself up," he told the officer. "I have stabbed a woman."

A short while later the three men returned to the house. Mr Martin was downstairs now and doing his best to comfort Betty's distraught mother. But sympathy seemed to be beyond him. "She deserved, it you know," he told his poor wife. "She was a little vixen." Mr Martin then turned to the policeman and poured out his soul. It was a mad tirade of regret and resentment that came to a halt only when Sam Johnson himself began to speak.

"We had been the best of pals up to two months ago,"

the killer remarked to nobody in particular as he looked down at Betty's lifeless body. "Oh – here is the knife I did it with," he added, pointing to a weapon which lay in the garden. About nine inches long and resembling a sailor's cutlass, its blade was caked with blood.

Sam Johnson was then arrested.

The inquest into Betty's death was held at Stretford District Council Offices. Medical evidence was given that she had received seven stab wounds in her neck and chest. One had almost entirely severed the main artery from her heart, causing immediate death.

Mr William Martin, Betty's father, admitted that she had not led a "straight" life. "Her habits," he told the court, "have not been right. She has been going out with different men for the last six years – since the Armistice."

"I put it to you that you did not tell the police that you were sorry your daughter was dead," said the coroner, Mr R. Stuart Rodgers. "Were your words not rather blasphemous and you expressed no regret?"

Mr Martin hung his head. "I said it was a blessing she had gone," he admitted. The coroner, studying the police notes of the conversation, observed that the actual words Mr Martin had used were, in fact, far stronger. But he allowed Mr Martin his new version, the man's actual words would have been too obscene to repeat in court.

Wearing deepest black, Mrs Mary Martin told the court that she knew the kind of life Betty had been leading and had often tried to reason with her, but this had not made the slightest difference. The girl was completely out of hand. For two years she had kept very late hours, but recently she had improved. However, for the past few weeks she had begun staying out late again.

In tears, she said that Sam Johnson had been a regular visitor to her house until about two months ago when Betty had suddenly told her she had tired of him. She had known nothing of Jack Hunter until after her daughter's death.

Then, in a barely audible voice, Mrs Martin told how on

the night of the murder she had tried to get Betty away from Johnson and into the house.

"I grabbed hold of my daughter to drag her in," she told the court, "but she and Johnson were struggling. Johnson then struck her several times with a knife or dagger in the neck and back. He never spoke. My daughter collapsed. I saw some instrument in Johnson's hand. I screamed for the police."

She identified the knife found in her garden as the one she had seen in Johnson's hand. Summing up, the coroner told the jury: "Here was a comely-looking girl hardly out of her teens who had begun living a life which could only end in physical and moral disaster. A woman who led such a life wanted more and more excitement, and it took a great deal to satisfy her craving."

It was, he concluded, "one of those passionate cases. In Southern countries such tragedies are almost daily occurrences, but it is not so here."

The jury returned a verdict of wilful murder and Sam Johnson was remanded in custody for trial. As he listened to their decision Johnson told the court: "I should like the case to be dealt with as quickly as possible." He was then informed that his trial would take place at the next assizes in November.

In Strangeways Prison whilst awaiting trial Johnson made it known that in preparation for his expected execution he wished to be confirmed into the Church of England. The chaplain got in touch with the Bishop of Manchester, who visited the prison a short time later to officiate at Johnson's confirmation.

On November 23rd, 1925 Johnson appeared at Manchester Assizes before Mr Justice Wright. It was to be one of the quickest trials on record. Johnson, wishing to die, made sure of that. To hasten the proceedings, he refused the services of a defence counsel. A reporter noted that Johnson entered the dock "almost at a run and stood close to the front of the bars as though regarding the trial as a mere formality which he was eager to see ended."

After Johnson had pleaded guilty to murdering Beatrice Philomena Martin, the judge asked him if he was defended by counsel.

"No," replied Johnson. "I don't want anyone to defend me. I refuse to be defended."

The judge frowned.

"Have you seriously considered the course which you are taking in pleading guilty?" he asked.

Johnson nodded.

"Yes, sir, I have considered it."

"You realise what you are pleading guilty to is..."

"Yes, sir," interrupted Johnson.

"Is of killing this woman," continued the judge speaking with deliberate slowness, "and intentionally with such purpose."

"Yes, sir," said Johnson.

"You realise," the judge went on, looking at him severely, "that, pleading guilty, the sentence which the law imposes upon you is not in any way affected?"

"Yes, sir," said Johnson, "I realise."

The judge sighed. "Very well," he said, signalling to the Clerk of Arraigns who then addressed Johnson: "You stand convicted of murder on your own confession. Have you anything to say why the court should not give you judgement of death according to law?"

Johnson, slipping his hands into the pockets of the heavy overcoat he wore, replied in a clear, steady voice: "No, sir."

As Mr Justice Wright donned the black cap and pronounced the sentence of death, Johnson seemed visibly relieved at having at last heard what he wanted to hear. As he quickly left the dock he paused to wave to a sobbing woman at the back of the court, whose identity was never made known. She was so overcome by the gesture that she fainted and had to be carried from the room.

The counsel who was to have prosecuted left the court without having got to his feet once during the entire proceedings. He could now say that he had attended one of the shortest trials in British criminal history. From the moment that Johnson entered the dock to the passing of the death sentence just four minutes had elapsed. This was also the first time a person had pleaded guilty in a murder trial in Manchester for 30 years.

There was no appeal against the sentence, but although Johnson seemed unconcerned about his imminent death, he was most upset about a photograph taken of him in court and later published in newspapers. It showed a coarse-featured, brutish-looking man who appeared quite capable of stabbing a woman to death on her own doorstep.

Johnson, who considered himself quite handsome, was deeply offended. To right the situation he had a photograph taken of himself while in Strangeways wearing his prison uniform.

Sam Johnson was hanged at exactly 8 a.m. on December 15th, 1925. The new photograph appeared in the newspapers that same day.

Just before he was executed Johnson wrote a long letter to his family:

Well, dear father and mother, as you know, when you receive this letter I shall have passed from this world and I am quite prepared for the next world. Remember that later on we shall all meet in the next world, which, as we all know, is far happier than this one... it makes me feel very happy to know that I am going to the land where my dear Betty has gone, for I am quite sure that she is happy where she is, and I know I shall be just as happy and that is how I want you to look at it, mother.

My one desire is that you will have no ill feelings against my friend Betty. Please remember that she has suffered through me, and I shall say this, there was no cause for it to be done.

10
PIGOTT

Florence died immediately when the bullet smashed into her skull. But the pistol had been fired out of love, not loathing.

It was a warm, sultry afternoon in August, 1876, when 17-year-old Florence Galloway first met 28-year-old George Pigott. She was a domestic servant in a Manchester suburb, and he was the driver of the tram she caught when making visits to her mother in Lawn Street, Lower Broughton, Salford. George found her bright innocence immediately attractive, while Florence was flattered by the attentions of an older man.

Soon they were meeting for walks in the park, and on her half-day visiting variety theatres in Manchester. As the romance flourished Florence expected George to propose. But though he often, and passionately, told her he loved her he never spoke of marriage.

Then one day he broke the news to her that he was giving up his job with the Manchester Carriage Company and going to try his luck in Birmingham, where he had friends. "But ... but what about us?" asked Florence, panic-stricken at the thought of having to part from him.

"But of course I want you to come with me," said George, taking her gently in his arms.

Florence was delighted. "Oh, wait till I tell Mother I'm going to be married," she cried, throwing her arms joyfully around his neck.

It was then that George explained, rather awkwardly, that he couldn't afford a wedding just at the moment.

However, as soon as he'd got a job in Birmingham and they'd found somewhere to live they would, of course, be married. If she had had any sense Florence would have been immediately suspicious at this suggestion. But what woman in love can ever be accused of having sense? She was far from happy with George's plan but she took him at his word.

Mrs Elizabeth Galloway, Florence's mother, was understandably appalled when she found out what her daughter intended doing.

"No decent girl could ever expect to hold her head up again if she did that," she warned. But the more her mother argued against it, the more determined Florence became to do what George wanted. One morning, without a word to either her employers or her mother, she packed her bags, and with Pigott at her side boarded a train for Birmingham. The girl was full of joy and hope. The future beckoned bright.

Seeing someone occasionally, however, is very different from living with them day in, day out, as Florence soon discovered. They had hardly set up home together before the strain of the new relationship changed George from the polite, attentive boy friend Florence had grown to love into a moody, difficult and often violent "husband", who preferred to spend most of his evenings drinking in the pub with his mates.

When George did eventually come home, usually the worse for drink, arguments would begin which often ended with Florence getting a beating. He had also become very possessive and would often, and for no apparent reason, accuse her of "loose behaviour", threatening to take her life if he ever found her with another man. At first a bewildered and unhappy Florence bore his ill-will with as much understanding and patience as she could, hoping that matters would improve. But they never did, and nor did the sound of wedding bells appear any closer. In fact, though George now had a good job as a tram driver and they had a comfortable home, he never even mentioned marriage now and she was too frightened of his moods to anger him by doing so herself.

After they had been living together for more than a year, something happened which changed the situation: Florence discovered she was pregnant. She didn't want her baby to carry the stigma of illegitimacy and was determined to be married to George before the child was born. So, when George came home from work that evening he found a nicer meal than usual waiting for him, as well as a glass of his favourite beer. He soon discovered why, when Florence broke the "good news" to him about the baby.

To her surprise and unease, George said nothing but just sat there, staring into space. "We must be married now," Florence went on anxiously, "you see that, don't you?"

George stared past her at the wall for some time. Then, in a cold, flat voice he said: "We can't, lass. You see, I'm... I'm already wed."

George Pigott explained that not only had he a wife but also three children who were at that moment living, unsupported by him, in the Ardwick district of Manchester. They were the reason he had wanted to leave Manchester so quickly, and why he could never marry Florence.

He began to sob, and taking her in his arms he pleaded with her not to allow this to change things between them. After all, he argued, he still loved her, nothing would ever change that, and he knew she loved him. To placate him, Florence pretended that all was still well between them. But, from the look in her eyes, it was clear that it was not.

The following morning, as soon as George had gone to work, she packed her things and pawning what few valuables she had, bought a train ticket for Manchester. Her mother, who had not heard from her daughter for 15 months, was delighted when she turned up on her doorstep and, pregnant or not, vowed that she would look after her.

When Pigott returned home from work and found Florence had gone he immediately went to Manchester in search of her. But when he knocked on the door of No. 20 Lawn Street it was not Florence but Mrs Galloway who opened it to him.

"Go back home to your wife and children," she shouted, angrily slamming the door in his face. Pigott then began a long, cold vigil, devoting all his waking hours to standing shivering on the corner of Lawn Street, waiting for Florence to come out so that he might speak to her.

On the evening of November 24th, Mrs Galloway, having eluded Pigott by slipping out through the back door, had taken Florence on a visit to see her closest friend, Mrs Hannah Wilson, who owned a draper's shop in nearby Lower Broughton Road. At about 7.30 p.m., as the three women sat in the kitchen talking and drinking tea, Mrs Galloway's son, who was minding the shop, suddenly rushed in and said, "Mother, you're wanted."

Going to the door which led from the kitchen into the shop, Mrs Galloway and Florence were astonished to see Pigott standing there. He leapt forward and, grasping hold of Florence by the arm, began pleading with her to come back and live with him again.

Mrs Galloway shouted at him to go away and, pulling her daughter after her, she hurriedly left the shop. But Pigott refused to be shaken off and, still gripping Florence's arm, he accompanied the two women down the road. Seeing she could not get rid of him, Mrs Galloway became so distressed that she fainted.

Pigott, at Florence's request, helped to carry her mother to the house of a friend who lived nearby. But when he tried to follow them into the house his way was blocked and he was asked to leave. Days passed, and neither Mrs Galloway nor Florence saw Pigott, although he continued to send letters to the house – letters which Mrs Galloway, recognising his handwriting, did not pass on to her daughter.

It was 5.30 p.m. on December 5th when a knock came at Mrs Galloway's door. She opened it cautiously and found a small, grubby-looking boy standing there holding out a letter. She took it and seeing it was addressed to herself asked the child if a reply was wanted. "No reply," cried the boy, who then ran off down the street.

Opening the letter, Mrs Galloway was surprised to find it was from her friend, Mrs Wilson. It read: "Mrs Wilson will be glad if Mrs Galloway and her daughter will come down about 7.00 p.m. this evening over some work" (Mrs Galloway and Florence both now earned their living by doing "plain sewing" for local drapers' shops).

At first Florence said she was too tired and didn't want to go, but after reading the letter she suddenly changed her mind. "Oh, we must go now, Mother," she said as she handed it back to her. At 6.30 p.m. the two women left the house together, Mrs Galloway glancing anxiously down the street just in case "he" might be about. But the road seemed deserted.

As they reached the corner of the street, however, Pigott suddenly stepped out in front of them. Despite her shock, Mrs Galloway was the first to speak. "You bad man," she scolded, "what do you want here? Go away."

"I want a word with you," replied Pigott.

"Well, I don't want anything to say to you, go away, go away to your poor wife and children," she cried, doing her best to pass him, but he refused to step aside.

"I only want to reason with you. You know how she is and I want to do something for her," Pigott added, with a glance at Florence.

"Well, I don't want to reason with you at all. Go about your business," shouted Mrs Galloway, her voice rising to a scream.

At this, Florence turned to her mother and said softly, "Hush, Mother, don't put yourself out, listen to what he has to say."

"Will you take charge of her?" asked Pigott, still refusing to allow the two women to pass. "Yes," replied Mrs Galloway defiantly, "every charge."

Pigott now looked at Florence. "Then you won't let me do anything for you?" he asked gently.

"No, no," said Mrs Galloway, putting both her arms round her daughter in case he might force her to go with him, or the girl herself might be persuaded into going.

At this Pigott raised his right hand close to Florence's head and said, "Take that."

A shocked Mrs Galloway heard a report and saw the flash of a pistol. She felt her daughter go limp in her arms and saw she was covered in blood. "Murder!" she screamed as Pigott turned and fled. "Murder!"

The next moment the street was alive with people who helped carry the girl back into her house.

Superintendent John Cole was one of the first policemen on the scene. It was not thought likely that Florence would survive the night, so he took her statement in which she identified George Pigott as the man who had shot her.

Two days later, however, Florence was still alive. Pigott was arrested and taken to Mrs Galloway's house to be formally identified by her daughter. When Cole and two other policemen escorting Pigott entered her bedroom they found Florence fully conscious and able to identify her attacker.

Meanwhile, a large crowd had assembled around Mrs Galloway's door. When Pigott emerged, they booed and jeered.

In that Lawn Street house Florence lingered on in agony for more than three weeks, eventually dying on December 31st.

The inquest was held at the Royal Archer Inn, Lower Broughton. A verdict of wilful murder was returned against Pigott.

George Pigott was tried at Manchester Assizes in January, 1878 where he entered a plea of not guilty.

It was a gruesome trial. George Pinder, the surgeon called to Florence's home when she was shot, appeared to relish shocking the court with his account of what he found. Not content with merely stating that she had been shot in the head he went into excruciating detail about the injury. He described how, through a splintered hole in Florence's skull her brain protruded to such an extent that when she vomited, which she did soon after the doctor's arrival, she forced a teaspoonful of "matter" through the wound. But despite the appalling injury her mind remained "tolerably clear".

After her death he had performed a post-mortem and discovered that her skull had been fractured behind the left ear by a projectile very similar to a pistol bullet. Evidence that the bullet had then entered the brain was confirmed by his finding what he at first thought was a piece of black felt (from Florence's hat), but which he afterwards discovered to be brown paper, blackened with gunpowder.

A ten-year-old boy described how Pigott had paid him a penny to deliver a letter to Mrs Galloway, and she – dressed in black and fighting hard to hold back her tears – told the court that, never having received a letter from Mrs Wilson before, she did not know her friend's handwriting. Asked how Pigott knew about her friendship with Mrs Wilson, she speculated that her daughter must have told him about it while they were living together. She then went on in a trembling voice to describe her daughter's shooting. Under cross-examination by the defence she recalled that although Pigott did not seem excited and did not appear to have been drinking on the evening of the murder, he did seem strange.

Peter Unsworth, a Salford barber, testified that Pigott had come into his shop in Chapel Street on the evening of November 5th, with part of his moustache on the right side of his face burnt away. There was also some blood on his face. Seating himself in a chair, he had instructed Unsworth to shave off the rest of his moustache and also his beard. After paying, Pigott had asked the way to Bolton – the town in which he was later arrested.

Counsel for the defence claimed there was no motive for murder as George had loved Florence and wanted her to come and live with him. So why should he murder her? It was the hostile intervention of Mrs Galloway which had driven Pigott to write the supposed letter from Mrs Wilson, in order to communicate with Florence. The girl still loved Pigott and had wished to see him again, the defence lawyer claimed, suggesting that Florence had in fact known Pigott had written the "Mrs Wilson" letter, having recognised his handwriting, which explained why she had suddenly changed her mind about going to see her mother's friend "as she greedily grasped at the opportunity of having an interview with her lover."

Pigott, his counsel continued, had only sent the letter in order to speak to the two women and he had no intention of hurting them. He had only fired the pistol to frighten Mrs Galloway into allowing Florence to go with him. He had no intention of killing anyone except, perhaps, himself. It was the sudden excitement on the part of the two women that had diverted his aim. It was an accidental shooting and not murder.

Summing up, the judge said that even if Pigott had meant to take his own life, but had taken another's in carrying through this act, he was still guilty of murder. Likewise, if he had meant to murder Mrs Galloway but had shot Florence instead, he was, in the eyes of the law, still guilty of murder. And if he simply intended to do himself an injury, or to frighten someone and death had ensued, it would be at least manslaughter. Only if it had been a complete accident would there be no case to answer. But it was clear that it was no accident. From the evidence it seemed probable that Pigott had meant to do some violence.

After an absence of twenty minutes, the jury found Pigott guilty of murder and he was sentenced to death. When the verdict was announced he covered his face with his handkerchief and began sobbing bitterly. And when the judge came to the phrase ". . . and that you hang by the neck until you be dead," Pigott fainted.

Awaiting execution at Strangeways Prison, he told his wife and parents that he was making no effort to obtain a reprieve and that he was resigned to his fate.

George Pigott was hanged on February 4th, 1878.

"Lord Jesus receive my soul!" were the last words he cried out on the scaffold as the white cap was placed over his face. Among his last written words were those in a letter to Florence's mother, penned a few days before his execution: ". . . I did not murder your daughter out of feelings of revenge but because I loved her."

11

THE BOTTLE KILLER

Isabella Cross was slain by having her head smashed in with a glass bottle. Her nine-year-old niece discovered the corpse.

Skipping happily to her Auntie Bella's sweet shop in Hulme Hall Lane, Miles Platting, Manchester, nine-year-old Stephanie Howard was surprised when she didn't find her aunt waiting to greet her. The child stood around for a moment and then peeped behind the counter. Then she saw her.

Stephanie's aunt, Mrs Isabella Cross, the shop's 57-year-old proprietor, was lying on the floor, her blue overall pulled over her head.

Running to the home of her married sister a few streets away, Stephanie burst in, crying: "Auntie Bella's dying!"

Her sister hurried to the sweet shop, accompanied by a friend. Stephanie had not exaggerated. Isabella Cross was dead. Stephanie had discovered the body at 4.30 p.m. on May 4th, 1962.

By 4.45 p.m., police were at the scene. They found that Mrs Cross had been battered to death, her attacker beating her about the head with five fizzy drink bottles. Fragments of glass from the bottles were strewn over the floor.

Neighbours soon suggested a motive. Mrs Cross and her husband were known to have tickets for the Cup Final. It was common knowledge that the couple planned to go to London the next day to see their team, Burnley, play at Wembley. Consequently, Isabella's mother, who lived with the couple, had gone to stay with another daughter. Perhaps the killer had known of the mother's absence, and had therefore chosen that particular day for the attack. Well, it was a theory, but Mr Cross, summoned home from his work at the Royal Ordnance factory in Patricroft, soon quashed it. He told detectives that he had the Cup Final tickets safely in his jacket pocket.

But there was still plenty of evidence that the attacker had been a robber, albeit of a more conventional kind. All the cash had been taken from the shop's open till, and a few coins were scattered on the floor. Open, bloodstained drawers were found in the living-room behind the shop. An unsuccessful attempt had been made to force the locked drawers of a desk, and the killer had apparently left by the back door, which bore traces of blood, as did the back yard gate.

Two days before the murder, Isabella's husband had been redecorating. On the edge of a recently painted door police found three fingerprints. They were not those of Mr Cross, Isabella, her mother or any friend they could trace. It was likely they belonged to the killer.

Shortly after the incident, detectives thought they had the whole case sewn up. They noticed a man loitering near the Crosses' back yard. Fragments of glass were embedded in the soles of his shoes. Taken to police headquarters, the man immediately admitted killing Isabella. Had it not been for the fingerprints, he might have been arrested. But the prints did not match and the man was swiftly eliminated from the investigation. He was a crank, police decided, and had just been seeking notoriety for a crime he hadn't committed.

Three weeks passed before detectives got the lead they needed. Officers in Edinburgh produced a match for the fingerprints found on Isabella's living-room door. The prints were those of James Smith, a 26-year-old former Edinburgh man with a criminal record. On moving to Manchester, he had found work as a rubber moulder in Failsworth.

Police mounted a watch on his home in Corfe Street,

Beswick, while other inquiries established that Smith was in the process of moving house and had already sold some of his furniture.

His shift at the firm of Ferguson Shiers on May 4th had finished at 12 noon, and one of his colleagues told detectives that he had accompanied Smith to a local pub that lunch-time. After having a drink, the workmate had left Smith at about 2.45 p.m. They usually caught a bus home together, and Smith would alight at the junction of Oldham Road and Hulme Hall Lane, near Isabella's shop. Two days after the murder, Smith had called at his workmate's home. His colleague had noticed a piece of sticking plaster on Smith's right hand. Smith said that he had cut himself on a spike in his back yard. Possibly, thought the detectives. On the other hand, maybe not.

At 8 a.m. on May 6th, the police knocked on Smith's door. It was opened by a tall, slim man who stared hard at the two officers.

"Yes," he admitted, "I am James Smith."

Inside the house the suspect was joined by his wife, their baby and two step-children.

"Do you know the sweet shop in Hulme Hall Lane?" asked one of the detectives.

Smith said he did.

"Did you walk past the shop on May 4th?"

"Yes, I walked past the shop on my way home that day, but I never entered the premises," Smith replied.

Arrested and charged with the murder of Isabella Cross, he said: "I had been drinking at a pub near my work until four p.m., then I went straight home. At four-thirty an insurance collector called at my house, so I paid him and he left."

The insurance agent confirmed that he had called at the house that day, but he said he arrived at 4.45 p.m. and he could not remember whether Smith was there or not. Police had established that Mrs Cross had been murdered between 4.20 p.m., when a cigarette delivery was made at the shop, and 4.30 p.m. when her body was discovered.

Smith could have committed the crime, with enough time to complete the 12-minute walk home before the insurance man arrived.

Asked how his fingerprints had come to be on Mrs Cross's living room door, Smith remained silent.

Searching his home, police went to work on his settee with a vacuum cleaner. As dust was sucked up from the side of one of the cushions, a tiny fragment of glass was collected. It was rushed to the forensic science laboratory near Preston for examination.

That settee was up for sale together with Smith's other furniture. Had it already been sold, what turned out to be a vital piece of evidence might have been lost for ever.

The four-day trial of James Smith began at Liverpool Crown Court on October 14th, 1962. He pleaded not guilty, but the jury preferred to believe the evidence of the fingerprints and that tell-tale fragment of glass.

In his summing-up the judge paid tribute to the work of the forensic team involved in the case More than 200 man-hours had been spent on painstakingly gluing together the pieces of those shattered fizzy drink bottles which had been the murder weapons. It had been time well spent. Convicted and sentenced to death, Smith assured his wife that he would not hang. His appearance, however, belied his show of confidence. His 6ft 2in frame shrank visibly as the weeks passed, and his brown hair turned white.

At 8 a.m. on November 28th, 1962, James Smith was executed at Strangeways Prison, two years before capital punishment was abolished.

12

HOLDEN

Rejected by his family and feeling all alone in the world, Joseph Holden's mind became obsessed with thoughts of vengeance and murder. "'Appen," he declared, as he gazed on the body of the grandson he had slain.

They say a poor man's riches are his children, but sadly for Joseph Holden this was not the case.

Always a man who liked his drink, the 57-year-old iron turner from Bury, Lancashire, had taken to it pretty badly after his wife had died. Soon he was good for nothing. He lost his job in the mill, and in next to no time he lost his home as well.

With neither home or job Holden looked to his eleven children for help, but they were now all respectably married and wanted nothing to do with their cantankerous, drunken father. Passing the time of day with him was all they could manage, and even that was a strain. As a result, Holden was forced to find what food and shelter he could within the grim walls of the local parish workhouse. It was not an arrangement he cared for.

"Eleven children, and no one who'll have owt to do with me. But I'll show 'em, I'll show 'em all," he'd mutter angrily to himself as he made his lonely way around Bury. Already in Joe's drink-sodden brain, strange, dark thoughts of revenge against his family were taking sinister shape.

In fact, things were not as black as Holden painted them. His children had not abandoned him entirely. His daughters called on him often and frequently they helped with gifts and money. But they had their own lives to lead and their own families to attend to. They couldn't give him the attention he wanted. In Holden's eyes this was unforgivable.

In August, 1900, one of his daughters, Mrs Dawes, arranged for Holden to come and live with her. But even this gave him no cause for comfort because it was only a temporary measure. It would last for as long as Mr Dawes was away in America, but not for one moment longer. As Mrs Dawes explained to her father that he would have to go back to the workhouse when her husband returned, Holden bristled. Even as he installed himself in her home at 18 Nuttall Street, Bury his mood did not improve.

Poor Joe still felt hard done by, and he was not shy in letting his daughter know his feelings. In the weeks that followed many bitter words were exchanged between father and daughter and the atmosphere in the Dawes's home grew increasingly tense. It was perhaps to his daughter's credit that she did not put a stop to it there and then. But Joe Holden didn't see it that way. Every day he would harangue her with insults and abuse, cursing her as often as he cursed all his other offspring. Whenever he left the house, she would breathe a sigh of relief. She'd cheerfully give him money for ale or tobacco just to see him go.

One warm afternoon shortly after he had arrived, Joe left his daughter's house saying he was going for a walk. He planned to visit another of his daughters, Mrs Eldred, who lived close by. As it turned out, however, she was not at home. But her little boy was. Nine-year-old George was playing outside in the street. He was all on his own, but seemed to be well occupied, and Joe stood for a while just watching him. Then a smile came to the old man's lips.

Joe Holden strode over to his grandson and asked the lad if he would care to come up to Birtle quarry with him. "I'll give you a pair of pigeons if you'll keep me company," he said.

The boy quickly agreed and the two set off together.

An hour and a half later, George returned home. But he was no longer the happy, smiling little boy who had been skipping down the street at his grandfather's side just a short time before. Now he was staggering along the cobbles and there was blood trickling down his neck from a wound to his head.

His horrified parents immediately hurried round for Dr France, the family's physician who, on seeing George, had grave doubts that he would live. But the child held on to life and in a feeble, faltering voice managed to tell his parents what had happened.

He described how Granddad Joe had come looking for his mother and on not finding her in, got chatting to him. As they both seemed at a loose end Joe had suggested going up to Birtle quarry.

George hadn't fancied such a long walk, but when Joe said he would buy him a couple of pigeons if he came with him, George agreed and they went on their way.

When they arrived at the quarry, an isolated, lonely place, Joe asked George to sit down on a stone and, handing the boy a knife, asked him to cut some tobacco for him. The boy gladly obeyed and busied himself with the task. In the middle of working, however, the lad looked up and was astonished to see his grandfather holding a stone as big as a football. Before George could dodge out of the way, Joe had thrown the stone and it had hit him hard on the head.

"Granddad, thee did that a'purpose," the boy screamed as tears of pain and bewilderment streamed down his young face.

Joe made no reply. He just stood there staring down at the lad. Then, taking out a handkerchief from his pocket he wrapped it quickly around the boy's head, and leading him to the road put him on a tram back to Bury.

Hearing this, Mrs Eldred put on her shawl and hurried round to Nuttall Street to confront her father. She didn't really know what to expect, but she was certainly surprised by what she found. Joe Holden was sitting in the kitchen calmly eating his tea. He seemed quite untroubled by what had happened.

He admitted that the boy had been hurt whilst they were

out together but vehemently denied it had been deliberate. "It were an accident," he told her angrily. "The blasted stone just slipped from me hands, that's all it were."

Incredibly enough, even though Dr France had stated quite firmly that her son had been hit with something which had been "thrown with some force", she took her father at his word. She refused to believe that he could have really meant to harm the boy. She cast her eyes to the heavens and returned to her home.

The next few days were an anxious time for the Eldred household. George's life hung precariously in the balance. Dr France called round regularly to check on the boy's progress and tend to his wounds. But it wasn't until a week had passed that he showed any optimism for the boy's recovery. The Eldreds did not inform the police, however. They managed to convince themselves it had been an accident and they didn't want to cause any fuss. If only they had done so, however, the tragedy that followed might have been averted.

It was a few weeks later, on the afternoon of September 5th, that Joseph Holden left his daughter's house in Nuttall Street once more. Things were now worse than they had been before and the two were hardly speaking to each other. Holden's mood was blacker than it had ever been and Mrs Dawes had to fight hard to control her anger.

Joe, as was now usual, slammed the door behind him as he stormed out of the house and marched off down the road as if he was ready to kill someone. And, indeed, he was. Twisted thoughts of revenge and hatred were now dominating his thoughts. He could think of little else.

Going round the corner to St Thomas's Day School, Holden collected nine-year-old John Dawes, telling his teacher that he was needed to go on an errand for his mother. The teacher watched them go. It seemed innocent enough. But John Dawes was never seen alive again.

At about 11 o'clock that evening Sergeant Arrowsmith was beginning his night-duty at Radcliffe police station. A short man with strange parchment-coloured skin came wandering in. Removing his cap, he calmly informed Arrowsmith that he had murdered his own grandson. He said he had come to give himself up.

Identifying himself as Joseph Holden he went on to make a complete statement as to what he had done and how he had killed the little boy.

"I took him to a disused quarry partly filled with water at Limefield. I picked the lad up by the scruff of the neck and the breeches and threw him down the quarry. I went to him and he seemed to be bleeding from the back of his head. Then I took him into the water. I wandered around for a bit. Then I decided I'd best come and give myself up."

The following morning a thorough search was made and John Dawes's battered body was found at the bottom of the quarry. He had evidently survived the initial fall of 40 feet, and had landed on some large stones. But then his body had been heaved into the water, where he had drowned. His cap and one of his clogs were found 20 feet away.

Joseph Holden showed no remorse for his crime nor did he stop feeling resentful of his family for their uncaring treatment of him. When Mrs Dawes, the dead boy's mother, identified Holden to magistrates and declared that he was indeed her father, the old man, swinging his cap idly, merely threw out the single ejaculation: "'Appen." The grief-stricken woman almost collapsed.

Holden remained unrepentant right up until his trial at Manchester Assizes, and even in the courtroom he expressed no remorse. Instead he used every opportunity to blame his children, saying it was their callous treatment of him which had led him to murder. More than once the judge had to order him to keep silent and not berate his family.

Understandably, the court refused to accept Holden's circumstances or the lack of care shown to him by his children as a mitigating circumstance for his crime. Indeed, they could find no reason for leniency at all. In delivering their verdict of guilty on the charge of wilful murder, not one member of the jury suggested any grounds for compassion.

There was the sound of muted cheers in the court as Holden received the sentence of death. The prisoner himself merely sneered as the judge declared that he would be hanged at Strangeways Prison, Manchester, on December 4th.

At first light on that fateful morning, despite the dull, rainy weather, the footpath in Southall Street opposite the prison wall was lined with people standing three or four feet deep waiting for the black flag to be raised that would signal that the execution had taken place.

Just before eight o'clock, James Billington, the executioner, entered the condemned cell and Joseph Holden was quickly pinioned. He made no protest. He was then led to his death.

Watched by representatives of the clergy and the prison authorities, and with a firm step, Holden mounted the scaffold, standing upright while the rope was adjusted around his neck, and the white cap fitted on his head.

At precisely eight o'clock – indeed, as the clock was still striking – Billington drew the lever, the drop fell and Holden was expertly dispatched into the next world. Two minutes later, the black flag was hoisted and the crowd outside slowly dispersed home.

Holden's body remained hanging for one hour before it was taken from the pit and placed in the mortuary. The prison doctor, Dr John Edwards certified that death had been due to the dislocation of the vertebrae and strangulation.

Ironically, though Holden had insisted that his children had shown a callous disregard for his well-being before the murder, after it and during his trial and imprisonment he could make no such claim. They went out of their way to help and comfort him. All of them, except Mrs Dawes, the dead boy's mother, visited him each day while he awaited execution. Furthermore, they did everything they could to get him a reprieve. Mrs Eldred even took her son, George – still bandaged and weak after the brutal attack on him –

to the prison and the papers of the day reported that the child spent, "a half-hour chatting happily to his grandfather in his death cell."

Joseph Holden thus died as he never would have thought possible – in the bosom of his family.

13

WALTER AND EMMA

*Walter Wood threatened to kill his wife unless she
returned to him. She didn't believe him, to her
cost.*

It was in 1886 that 35-year-old Walter Wood made the fatal
acquaintance of 29-year-old Mrs Emma Ford. He had been
hired to install machinery at Chesham Fold Mill in Bury,
Lancashire, where Mrs Ford was employed. He was immediately attracted to the buxom, cherry-cheeked widow and
was soon asking her if she would "walk out" with him. She
cheerfully agreed. One thing led to another and soon there
was talk of marriage.

Wood, himself a widower, had two sons – Walter junior
aged 10 and Reuben aged six – for whom he was anxious to
provide a mother. But there was another reason for his
interest in Emma. Her late husband, James Parkinson, had
left her not only a quantity of good household furniture, but
also a tidy sum of money in The Bury Co-operative Society.

For her part, Emma was not averse to remarrying as she
too was struggling to bring up a child alone. Her daughter,
Ellen, aged 10, was illegitimate, having been born before
her marriage to Parkinson. This was why she always
referred to herself by her maiden name, Ford, even after her
marriage.

Emma and Walter were married in October, 1886, and
Wood immediately found new employment in a mill at
Darwen, near Bolton. Twelve days later he had to leave his
job – due, it was later claimed, to his entanglement with
another woman. Thereafter he found no more work and
started to drink. He also began to abuse and ill-treat Emma

125

and accuse her of all sorts of indiscretions, infidelity in particular. He was certain that she was seeing another man.

In due course finances became so dire that they had to leave their home. Thus Woods, with his family in tow, moved to a new house in Brooklyn Street, Bolton.

While the furniture went on ahead in a van, the Woods, to save money, made their way to Bolton on foot. During the journey Wood was so out of temper that he began kicking and beating his wife. A lamp she was holding got smashed and she badly cut her hands. But Walter paid no attention. Instead he dealt her such a blow to the side of her head that she was sent reeling against a wall. Her screams soon roused people along the way and Wood was rebuked for his behaviour, but it did no good. And when little Ellen also joined in shouting at her stepfather to stop beating her mother, he turned on her too.

Life did not improve for the family after they moved to Bolton. Wood still could find no work and the family was forced to make do on the 10 shillings a week unemployment benefit he was entitled to claim from the Amalgamated Association of Engineers, of which he was a member.

In marrying him, Emma had hoped that she and her daughter would have a better standard of living. Instead, she found herself scraping by on less than she had before.

The couple quarrelled endlessly, matters coming to a head when Wood ordered his wife to hand over some of her Co-operative Society money. When she refused, saying that what little money she had she needed, he became enraged.

"If you don't give me the money," he shouted, "I will take your bloody life".

When she still refused he threatened to kill both her and her daughter and then burn down the house, though not before he had taken a hammer and smashed up every piece of her precious furniture. But Mrs Wood was not to be intimidated, especially by a man she no longer respected. She told him he could threaten all he wanted but she would not part with a penny. At that Wood stormed out of the house. Sinking into a chair, Emma decided it was time to leave her husband. She feared that sooner or later he would force the money out of her. Besides, she was tired of living on next to nothing and hoped that by going she might shock him into finding work. The following day, after Wood had left the house, Emma packed her things and went with her daughter to live with her parents at 35 Clarendon Street, Bury. Afterwards her brother, Fred Ford, returned with her to Bolton to remove her furniture, taking it for the time being to his own house in Henry Street.

Finding that both his wife and furniture had gone, Wood went to his brother-in-law's house and asked Fred if he could speak to Emma. He asked her to return to him, but she refused. "If you do not come to terms it will prove fatal," he warned her, but Emma didn't seem to take him seriously and laughed. "Oh, don't make light of it, Emma, for my sake; if you don't come to terms this night I will kill you," he said. Emma continued to smile.

During their separation Wood sent his wife two or three letters a week, begging her to return to him. As she could neither read nor write, her daughter Ellen would read these out to her and, if necessary, write a reply which her mother would dictate. Sometimes in his letters Wood claimed he had found work, but when Emma went to see him at his mother's house in Thynne Street, Bolton – where he and his two sons were now living – she always found this was not the case. Wood also frequently wrote asking her for money, but each time Emma refused him.

On the morning of February 17th, Walter Wood rose early, full of optimism that this was the day he would succeed in getting his wife back. With this in view he set out armed with a glowing reference he had managed to obtain from a former employer, and headed for a mill at Guide Bridge, near Ashton-under-Lyne. The reference duly impressed the mill foreman, who immediately hired Wood as mule overlooker. Jubilant, Wood headed home to Bolton. His mood soon changed, however, when he read the strange letter he found waiting for him.

Walter Wood,
You will have to excuse me for not writing sooner, as I could not.
Some nice news I got when I did come home. Jim is about to put
you to further trouble to make you prove your words and I hope
he will. For if he does not I will. Jim has been to my mother's
several times trying to see me, but he has not seen me yet. I shall
be very glad if you will come over and show me the woman who
has been the cause of all the scandal, and take her before her
betters to make her prove her words. I have no need to come to
Bolton again as the woman lives in Bury. I shall be glad if you
will come over and bring the woman with you and if you don't
come over I shall have to come to 73, Thynne Street, Bolton. No
more at present,

Emma Wood

This letter would have been unintelligible to most people. But to Walter Wood it made perfect sense. Emma was
teasing him, and teasing him very cruelly. It referred to
Wood's accusation, which Emma always denied, that she
was seeing another man. But now Emma was giving him a
name: Jim. Wood was certain that if he didn't act quickly,
Emma would be off with her "new man". He immediately
ran to catch the train to Bury.

Once he had arrived Wood found a lad who agreed to
deliver a letter to Emma's parents in Clarendon Street.
Ellen read it for her mother when it arrived:

The person you call Walter Wood is waiting to see you beside the
Washington Inn, Walmersley Road. Come at once as I have a
good place of work and I have no time to wait.

Walter Wood

"There is more trouble coming again," sighed Emma.
"But I will go and see what he wants." She told a friend:
"I'll bet he's come to settle this matter about Jim... I will
prove my innocence if it costs me £5 [the cost of sending

a solicitor's letter to Wood to prevent him spreading more unfounded rumours about her and Jim]. But I will clear myself whatever the consequences." With that she put on her shawl and went off to Walmersley Road to meet her estranged husband.

At 2 p.m. Emma arrived back at her parents' house to change into her best clothes. She had Wood with her.

Both her father and mother begged her not to go with him, but Emma wouldn't listen. The couple set off towards Huntley Brook for a walk in the countryside.

A farmer they passed on the way noted how silent they were and what a strange look Wood had on his face.

It was 3.45 p.m., and Mrs Jane Kay was in her cottage at Huntley Brook, when she heard someone scream: "Murder! Murder! Murder!"

Through her window she saw a woman running down the lane. Blood was pouring down the front of her dress. Mrs Kay went outside and asked: "What's to do?"

"My husband has cut my throat! My husband has cut my throat!" repeated the woman, her eyes wild with fear as she desperately clutched the wound in an attempt to stem the flow.

Mrs Kay led her to the dairy nearby, calling out to the farmer's son to fetch a doctor. Emma collapsed on the dairy floor.

Meanwhile, the farmer's son had located Dr Kerr on nearby Rochdale Old Road and sent him hurrying up to the farm. He arrived a few minutes later and on examining Emma was horrified to discover that her throat had been practically slit from ear to ear. He was amazed that the woman could still speak.

"Please help me," she implored. "My husband did it."

"I will do all I can," Dr Kerr assured her. But though he tried to stop the haemorrhage she died about two minutes later.

Police called to the farm searched the area for Wood, but he had vanished. Hearing of the murder, crowds besieged the farm to stare at the bloodstained floor of the dairy and view the body, which had now been carried into the farmhouse. So many people gathered that policemen had to be put on duty to keep them away.

Meanwhile Ellen Ford was coming out of St Paul's churchyard after attending a funeral, when a lad she knew ran up and told her that someone had cut a woman's throat at Huntley Brook Farm. Ellen ran off at once to the farm, fearing that it might be someone she knew. When she got there a man in the crowd outside the farmhouse lifted her up to a window. Looking through she was horrified to see her mother lying dead inside.

At first it was thought that Wood might have drowned himself, and part of the River Roach, nearby, was dragged by the police, who also kept a watch on his mother's house in Bolton. But they found nothing.

At 8.10 p.m. on February 19th, two days after the murder, Mrs Wood heard a knock on her back door. At the time her two young grandsons and two of her neighbours were in the house, keeping her company. Lighting a candle she went into the yard and opening the privy door, she saw a shadow move.

"Mother, it's only me," said Wood, cautiously coming out into the light.

Hurrying back into the house, Mrs Wood excitedly told the others, "My God, it's our Walter." A few moments later he followed her in. But as Walter junior rushed to hug his father the younger boy, Reuben, was so terrified that he began to scream hysterically.

"What's wrong?" asked Wood. "You know I never hurt you." But the child continued to cower behind his grandma's apron.

"Mother, can I have some dry things?" Wood asked quickly. "Where have you been?" asked the old lady, noticing that he was dripping wet from head to foot.

"I've been lain down at the bottom of a pit," he said. "They'd never have find me there for six months."

His mother told him that upstairs he could find some old flannels and shirts belonging to his brother. Throwing off his wet outer clothes, he rushed upstairs. Alas, almost immediately there was a loud knock at the front door and Sergeant Miller and Police Constable Worrall, who had been watching the house, entered. Creeping as quietly as he could up the stairway, Miller surprised Wood as he was washing himself in the front bedroom.

"Walter Wood," he said. "You are wanted at the police station."

At Bolton Town Hall Police Station, Wood lamented: "Oh, I wish I had never gone to Bury. If I had not gone to Bury, this would never have happened. She was the worst-tempered woman in the world. I wish I had never seen her."

At 10.20 that evening Wood was handed over to Bury police, who took him there by cab, arriving shortly after midnight.

"Notwithstanding the lateness of the hour," reported the *Bury Times*, "there was a large crowd in front of the police station and when the cab drove up Wood was greeted with a storm of groans and yells, and an ugly rush was made for the cab amid cries of 'Let us get at him' ".

The cab door was pulled open and hands grabbed hold of Wood, who screamed in terror, as an attempt was made to pull him out. But the police managed to drive back the mob and regain control of the vehicle. The crowd was still so threatening that the cab had to be quickly driven into the yard of the Derby Hotel (next door to the police station). The yard gates were immediately closed, and Wood was then taken into the police station by the back door.

On May 9th, 1887, Walter Wood's trial opened at Manchester Assizes. Looking pale and haggard, he pleaded not guilty in a husky, but quavering voice. Only once did he break down and weep, and that was when Mr M'Keand was addressing the jury in his defence, telling them that although Wood had murdered his wife it was not a premeditated act. Emma Wood had, despite Wood's pleadings, refused to return to him and he, "lashed into a frenzy by her refusal...whipped out his pocket knife, but," argued M'Keand, "without any real intention in his mind of inflicting grievous bodily harm or murder." He hoped the jury would accept this and thus reduce the crime from murder to manslaughter.

Mr Justice Wills, however, would have none of it. He told the jury that if Wood meant to kill his wife at the time he cut her throat then he was guilty of murder and that was that. There must be proof of provocation to reduce the crime to manslaughter and in his opinion none was given in this case.

It took the jury only five minutes to convict Wood of murder and he was sentenced to death. As he left the dock a whistle was heard from the gallery and looking up, Wood kissed his hand to his brother, who shouted back in reply, "Goodbye, Walter."

Just as Bury had rallied to the memory of its daughter, Emma Ford, wanting to tear Wood limb from limb, so did Bolton rally in support of its son, convicted killer though he was. A petition seeking a reprieve, signed by 2,400, was sent to the Home Secretary, but it was to no avail. The sentence would not be overruled.

Awaiting execution, Wood wrote two self-justifying letters in which he blamed Emma's unfaithfulness and bad temper for their fate. The first letter was to his mother:

If the one who has left the world a little before me had done to me as she ought to have done, how happy we might have been enjoying all this world could afford. Oh, how foolish she had been, standing in her own light from beginning to the end, and brought us both to an early grave through the want of proper love towards her husband...

The second letter was to his brother:

He (God) has forgiven me for my sins and wickedness. And it leaves me thinking it is my duty to forgive my wife, who has so falsely deceived me and laughed me to scorn and treated me in a very improper manner I was not deserving of and I loved her so dear as my own life...

The reaction of Walter Wood's mother to the plight of her son was that of one whose son could do no wrong. Emma had been a dirty, careless woman who had used her husband and children very badly, she told reporters. Emma had never washed the bedding and Wood had frequently worn shirts a month at a time, "his wife being too idle to wash them."

At Strangeways Walter Wood met his end bravely. He made a great impression on James Berry, the executioner, who later recalled the occasion in his memoirs: "This execution affected me deeply. The man was fully conscious of the hideousness of his crime and sincerely repented. He assured the chaplain that he beheld the world and all things in a totally new light and that the consciousness of his crime had changed his whole character. What would have been the fate of such a man if he had been allowed to go free?"

14

MURDER AT THE BARRACKS

A great deal is said of the friendships that are established during military service. But hatreds develop too, and between Gunner William Hudson and Bombardier Harry Short that hatred led to murder.

William George Hudson of the Royal Field Artillery was put on trial for the murder of 23-year-old Bombardier Harry Short on Friday, April 24th, 1903. Standing in the dock of Manchester Assizes, he was a sorry sight. Looking much younger than his 26 years, his head was bowed and his hands were trembling. At first it seemed inconceivable that this man could have shot dead his superior officer. But all the evidence, circumstantial though it was, established his guilt beyond doubt. Hudson was a murderer.

William Hudson was originally from Birmingham, where he spent his childhood and found his first job as a market porter. It was there also that he had married, and for a brief while nurtured that simple dream of having a home and a family. This, however, was not to be. Then, as later, he made the wrong choice. Hudson and his wife were ill-suited. They quarrelled almost continuously, and after one particularly heated row, she left him. Hudson thus found himself unloved and alone and with very few prospects for the future. It was then, in 1899, that he resolved to start his life anew and enlisted in the Army.

Hudson saw some years of active service but, after being posted to India he was wounded and invalided home to Netley Hospital. He remained in the hospital for some weeks before returning to duty at Fulwood Barracks in Preston, Lancashire where, on December 24th, 1902, he met Bombardier Harry Short.

Why Hudson should have taken such an instant dislike to Short still remains something of a mystery. Was it simply that he was envious of the man? Was he resentful that Short, though three years his junior, was his superior? Or did their antipathy have a deeper root? Later there was some speculation that the two had known each other before, though the truth of this was never established. But whatever the reason, their mutual antipathy was intense and clear for all to see.

Hudson would provoke the Bombardier and deliberately antagonise him with his surly and insubordinate behaviour. Short, for his part, would respond with punishments; many unnecessarily severe, some entirely unwarranted. Matters came to a head on January 27th, 1903 when Short lodged a charge against Hudson for disobeying orders and for striking him. The soldier said it was all a lie, a product of the bombardier's fevered imagination. Nevertheless, a week later, Hudson was up before the court-martial.

There was no evidence to back up the charges, it was simply a question of man's word against another. The authorities listened patiently to Bombardier Short's allegations and then to Gunner Hudson's denials. It says something for military justice, that, in the end, the charges were dropped. Hudson was acquitted without a stain on his character. Short, by contrast, had had his authority undermined. And yet, as the proceedings drew to their close it was Gunner Hudson and not Short who was seething with resentment. As he walked out of the courtroom and back on to the barrack square he was still livid. He angrily confided to his friend, Gunner Henry Brown, that the Bombardier was not fit to bear stripes. He vowed then that he would get his own back one day.

Shortly before midnight on Monday, February 16th, 1903, Hudson and two comrades, Gunners Matthews and Foster, returned to barracks very much the worse for drink. Having consumed no less than fourteen beers and five whiskies each, they were barely in control of their senses and as they staggered clumsily across the barrack square, they were all verbose and rowdy. Hudson, however, seemed more affected than the others and suddenly became very angry and loud. He declared to all and sundry that he was going to get even with Short there and then. "I will do for him," he bellowed.

To his friends' alarm, Hudson then made towards the block in which Short slept. Matthews, fearing trouble, tried to restrain him and called out to Foster for help. Foster obliged. He seized Hudson by the scruff of the neck and together they carried their drunken comrade back to his block. Begging him to be quiet, they heaved him into his bed and watched him curl up. They then went to bed themselves.

It was at 7 a.m. the following morning, just as reveille was being sounded, that Bombardier Short's body was discovered. He had been shot in his sleep and had died instantly, the bullet having passed right through the back of his skull. That deadly bullet was later found under the bed.

From its trajectory, it seemed likely that the shot had been fired from the doorway and the killer must have been a crack marksman. There was no way to tell who that had been, but the bullet provided a major clue. It was a Martini-Metford, which could only have been discharged from a rifle of the same make. Records quickly revealed that there was only one such rifle in that part of the barracks – the others were all Martini-Henris – and that rifle belonged to Gunner Jerry Owen.

Owen was immediately arrested and, though vigorously protesting his innocence, he was taken to the guardroom cells. A check of his rifle revealed that it had indeed been recently fired.

The Army authorities had already informed the local police and, in due course, Inspector M'Lennan arrived at the barracks to investigate the crime and interrogate the suspect.

He began by talking to the eleven men who shared the same room as Bombardier Short. He was staggered by the way that almost all of them had heard the shot but none seemed to have been disturbed by it.

Gunner Finnerin told the inspector that he had been awakened at about 12.30 a.m. by what he took to be the discharge of a rifle. In the darkness he saw a flash of light. Alarmed, he had shouted out: "What's that?" But he got no reply. There was no light in the room and he heard no other sound so he went back to sleep.

Gunner William Baggott, who also slept in the room, told M'Lennan that he too had been awakened by a noise on the morning of the murder, and heard Gunner Brown in the next bed shout out, "What's the bloody game?" He added that though the room was dark, he was certain he would have seen someone if they had been up and about. But he did not see anybody nor did he hear anything more.

Driver Hughes, who had been on sentry duty, told M'Lennan that he had heard a sound coming from the direction of Short's quarters at about 12.30 a.m., but at the time had thought it was merely the banging of a door and had taken no action. He certainly had not thought that the noise was the sound of gunfire.

All the men agreed that Short was well liked generally, but that his position as bombardier made it inevitable that he would have enemies. In particular they mentioned the well-known animosity that lingered between Short and Gunner Hudson.

M'Lennan then went to the guardroom to speak to Jerry Owen. The soldier told the inspector that on the evening prior to the murder he had hung up his Martini-Metford rifle in a rack near his bed, clean and ready for inspection the following morning. However, when he awoke at reveille it had gone. At that time he had no idea what had happened to it and no notion that someone had been shot. He was merely concerned that the rifle had gone missing. He searched his room and, when he still could not find it, he had gone across to the room opposite. There he asked if anybody had got the weapon.

According to Owen, Gunner William Hudson had

immediately owned up to the theft. "It's all right, Jerry," he had volunteered, "I've got it." He then asked Gunner Foster for a "pull-through" (a rag with which to clean the muzzle of the rifle). Hudson then cleaned the rifle and handed it back to Owen.

M'Lennan realised that if what Owen said was true, then Hudson had been in possession of the weapon at the time of Short's murder and it was Hudson, therefore, who would be the prime suspect. All in all this made much more sense. Having already heard of the enmity that existed between Hudson and Short it seemed far more probable that this soldier was the villain. Hudson had a motive for the murder. Owen, by contrast, appeared to have no motive whatsoever. Indeed, Owen and Short were on good terms, almost friends. Still, M'Lennan continued to question the soldier for a while longer and listened as Owen, now close to tears, not only continued to deny the killing but informed him that he could not have fired the shot in any case. He explained that he had only had the weapon for six weeks and still had no ammunition for it.

M'Lennan decided it was time to speak to Hudson.

Hudson was also being detained in the guardroom cells, though it was nothing to do with the murder. An eagle-eyed officer had seen him and his friends returning the previous evening and had noticed he was not in his uniform. Hudson was thus being punished for this relatively minor transgression of army regulations. He greeted the inspector's questions about Short's death with astonishment.

No, of course he had not gone into Short's room and neither had he taken Owen's rifle. What was more, he had no grudge against the bombardier. True, he had no particular liking for the man. But he had no cause to hate him and certainly no reason to wish him dead. No amount of questioning would shift Hudson from his claim of total innocence. Eventually the Inspector gave up. In his soul, however, he was still certain that Hudson was the guilty man.

As the days passed the investigation proceeded very

slowly. Almost everyone on the barracks was questioned, but no one would talk. Even Gunner Owen would not add to his statement. M'Lennan felt that this silence was not caused by fear, but by a soldierly loyalty to Hudson and could not fail to be impressed by it. At the same time, however, he knew that if he was ever to get at the truth he would have to break through this code of honour.

He began by speaking again to Gunner Foster, who had been out with Hudson on the evening prior to the murder. He, like the others, had said little at their first meeting. But now M'Lennan pointed out the terrible consequences for Owen if the truth were to remain concealed. The man would surely hang, he said. Could he allow a fellow soldier to suffer like that for a crime he didn't commit?

Foster thought this over. He knew the inspector was telling the truth. By not speaking he was protecting a friend but he was also condemning an innocent man to the gallows. How could he ever forgive himself if Owen was to hang? Finally, after a thoughtful silence, he agreed to talk.

Foster told M'Lennan of how he, Matthews and Hudson had arrived back at the barracks, very much the worse for drink. He admitted that Hudson had made threats against Short and had threatened to kill him. He also related how he and Matthews had bundled their comrade into his bed. Foster sat Hudson down on the bunk and removed his boots. The soldier went on to say that Hudson had not gone straight to sleep. Instead, he had sat bolt upright on the bed and repeated his threat to kill the bombardier. "I will do for Short!" he had cried out. He remained sitting for some time, Foster remembered, and then, still in his stockinged feet, he got up and took something out of his box. Foster asked him what he was doing, and Hudson said he was getting some supper. But Foster could see nothing in his hand.

Hudson had then left the room for five minutes and when he returned he told his comrade, "I've done for Short." Foster saw that he was carrying the Martini-Metford rifle, which he cleaned and placed on a nearby rack. He then got into bed.

At about 9 a.m. next morning, after the murder had been discovered, Hudson said to him, "Don't give me away." Foster reassured him: "You needn't be frightened of me because I don't believe you've done it."

"Oh yes, I have," announced Hudson with a chuckle. "Old Short cocked up his legs and began screaming."

Foster maintained that he didn't believe Hudson had committed the murder, and this was the reason he had not spoken up earlier. The inspector looked at him scornfully and then dismissed him from the room.

M'Lennan next spoke to Gunner Matthews. He too wouldn't say much to begin with, but he finally admitted that on their return to the barracks, Hudson had made several threats against Short. At 7.15 a.m. the following morning, Matthews went down to Hudson's room for a glass of whisky which had been promised to him the night before. As he was drinking it, Owen came into the room, looked around and asked, "Where's my rifle?"

Matthews noticed that his gaze was fixed firmly on Hudson, who was sitting on the bed in his drawers and boots. Obediently, his friend got up and went over to some spare beds, picking the rifle out of the arm-rack on one of them. He cleaned the rifle and handed it back to Owen, who then returned to his own room.

After Owen had gone, Hudson confided to Matthews that he had "done" for Short with Owen's gun. Kneeling down, he demonstrated with his own rifle how he had fired at Short's bed. Foster was also in the room, but Matthews wasn't certain if he heard what Hudson said or understood what was going on. Like Foster, Matthews also claimed that he had not told the inspector the full story before because he did not believe Hudson was really the murderer.

On Saturday, February 21st, Hudson was formally arrested on the charge of murdering Bombardier Short. All he would say to the charge was: "I know nothing at all about it." Two days later Gunner Owen was released from custody and cleared of all suspicion.

Hudson's trial began at Manchester Assizes on Friday, April 24th, 1903, before Mr Justice Lawrence. The prosecution was led by Mr Sutton and the defence by Mr Jordan. Hudson pleaded not guilty.

Dr McKeague, who had performed the post-mortem on Short, told the court that in his opinion the bullet which killed him was fired from a kneeling position, probably from the doorway, and that the result would have been instantaneous death. He added that he felt it highly improbable that the dead man would have screamed out after being hit.

William Matthewson, a foreman in the Army Inspecting Department, testified that the day after the murder he had examined 13 rifles. Twelve were perfectly clean, but one, the Martini-Metford owned by Gunner Owen, showed signs of having been recently fired.

Gunner Matthews then repeated his account of Hudson's confession and gave the court a demonstration of how Hudson claimed he had fired the shot. One reporter in court noted how ill at ease Matthews seemed to be while giving evidence against his friend and comrade. "Embarrassment was written on every line of the gunner's face," he wrote, "as with soldierly precision he answered the abrupt and searching questions put to him by the prosecution."

Matthews concluded his testimony by declaring that he did not personally believe that after 14 beers and five whiskies, Hudson would have been in any condition to fire the shot. Though Hudson had indeed made the confession, he still believed him to be innocent of the crime. This opinion, however, was dismissed by the prosecution.

Gunner Foster was the next to be called to the stand and he told the court how on the fatal night he saw Hudson take something from his box, claiming it was his supper. He also repeated his earlier evidence to the police where he had testified that Hudson left the room for a few minutes and when he returned he was carrying Owen's rifle claiming: "I've done for Short." The prisoner had told him: "Keep your mouth shut". Foster added that, as Hudson was getting into bed he had also said to Thomas Kelly, one of the other men who shared the room: "Don't say anything."

Kelly was then called to give his evidence, corroborating Foster's last statement.

Gunner Owen then told the court that when he enquired about his missing rifle, Hudson had said, "Jerry, I did it. Don't say anything." Shortly afterwards, Hudson returned the rifle. Owen swore that he had never used the weapon himself.

Called for the defence, Captain Francis A. Tighe, commanding officer of the depot, said he thought it unlikely that a man standing in the doorway on a dark night (there was no light in Short's room) could have fired such an accurate shot. He said there was a tendency on the part of people shooting in the dark to aim high and therefore miss their target. During his extensive experience in the Boer War, this had been a common problem. Mr Sutton, for the prosecution, then asked him if it wasn't true that all his men would have known this. Tighe replied that the men under him were mainly recruits and "would not know much about it." However, Sutton challenged, Hudson was not a recruit. Tighe agreed that the defendant had been posted to India, but argued that he had seen little active service.

Tighe's testimony was the only evidence which seemed to be in Hudson's favour and even this was undermined by the prosecution. Sutton pointed out that although the faces of the people in Short's room could not be distinguished in the dark, it was still possible to see whether or not a bed was occupied. It was also revealed that Hudson had often visited Short's room to see his friend, Gunner Brown, and knew exactly where the bombardier slept.

The prosecution concluded their case by claiming that although no one had actually seen Hudson go into Owen's room or fire the shot which killed Short, he had nevertheless told many people that he would "do" for the bombardier, and later, after the murder, that he had "done" for him. As to the argument that Hudson was drunk and therefore unaware of what he was doing, Sutton said, "I do not see, supposing a man had had considerable drink, how his condition could be any excuse for using such a deadly weapon."

Mr Jordan, in his closing speech for the defence, said the evidence against Hudson was highly circumstantial. He told the jury that they must not return a guilty verdict if they felt the slightest doubt. It was, he said, preferable that 99 guilty people should be acquitted than that one innocent man be punished. Then again, even if Hudson had fired the fatal shot, it had been proved that he was "in liquor" at the time, and despite the prosecution's claims, he probably didn't know what he was doing. This could reduce the charge to one of manslaughter.

But there was, he argued, no firm evidence that Hudson had taken a bullet from his box, or indeed that he'd had such a bullet or cartridge in his possession. Matthews and Foster had also been drinking on the night when Hudson told them he would "do for Short". Could they, under these circumstances, have remembered clearly what was said?

Jordan again reminded the jury that no one had seen Hudson go into Owen's room and, most importantly of all, no one had seen him kill Short. In the end the only real evidence against Hudson was that he had the Martini-Metford rifle in his possession the following morning. A fact, Jordan stressed, of which the accused had made no secret. "He did not hide it or guiltily dispose of it, but left it in its proper place in the rack in his own room."

Jordan did his best to plant seeds of doubt in the minds of the jury members. Why did Hudson use Gunner Owen's Martini-Metford rifle when all his comrades, himself included, had Martini-Henris? Why, when he had used it, did he keep it? Why didn't he return it to Owen's room, or hide it somewhere, or simply leave it at the murder scene? After all, his possession of the murder weapon was the most damning evidence against him. Of course, if he was the worse for drink that night then this would undoubtedly have hampered his reasoning powers. But again, if he was so drunk was it right to judge him on a charge of murder? Would not manslaughter be more appropriate?

The defence's efforts to save Hudson's neck were valiant, but they were largely wasted. In his summing up the judge made no secret of his feelings about the case. The evidence, though largely circumstantial, seemed plain and conclusive. And the claim to manslaughter was simply a red herring. The fact that Hudson might have been drunk at the time of the murder did not free him from responsibility for his actions. Therefore the jury did not need to trouble itself about any distinction between manslaughter and murder. If they believed it satisfactorily proved that Hudson had fired the shot then he would be guilty of murder plain and simple. There could be no other judgement.

Mr Justice Lawrence also roundly criticised the system which allowed soldiers to return to barracks whenever they liked, and in whatever condition they chose. In his day, he declared, curfew was 10.30 p.m. and if a soldier was late he was flogged. To everyone in the court it was clear that Judge Lawrence believed it was a mistake that this regime had ever been slackened.

After an absence of just 13 minutes the jury returned to court with a verdict of wilful murder, but with a recommendation for mercy on account of Hudson's youth. Asked if he had anything to say, Hudson replied: "I have nothing to say – only that I am innocent." The judge then passed sentence of death. As he was led away, Hudson waved to his father and brother who were among the spectators in court.

William Hudson was executed inside Strangeways Prison, Manchester, at 8 a.m. on Tuesday, May 12th, 1903. It was reported that he met his death with cool courage, and that he gave no trouble to the executioner. He made no confession.

After his conviction he had been discharged from the Amy and, as a consequence, he was in civilian clothes when he was hanged. There was no black flag and no passing bell, both having recently been abolished. An official notice nailed to the main door of the prison was the only outward sign of the tragedy being enacted within. Yet from 7.30 a.m. a fairly large number of people began gathering around the prison door. It was noted that they were mainly working people – both men and women – who had stopped on their way to work, and that their behaviour was remarkably restrained and quiet. The prison doors remained shut from a few minutes around the time of the execution. Not even prison officers arriving for work were allowed in. Then at about 8.10 a.m., the outer door creaked open and the crowd, knowing it was all over, immediately began to disperse.

But that was not quite the end of the story. Shortly after noon on the day of Hudson's execution, Gunners Owen, Matthews and Foster were formally drummed out of the Army. It was felt by the authorities that they had withheld vital evidence about Bombardier Short's murder, and in so doing had rendered themselves unworthy to wear the uniform of the regiment. The loyalty they had shown to their comrade, a virtue in which the Army usually takes pride, cost them dear.

15

AN AMERICAN CONNECTION

*After they first met in a Philadelphia saloon the
fates of two men became curiously intertwined.
They would meet again at the gallows.*

It was chance that brought two Lancashire men together
in a Philadelphia saloon in the spring of 1883 but sharing
a fascination with America, 50-year-old Harry Swindells
from Oldham, and 24-year-old Kay Howarth from Bolton,
quickly took to each other. They spent the next month
sharing their dreams and with what little money they had,
exploring the city.

Then Swindells, his money all but gone, decided he must
return to Oldham to see if he could salvage his broken
marriage. As the two men parted, it seemed unlikely that
they would meet again. But they did, in a way which makes
fact stranger than fiction...

Suzannah Wild had been widowed in 1877, with two
daughters – Mary, aged 14, and Edith, just two years old –
but had been well provided for by her yeast-merchant
husband. He left her not only his business but also £2,500,
a small fortune in 1877.

A year later Mrs Suzannah Wild, still young and attractive, had met and fallen in love with Harry Swindells, a
book-keeper in the offices of the Oldham iron foundry in
which most of her money was invested. He proposed and
she accepted. They were married in December 1878, and
soon afterwards Harry Swindells left the iron foundry to
help his wife in the family yeast business.

Their quarrels began soon after. They centred on

Suzannah's inheritance from her first husband. Swindells wanted that £2,500. She wouldn't let him have it. She told him under the terms of her late husband's will she only had the use of the interest during her lifetime: the capital must go intact to her daughters. In fact, this was a lie. Suzannah's first husband had made no such will.

After many bitter scenes, she finally agreed to hand over £500. Swindells promptly spent this on what his wife regarded as "riotous living" and it was soon gone. Thereafter she allowed him £1 a week. This, he declared, was nowhere near enough. He wanted more. In fact, he wanted the whole lot. Mrs Swindells now had no doubts that her husband only wanted her for her money and had married her simply to get his hands on it. In this she was not far from the truth, but the knowledge did her little good.

Soon enough George Swindells began to drink heavily and also to womanise and things went from bad to worse. It reached a peak when, one day, a young lady came to see Mrs Swindells and angrily informed her that George had promised to marry her sister, who was in the "family way" by him. Suzannah was distraught. Enough, she thought, was enough. That day she left her husband, and taking her two daughters with her she moved into another house.

It was when Swindells found his wife had left him that he decided to sail for America. But he didn't remain there long. Three months later he was back, begging his wife for a second chance.

Suzannah was moved by his entreaties and consented to try once more. But the arguments soon recurred. And now their marriage was also facing other problems. Mary, Suzannah's eldest daughter, had turned 16 and was proving to be openly rebellious to her stepfather. She resented his authority and hated the way he quarrelled with her mother. After one particularly violent scene she left the house and went to live at the home of her uncle, 59-year-old James Wild. This, however, did nothing to improve relations between Harry and his wife. In fact, things got even worse.

One day Swindells came home drunk and threatened

Suzannah with a revolver. Managing to get the weapon away from him, she fled to a neighbour's house and the police were called.

It was after this incident that the final separation took place. Swindells sailed again for America and during the second visit made the acquaintance of Kay Howarth.

Meeting a fellow-countryman of half his age was a pleasure. Many had made good in the United States, and both these Lancashire men were ambitious to get rich quick. Yet as Swindells and Howarth whiled away their days in the simple camaraderie of fellow-exiles, what chances there were for making a swift fortune always passed them by. Eventually they both had to face up to reality.

It was with some regret that Harry Swindells decided to cut his losses and go home. He was broke, but he had enough money left for his passage home. He hoped that, once he returned, he could again prevail upon Suzannah to have him back. She had done so before, and he was certain he could use his charm on her a second time. But he soon found out he was wrong. On his return to Oldham in the June of 1883, he called at her house in Henthorn Street.

"Never again," she told him, impervious to his begging. She slammed the door in his face and left him on the street.

Harry Swindells had pinned all his hope on Suzannah taking him back, and was now at a loss. It was obvious that pleading with her would not make any difference, but surely she could still be persuaded. He felt that being her husband still gave him some rights. He was reluctant to let her – and more importantly her money – go.

A few days later he was back. This time he asked her to give him back his revolver. Suzannah had had the gun ever since the evening he had threatened her with it and, understandably, she refused to hand it over. "Oh, that's all right," he told her. "I have another one and I mean to use it." Suzannah ordered him to leave her house. Swindells obliged. "I will return once more, and only once more," he warned as he shut the door behind him.

At midday on July 16th, Mrs Swindells and her daughters

had just returned home after spending the morning shopping when they heard a knock at the back door. Mrs Swindells unlocked the door, and opening it slightly, peeped out. As she did so, Swindells pushed past her and marched into the kitchen.

"What do you want?" she demanded.

"I've come for my revolver," he shouted. "Get it for me."

"No, I will not," she told him.

Swindells swore at her, then he sat himself down at the bottom of the stairs and refused to budge. Suzannah was both angry and terrified. She sent her younger daughter to fetch Uncle James, who lived in nearby Shaw Road, and as she waited for him to come, she stood at the open door ready to run out should Swindells become violent.

She saw her neighbour, Mrs Elizabeth Street, come out into the yard the two families shared. "Mrs Street," she called out, "is your husband in?"

"No, he's gone back to work," replied the woman.

"What do you want him for?" demanded Swindells.

"I think I ought to have a policeman for protection," replied Suzannah.

A few minutes later Mrs Swindells's younger daughter returned with James Wild. "What right have you here?" he shouted, furious at Swindells's intrusion.

"More than you have," retorted Swindells.

Wild told Mary, the older daughter, to fetch a policeman.

A short while later Mrs Street, who was still standing in the yard, heard two loud noises coming from the Swindells' kitchen. Concerned, she ran to their back door, which was now closed. Pushing it open, she saw James Wild and Swindells struggling violently at the bottom of the stairs. Wild had Swindells by the collar.

"Eh, Wild, come out," she cried, fearing he was going to come off worst in the fight. But Wild did not speak.

The next moment she heard a pistol shot. Wild loosened his grip on Swindells, staggered through the back door and collapsed in the yard, blood pouring from his mouth.

Screaming hysterically, Mrs Street saw Swindells put something into his pocket – she did not see what – before hurrying past her into the yard and out into the road where his pace slackened. Neighbours hearing Mrs Street's cries came running from their houses. One of them, seeing Swindells, asked, "What's to do, Harry?"

"Oh, it's some women falling out," he replied, walking on at an ordinary pace. But once he'd passed the crowd he started to run. He knew he had to get away fast. Swindells had fired at two people and, for all he knew, he had killed them both. In fact, only Wild died. Suzannah had received only a flesh wound and soon recovered.

The police soon started to search the neighbourhood but they were too late. Swindells had already vanished. It was later discovered that he had taken a train to London and from there sailed for America.

It seemed unlikely that he would be seen again, but on August 4th, 1884, police heard that he had been sighted on the road from Ashton-under-Lyne to Oldham.

When he was arrested, Harry Swindells was dressed like a tramp in filthy old rags. The only money he had on him was coppers.

Suzannah could not give evidence at his trial because, under English law a wife could not testify against her husband. So it was left to others to describe James Wild's murder.

The surgeon who had carried out the post-mortem examination of Wild's body told how he had found four bullet wounds. Nine-year-old Edith described how Swindells had followed her mother to the front door when she tried to run from the house, and had shot her. Mrs Street said that although she had not seen a revolver in Swindells's hand, Wild could not have fired the shots because when they rang out he was gripping Swindells with both hands.

Evidence was given that a tin belonging to Swindells had been found to be six bullets short of its contents of 50. Six bullets altogether had been recovered at the scene of the murder. A gunsmith testified that those bullets were similar to the ones remaining in Swindells's tin.

For Swindells's defence, it was argued that the gun could have gone off accidentally. Swindells himself denied that he had gone to the house intending to shoot anybody. It was a claim that no one believed.

Found guilty and sentenced to death, he was taken back to Strangeways Jail. It was there, taking a turn in the exercise yard, that he saw a familiar face. Also stretching his legs was Kay Howarth! They greeted each other, shaking hands warmly. In Philadelphia they had shared a passion for America. Now, they found they had something else in common. Both were awaiting execution.

Howarth's career following his return from America had been a different story, though it was to lead to the same sorry conclusion. It began on the morning of October 3rd, 1884, when two men were sitting drinking together in the Fleece Hotel, Bradshawgate, in the centre of Bolton. One was Richard Dugdale, a 37-year-old commercial traveller from Wakefield, Yorkshire. The man with him was an old friend, Robert Hall, a Bolton oil merchant. Dugdale had arrived in Bolton the previous evening to do business with various landlords in the town on behalf of his employers, a firm of brewers. This business involved the collection of quite large sums of money.

Hall had hardly sat down with Dugdale when Kay Howarth wandered into the pub. Spying Hall, whom he knew, Howarth came over to say hello. Hall was not pleased to see him as he thought Howarth a loafer and sponger. It was also rumoured that he had recently resorted to thieving. The merchant was therefore very cool in his greeting, and tried to make it clear to the intruder that they didn't want his company. But Dugdale seemed to take an instant liking to the man, and not only offered to buy him a drink but also asked him to join them.

Subsequently, the three men visited several pubs, Hall or Dugdale paying for the drinks, Howarth saying he had no money. Every now and then Dugdale left the other two to see various landlords and collect money from them. Returning from one of these expeditions, he showed Hall and Howarth a cheque for £8 and a number of gold sovereigns.

By 6.15 p.m. Dugdale was very drunk and Hall, who had to keep a business appointment at the Crown and Cushion in Mealhouse Lane, asked Howarth to take him to the Wheatsheaf Inn, where he was staying.

At about 8 p.m. Howarth rejoined Hall at the Crown and Cushion. Hall asked him about Dugdale, and Howarth replied, "Oh, I left him at the Balmoral Hotel."

"Why didn't you take him back to the Wheatsheaf?" Hall asked.

"We went there for a drink," Howarth explained, "but Dugdale began calling me names because I couldn't stand my corner. I didn't like it so I left."

Worried about his friend, Hall said he would go to the Balmoral and see him.

"Oh, he's not there," added Howarth quickly. "He followed me out and the last time I saw him he was going by the end of Mawdesley Street Chapel."

Still concerned, Hall decided to pop into the Wheatsheaf "to see if he's landed." But as it was now quite late and as he was expected home he changed his mind and caught the 8.45 p.m. tramcar to Eagley, where he lived.

At 9.00 p.m., William Quinn came out of his house in Silverwell Lane to dispose of some old bottles on a piece of nearby waste ground. Suddenly he stumbled across a man lying sprawled on the ground. At first he supposed he was a drunk sleeping it off, but when Quinn threw the bottles against a stone and the man failed to move as they smashed, he went to have a closer look. The man's face was both dirty and bloody. Alarmed when he still showed no signs of life, Quinn hurried to fetch a neighbour, who returned with him to the body.

Lighting a match and putting his hand on the man's head, the neighbour exclaimed: "Why, he's quite dead and cold, and it looks as if his eye is knocked out."

Quinn ran for help.

Arriving at the scene, police found the dead man lying on his back drenched in blood. His right hand loosely held a bloodied knife, the cutting edge towards the body. His throat had been slit wide open. In the man's breast pocket police found a note-book with the name Richard Dugdale written inside. Scrawled on the flyleaf was a suicide note.

The note-book indicated that Dugdale had spent the day collecting payments from landlords in the town and had received a considerable sum of money, yet he had only eightpence on him. The suicide message was not only in a completely different hand to that which had made the entries in the rest of the book, but had been written with a black-leaded pencil and not the blue pencil with which the rest of the entries had been made. The injuries to the body also suggested this was no suicide. Besides having had his throat cut, the man had been so severely beaten that one eye now hung grotesquely from its socket.

Calling at the pubs which the notebook indicated Dugdale had visited, police learned that he had been in the company of Robert Hall. At 4 a.m. they banged on Hall's door.

Hall told them that Kay Howarth had been the last person to see Dugdale, and gave them his address. Shocked by the news of Dugdale's murder, and feeling he had let his friend down by not seeing him back to his hotel, he accompanied police as they set out to question Howarth.

"I know nothing about it," Howarth told the police when they roused him from his bed. Searching his room, police found a gold watch and chain with some spots of blood on it, and a number of bills with Richard Dugdale's name on them. There was also blood on Howarth's clothing.

In his pockets was £32.10s. in gold and 18 shillings in silver. The police also found a cheque for £8, which Hall identified as the one he had seen in Dugdale's possession. He also identified the gold watch and chain as belonging to Dugdale. Shown the supposed suicide message in Dugdale's note-book, Hall said the handwriting was Howarth's.

Howarth didn't deny that the watch and chain and

money belonged to Dugdale. They had been handed to him by Dugdale for safe-keeping until the next day, he said. Dugdale had realised he had drunk too much and feared he might be robbed.

At Dugdale's inquest, Hall identified the knife found in the dead man's hand as one which he had seen Howarth using to cut tobacco. The barmaid at the Balmoral Hotel said that neither he nor Howarth had visited the hotel on the day of the murder. Three witnesses described how they had seen an obviously intoxicated Dugdale being assisted by Howarth as the two made their way towards the waste ground where the body was found.

A barmaid at the Crown and Cushion recalled Howarth entering the pub alone at about 7.50 p.m. on the night of the murder. He told her he was going to America and asked her to accompany him. "Oh, yes," she had laughed, "and where's your money?" To her astonishment, he had produced a handful of sovereigns. Howarth's landlady said he had returned to his lodgings in a very jolly mood that night, showing fellow lodgers a number of sovereigns and saying he had won them playing dominoes.

Committed for trial, accused of Dugdale's murder, Howarth was subsequently found guilty and sentenced to death.

At Strangeways Jail, fresh links were forged in the chain of events connecting Howarth and Swindells since their Philadelphia encounter. Although both had denied committing murder, each confessed his guilt on the eve of execution. They were hanged together at 8 a.m. on November 24th, 1884, and they ended their long journey from Philadelphia sharing the same grave in the prison precincts.

16

CHINESE HONEYMOON

The new bride lay dead on the path. A cord belonging to blinds from her hotel was wrapped around her neck.

Two pieces of blind-cord and a small piece of string were knotted around the delicate throat of Wai-Sheung Siu, a diminutive Chinese bride, when her body was found by a bathing-pool near the Lake District village of Grange-in-Borrowdale. It was one of the strangest murders of the 1920s, for the girl had arrived at an hotel there on honeymoon only a few hours before.

Wai-Sheung Siu was the daughter of a wealthy Macao merchant and had travelled widely in America, China and Britain. After her father's death she ran an art shop in Hong Kong and whilst she was in New York, on a buying trip in October, 1927, she met Chung Yi-Maio. He was a handsome law student whose family originally came from Shanghai.

Chung Yi-Maio fell in love with her almost immediately and she with him. Within six months, on May 12th, 1928, they were married. They had a leisurely honeymoon, first in America and Canada, then in Scotland, later moving south to Grange-in-Borrowdale in the Lake District. Arriving on the afternoon of June 18th, they spent their first day in the hotel and the next morning strolled around the locality. That afternoon they were seen going for a walk towards the bathing-pool. And then a maid at the hotel noticed that Chung had returned alone. When she later asked whether his wife would be returning for tea, he replied: "She's gone to town to do some shopping and won't be back until 6 o'clock."

Chung Yi-Maio dined alone at 7 o'clock in the hotel restaurant. When a woman guest asked him where Wai-Sheung was, he said: "She's gone to Keswick to buy some warm underclothes." By then, however, the shops would have long since closed.

It was 10.30 p.m. when, with still no sign of his wife, he began to agitate. He asked one of the servants: "Should we inform the police?" The servant told him that this couldn't be done until Miss Crossley, the hotel proprietress, returned. Meanwhile, a farmer walking along the path near the bathing-pool found the woman lying dead on top of some roughly piled stones. She was wearing an extremely expensive fur coat.

The farmer rushed to the village to tell of his discovery and, in a short while, he was returning back to the path in the company of a local bobby and Detective Constable William Pendlebury, a Southport policeman who was in Keswick on holiday.

Pendlebury examined the corpse. Wai-Sheung had been strangled with a long piece of green blind-cord, then with a second piece wound several times around her neck and tied with a reef knot and, finally, with a tightly twisted loop of string.

She lay on her back, her petticoat pulled up, suggesting at least an attempt at rape. Though a diamond-studded watch remained on her wrist, there were signs that her wedding ring had been torn off.

The detective recognised the victim as a guest at the hotel and, after the body had been photographed and taken to the mortuary, he went to search out her husband. Pendlebury arrived at the hotel in the company of an Inspector Graham from the local force to give Mr Chung the sad news.

"I am afraid a body has been found near the bathing pool," said Inspector Graham, "we believe it may be your wife."

Both policeman were surprised by the man's reaction.

"That's terrible," uttered Chung, " my wife assaulted, robbed and murdered!"

Neither policeman had said anything about the way Wai-Sheung had died.

Chung's room was searched. The police found a locked jewel case in which Wai-Sheung had kept a valuable pearl necklace and other items worth about £3,500. The keys to the case were found inside one of Chung's shirts in a suitcase. Later, the bride's diamond ring and wedding ring were found hidden inside a spool of camera film that was also in the case.

Chung was taken to Keswick police station on suspicion of having caused his wife's death. Later he was formally charged with the murder.

Chung Yi-Maio's trial at Carlisle Assizes in November 1928, lasted three days. Leading for the Crown was Mr. J. E. Singleton, KC, who suggested that Chung had deftly strangled his wife as she sat on a rock, death being almost instantaneous. Chung, he said, had also attempted to create an appearance of rape and violent robbery.

A local doctor, giving evidence, said he believed that the woman had been killed at about 6.30 p.m. but no later, for he had examined the body at 9.30 p.m. and blood was still flowing from her left ear. As a rule, blood would not flow for more than three hours after death. He also confirmed that the ligatures around the dead woman's neck that caused her death appeared to be of the same cord as the hotel's blinds.

Professor John McFall, from Liverpool, said that there was a tear in the victim's bloodstained knickers. "I have seen many of these cases. And it is a very good imitation of an assault. This can be discerned from the manner in which the material has been torn." McFall was also certain that a bloodstained left-hand glove, found partially inside-out near the body, had been removed after death. There were, in all, ten bloodstains on the girl's skirt. "The ten smudges were the result of one large smear, as if the material had been gathered up by a bloody hand," the professor explained. "When it is opened out, you can see the smudges. It was therefore made by someone tampering with the body after the injuries were inflicted."

Cross-examined by Mr J. C. Jackson, KC, Chung's chief defence counsel, Professor McFall persisted in claiming that rape and assault appeared to be something of a sham. But he also added that other forensic evidence did not point to the victim's husband as being her assailant. He admitted that there were no traces of either wet or dry blood on Chung's clothes. Nor was there any evidence that he had tried to wash off any bloodstains at the time.

Mr Jackson stressed that Wai-Sheung had considerable wealth and had a passion for costly jewellery, which she always wore and was wont to show off, even to comparative strangers. As she had mingled in New York society, her recent marriage had been extensively reported there as were her honeymoon plans. She was a target of international jewel thieves, he pointed out, and it was quite possible that they were responsible for the attack. Mr Chung, he said, had already expressed concern to his wife that two Orientals seemed to be following them on their honeymoon. He had even seen them in Grange-in-Borrowdale.

In his evidence, Chung stated that on the morning of June 19th, his wife was wearing her two rings at breakfast. After lunch, he added, he saw her put them in the spool carton of camera film. He was not surprised at this, he said. His wife often put her jewellery in odd places. Sometimes she even put her jewels on top of the wardrobe.

Wai-Sheung had suggested going into Keswick by herself, he said. She was going to get some medicine for him – Chung said he had developed a cold – and some warm underclothes for herself. She said she would be back at supper time-and that was the last he saw of her. Under cross-examination, Chung admitted that, in talking to the police, he had initially told them that his wife was wearing a diamond ring and then changed his statement to question whether she was wearing any rings at all.

"So why did you tell the police officer, 'Rings–I do not know,' if the last thing you saw her do in the house was to take off the two rings and put them in that spool carton?" asked Mr Singleton.

"She sometimes kept loose jewellery in her bag–and she may have put on others when I was not looking," Chung replied.

Mr Singleton then pointed out Chung's immediate reaction to the news of his wife's death: "assaulted, robbed and murdered." How did he know his wife had been murdered?

Chung now swore that he had never said, "Robbed and murdered," but "Rudely murdered." Moreover, he had never used the word "assaulted."

Could he explain how her keys were found in his bag, proving that he had access to her jewel case?

Chung replied that several of her belongings had been packed by the police into her bag. There could have been a mix up. Also, he claimed, just like his wife often put jewellery in odd places it appeared that she also did the same with keys. Chung said she hid her keys all over the place, even inside his shoes.

Mr Jackson then took up a key point in Chung's defence–the fact that "two Orientals" had been seen either following or watching the honeymoon couple.

A chemist on holiday in Keswick recalled seeing "two men whom I took to be Chinese" outside a Keswick hotel at about 10 o'clock on the morning of June 19th.

A local farmer said he saw another Chinese about half an hour later, two miles from Keswick, walking towards the town. When cross-examined, he agreed that the man might have been a Japanese. He did not know that, in fact, a Japanese was staying at a house quite near his farm.

Another farmer said he'd passed two Orientals coming into Keswick at between 11 and 11.30 p.m. on the day before the murder. He saw them again about an hour later. Another witness said that, at about 2 p.m. that day, a "foreign-looking man" called at a house about four miles from Grange-in-Borrowdale and asked the way. Upon being directed, he made off towards Keswick, which lay between the house and Grange-in-Borrowdale. He had wanted to know the quickest way, as he had to catch a bus in Keswick.

Two further witnesses said that they each saw two Orientals leaving Keswick station on the morning of June 20th. The first witness saw them on a train to Carlisle, the second on a train for Penrith.

In his closing speech for the defence, Mr Jackson asked what possible motive there could be for Chung to commit murder. Both the newlyweds had been happy and devoted and well-off. "And even if the prisoner had wanted to murder his wife, why come to England to do so?" he asked. "Why not simply push her into the sea from the ship while they were crossing the Atlantic?"

He said it had been shown that Wai-Sheung had been rather vain about her valuable jewellery, which made her a very tempting target for crooks. What were those Oriental persons doing in Keswick at the same time as Mr and Mrs Chung were staying in Grange-in-Borrowdale? Many witness had testified to seeing them. They obviously weren't a figment of Mr Chung's imagination.

The police, Jackson suggested, had arrested Chung when the only evidence against him was that he had been seen with his wife in the afternoon. Since then, they had simply tried to build up theories. Mr Jackson suggested that there was no proof that Wai-Sheung was murdered where she was found. She could have met her death almost anywhere and her body could have been carried over the low wall near the path, where the scene had been clumsily staged to suggest motives other than robbery.

In his summing-up to the jury, Mr Justice Humphreys noted that the police and the defence had not been able to trace anyone who saw the woman actually going to Keswick. He added: "She had been killed in what I think may be described as a remarkable manner. The defence is suggesting that the murder may possibly have been committed by

William Burtoft (below right) battered Fanny Levine to death as she lay dozing on the settee in her living-room. Crowds gathered as the old lady's funeral cortège passed by her home in Cheetham Hill Road, Manchester.

The Manchester Settee Murder

The X marks the spot on the doorstep of the house in Wingfield Street, Gorse Hill, Stretford where Samuel Johnson (above left) stabbed to death Betty Martin (above right).

The Killing of Betty Martin

John Jackson (above) escaped over the rooftops of Strangeways prison after killing Warder Webb (left)

Escape from Strangeways

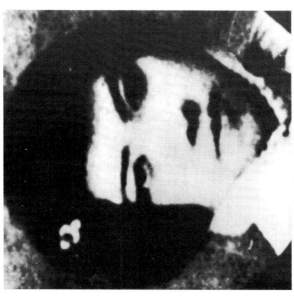

Chung Yi-Maio (left) strangled Wai-Sheung Siu (right) with the blind cord from their hotel. She was his wife, they were on their honeymoon.

Chinese Honeymoon

Strangeways was the last resting place of many of Britain's villains. Amongst them was Mary Ann Britland (inset), the notorious Lancashire poisoner.

The Lancashire Poisoner

An early photograph of suspected killer Henry Jackson. Because his landlady, Mrs Rimmer (above left) backed up his alibi he was not arrested for the murder of Dorothy Allen (above right).

The Southport Landlady

Jerome Caminada was one of Manchester's finest detectives who brought many criminals to justice. This photograph, taken in 1890, shows him with his mother and family.

The main gates of **Strangeways Prison**

robbers – people who were after this woman's jewellery. She was found to have been killed by the application very tightly round her throat of a piece of cord which had been twisted, so as to make it double. Who did it? Can you imagine a robber killing a woman in that way?

"This was a little woman, only five feet tall. Do you think a person who wanted to take her jewellery would have got so near to her without her knowing it? To put the cord round her neck and strangle her? Of course, if the person who did it was a person in whom she had every confidence, you may think she would have no objection at all to his putting his hands round her throat, or doing anything else he liked – and that it would be quite easy for such a person to put his hands on each side of her throat, with a piece of string between them, then suddenly draw it tight when, we are told, the result would be almost instantaneous unconsciousness and very shortly death...

"She was a young married woman on her honeymoon. Do you think it likely, do you think it possible, that she would have allowed any strange man to walk with her in such a place as that?

"According to the prisoner she was on her way to Keswick. That is not the way to Keswick – to go through that wicket gate and down that path to the bathing-pool."

Mr Justice Humphreys further asked the jury: "Do you think the prisoner is the unfortunate victim of circumstances? Do you accept his explanation that there was a misunderstanding on the part of a number of persons, or do you take the view that he is a man who had committed a foul murder, who was clever enough to feign emotion, clever enough to try to cover his tracks-and who has given plausible, though not acceptable, explanations of the evidence?" He pointed out that the police had made inquiries for any Orientals in the neighbourhood, but had found no trace of those persons in Grange-in-Borrowdale on June 18th or 19th.

He declared: "It is suggested that there were policemen on point-duty in Keswick who might have seen these

Orientals. But I should think you will not doubt the truth of these persons for the defence – that there was some Chinese or Japanese. Indeed, it is suggested by the prosecution that there was a Japanese staying at a boarding-house. The question is whether you think that helps you in the solution of this case – that there may have been either Chinese or Japanese in a place four miles away from Grange-in-Borrowdale."

The judge asked the jury to note that, though the bride was wearing her rings at breakfast on June 19th, they were found after Chung's arrest, not slipped into the spool carton, but carefully wrapped in silver paper on the metal end of the spool.

After an hour's discussion, the jury brought in a verdict of guilty. Before the death sentence was passed, Chung said: "Now you have tried me for my life and the verdict is that I am guilty. If I did that, I must be very nervous. Now, you see, I am not nervous..."

Chung took the case to the appeal court, insisting that, as a holder of the degree of Doctor of Law in the USA, he wanted to conduct his own case. This was granted – as was also his unusual request to call fresh evidence.

One of his "new" witnesses was a holiday-maker in Keswick at the time of the murder, who remembered seeing an Oriental at about 4.30 p.m. on the day in question at a spot about half a mile from the place where the body was discovered. The Oriental, hatless and coatless, was "hurrying." Two women from London, also in the neighbourhood on holiday, recalled seeing two Orientals about half a mile from the bathing pool between 3.30 and 4.30 on the same afternoon – when Chung would have been back in the hotel.

Chung alleged that the police had never tried hard enough to find the real murderer, although he knew that two Orientals had followed him and his wife from Glasgow. He suggested that the murderers tore his wife's clothes in taking her body by car to the place where it was found. If he had tried to kill her, she would have struggled, but his face was unscratched and his clothes untorn.

He said that, under Chinese law, the wife's effects become the husband's property immediately after marriage. But after her death he could not reach any property in the hands of her relatives. So he had no motive to rob or kill. Indeed, it was against his own interests.

Dismissing the appeal, the Lord Chief Justice stressed the finding of the rings so carefully and elaborately concealed. "It may well be that in this case the jury thought that his cupidity had got the better of his cunning."

Chung Yi-Maio was hanged at Strangeways Jail, on December 6th, 1928. He died instantly.

Three months later an article in the *Sunday Express* suggested that Mr Chung may have been telling the truth all along. He had not killed his wife for her jewellery. But he had killed her all the same. The article revealed that Wai Sheung Siu had been unable to bear children. It was this, they suggested, rather than greed, that led Chung Yi-Maio to murder.

17

WHERE IS ANNIE FARNWORTH?

*The murder of little Annie Farnworth was one of
the worst crimes in Manchester's history. Worse
still because the culprit was a teenager.*

Tuesday, March 22nd, 1932, began like most other days
in the Farnworth household with Henrietta Farnworth
sending six-year-old Annie off to school.

The child arrived at Highfield Infants School in plenty of
time for her morning lessons. At midday she went with the
other children to neighbouring Vernon School for lunch.
Sometimes, if time allowed, Annie went home to Kay Street
to play before going back for her afternoon lessons. On this
particular day, though, Henrietta Farnworth saw no sign of
her daughter and presumed she had not had enough time
to run home.

But Annie Naomi Farnworth had started for home that
day – she just never made it to the front door.

At 5.10 p.m., when Annie should have been home
almost two hours, she had still not returned. Initially, the
Farnworths imagined that she had called in on a relative, or
had perhaps run an errand for a neighbour. But by 6 o'clock
they were at their wits' end and began calling on everyone
they could think of who might know where Annie was.

The Lancashire cotton town of Darwen had a population of 36,000 in 1932 but it was still a friendly place, and
no sooner had word got around about Annie's disappearance, than the close-knit community pulled together in
their search for her. Many people knew Annie, not only
because of her sunny good nature but because of her
willingness to run errands. School friends, Boy Scouts,

neighbours and relatives joined in to look for the missing girl, but Annie was nowhere to be found. So Albert and Henrietta Farnworth went to the police to report her disappearance.

By the time dusk settled on the town, extra police had been called in. At the instigation of Annie's parents, a description of the girl was broadcast over Manchester's BBC radio. She was described as having very fair hair, a fair complexion and uneven teeth. She had last been seen wearing steel-rimmed spectacles, a blue dress, brown coat, blue hat and fawn stockings. In the appeal it was stated that Annie had been missing since 6 o'clock. However, further police enquiries determined that she had in fact been missing since lunchtime. The headmistress of Annie's school said the child had not returned for lessons that afternoon, and she had assumed Annie was ill and had been kept at home.

A temporary halt was called to the search, which was resumed at first light the next morning. Out of the way places like Sunnyhurst Woods were scoured without finding a trace of the child, and it was not until Thursday morning that the police got the break they were hoping for. In what initially started as a routine house-to-house enquiry, they were provided with some useful information by 13-year-old Doris Sharples, who lived in Kay Street. Doris told the police she had seen Annie at a local fish and chip shop buying tripe and chips at around noon on the day she disappeared. And a white jug the girl had in her hand Doris recognised as belonging to Charles Cowle, who lived next door but one to the Farnworths.

Doris said that around 6 o'clock that evening, she had spoken to Cowle on his doorstep. He asked her if she had heard about little Annie going missing and when Doris said that she had, Charles Cowle told her darkly, "You will be next!" Although Doris had not taken his remark seriously at the time, she now thought she had better report it to the police.

At 9.45 a.m. two uniformed officers went to 82 Kay

Street. The door was promptly opened by 18-year-old Charles. He eagerly invited the officers inside, explaining that his parents were out at work. The policeman got straight to the point and asked him if he had seen Annie on the day of her disappearance. "Yes," he said, "I asked her to run an errand for me to the local fish and chip shop. She brought back tripe and chips, and stayed on for a couple of minutes before leaving." He said he did not know where Annie went after leaving his house.

Charles Cowle seemed anxious to help the police and he appeared to be telling the truth. But the officers were suspicious. Not only had the young man said nothing before he had been approached, despite all the appeals for help and information, they also knew that Cowle had a criminal record. Moreover, his violation of the law had involved violence against a child.

The police didn't take their interrogation further, however. Instead they gave Cowle the impression of being entirely satisfied with his story. They wrote down what he had said, asked him to sign the statement and left.

Detective Sergeant Kenyon and Inspector Kay listened to their subordinates' account of their meeting with Cowle with growing concern. Looking up the young man's record, they saw that he was a nasty character indeed. At the age of nine he had smashed a two-year-old boy over the head with a brick, and left him for dead in a pool of water. Had it not been for a passer-by coming to the rescue, the infant would have died.

When he was apprehended for that crime, Cowle, young as he was, showed himself to be an accomplished liar. Immediately he tried to blame a fictitious man for the attack. There was no doubt, however, that he was the culprit and, on being found guilty he had been sent to borstal for five years. The detectives reasoned that, if he had harmed a young child then and lied about it, he could be doing exactly the same thing now.

Within an hour of the police paying their first visit to Cowle's house, the youth found himself facing a further visit from the law. However, on this occasion his visitors were Inspector Kay and Sergeant Kenyon.

"Are you sure you told us the truth?" Kenyon asked. "Did Annie stay for only a few minutes? Are you certain she left the house? Did anything untoward happen? Have you seen her since?"

Faced with such blunt questions, Cowle began to change his story. "Annie came back from the shop and I gave her some of my chips wrapped in paper," he said. "She ate the chips and stayed in the house for twenty minutes before leaving." Cowle went on to say that he chopped wood for the fire before leaving the house himself at around 2 o'clock that afternoon. He had then gone to visit a friend of his who lived around the corner.

Inspector Kay did not give Cowle time to draw breath before saying, "I don't believe you. We are going to search the house."

During their search of the downstairs rooms, Cowle appeared indifferent to what was going on. When they started to go up the stairs, however, his mood rapidly changed. As the inspector turned the knob to the bedroom door, he could maintain his bluff no longer.

"She's in there," he stammered, pointing out a tin trunk covered by a cloth which stood beneath the bed. "I strangled her."

The inspector knelt on the bedroom floor, opened the trunk and reeled back in horror. Annie had died in atrocious circumstances. Her tiny hands were clenched tightly, even in death. She had been strangled, and there were clear signs of rape. She was naked from the waist down. Bruising on her arms and lips showed how wildly she had struggled during the assault. The sight of her bruised and bloodied genitals made the officers squirm.

Wound tightly round her neck was a six foot cord which had been looped five times and pulled as tight as it would go.

Inspector Kay had seen enough. He arrested Cowle on the spot. In marked contrast to his earlier garrulous behaviour, the youth shrugged and said, "I have nothing to say."

It was only a matter of time before a police doctor confirmed the inspector's opinion. She had indeed been savagely raped. Her time of death was estimated to be around 3 o'clock in the afternoon.

At the post-mortem it was discovered that Annie had eaten potato hash from her school meal, and chips with which Cowle had lured her into his house.

At the local police station the beleaguered suspect began to admit his guilt. "After I gave Annie chips, I went funny in the head. I carried her upstairs but she was screaming, so I put my hands around her throat to stop her noise. Then she went quiet."

As the investigation continued and the evidence began to mount detectives were amazed by both the callousness of Cowle's crime and also the absurdly ineffective way he had tried to cover it up. He had hid the body where he must have realised it would be discovered at any moment. Mrs Cowle confirmed that the front bedroom was shared by herself, her husband and Charles. The trunk under the bed was used to store clothes. It was a miracle, she said, that she had not opened it in the past three days.

When forensic experts delved more thoroughly, they discovered yet more incriminating evidence in the bedroom. Under one bed lay a small suitcase. It contained Annie's knickers, coat and hat. Cowle's bed linen was speckled with bloodstains which could only have belonged to Annie, and his clothing was examined and found to be spattered with blood and semen.

It added up to damning evidence – but Charles Cowle's reported behaviour immediately after the murder was equally incriminating.

On the day of Annie's disappearance, Cowle called at his friend's house in the late afternoon. James Foster had not been at home at the time, but his mother was. Mrs Foster remarked to Cowle that he had been a long time doing his chores, but it was Cowle himself who brought up the subject of Annie's disappearance.

"Annie Farnworth's missing," he stated, as if waiting for a reply. At this juncture Hames Foster came in and suggested that they should go and help look for her. Cowle seemed to view the idea with glee. They spent half an hour searching Sunnyhurst Woods before returning to the Foster home. There was an absurd grin on Cowle's face the entire time.

For the rest of the evening James and Charles played their usual game of dominoes. According to Mrs Foster, Cowle's conversation was full of talk about the little girl's disappearance.

Despite the deluge of information now arriving at police headquarters, the more the investigators delved into the case the harder it became to fathom Cowle's psyche. Even his father went as far as to say that he had always regarded his son as "dull."

"There is something lacking in our Charles," he declared. "From the moment he left borstal, he hasn't been able to hold down a job for more than two weeks. In the end, his mother and I left him to look after the house while we went to work."

The police also contacted the former headmaster from Cowle's reformatory school. "Charles was a loner," he said. According to a report he had written at the time of Cowle's incarceration, the lad was small in stature with a tendency towards plumpness. He didn't have many friends and rarely mixed with the other boys. All in all, however, he seemed relatively normal although, the headmaster had noted, for some reason he had always kept himself more than scrupulously clean. Still, he concluded, the boy never displayed any signs of insanity.

"No outward signs of insanity," was the last thing Cowle's solicitor wanted to hear. His own investigation revealed that there were a great many abnormalities in his client's family and this, he believed, might save the boy's neck. For instance Cowle's grandmother was described as "going funny" before dying at an early age. Then there was his grandfather, who had spent quite some time in an insane asylum. Moreover, his grandmother's sister and brother had both died in asylums. This, the solicitor thought, was good ammunition for a plea of insanity. But, unfortunately for Cowle, on its own, a family history of madness would not be enough.

The psychiatrists brought into the case went so far as to agree that Charles was a high-grade mental defective. In layman's terms, he was retarded. But they refused to declare him mad.

The trial began on April 26th, 1932. Charles Cowle stood in the courtroom at Manchester Assizes, smirking and standing deliberately to attention. He gave the appearance of being nothing more than a naughty school-boy who had been caught smoking behind the bicycle sheds.

Unusually, his defence counsel was eager to air his client's past record of violence. In fact he positively high-lighted Cowle's odd behaviour. It was the defence who called Doris Sharples to give evidence about Cowle's remark, "You will be next," and they dwelt at length on the prisoner's bizarre behaviour in looking for Annie even though he knew full well where she was hidden.

But despite the valiant efforts of his counsel to convince the jury that Cowle was insane, it didn't work. The jury returned with a verdict of guilty.

Before passing sentence, Mr Justice Humphreys vented his feelings on the horrible crime which he described as "terribly sadistic." He then donned the black cap. Cowle, however, did not react.

Both during and after the trial, Charles Cowle never wavered from his matter-of-fact attitude – not even when his father tried to comfort him. "What are you bothering about, Dad, I'm all right," remarked the bewildered youth. His puzzlement at the fuss being made would last until the day he died.

On May 18th, 1932, Charles Cowle, now 19, was led to the gallows at Strangeways. Only then, seeing the wooden death instrument before him, did he appear to comprehend his fate and show fear.

Abolitionists were appalled at the prospect of hanging a youth with the mental age of a child. Nevertheless, the execution went ahead, and the people of Darwen had little sympathy for the teenager's demise.

On the day of the execution only one set of curtains was drawn in Kay Street, those of his parents. The rest of the townsfolk reserved their pity for Albert and Henrietta Farnworth.

18

ESCAPE FROM STRANGEWAYS

*John Jackson idolised Charlie Peace and vowed
to follow his hero's life of crime. He succeeded,
but only in so far as he too ended his days in the
hangman's noose.*

"Charlie Peace hanged! Charlie Peace hanged!" On
February 25th, 1879, the notorious criminal Charles
Frederick Peace was executed at Armley Prison, Leeds. It
was cause for celebration. Peace had been the terror of
Britain for many years.

Hardly had the rope tightened round the neck of the
arch-thief and murderer, however, when one man turned
from the prison gates angry and resentful at what had
happened. His name was John Jackson, a 24-year-old
plumber from Birstall, near Bradford.

All his adult life this sometime bully and social misfit had
idolised Charlie Peace and his defiance of the law. Peace
was his hero and if Jackson had one wish it was to be just
like him. Now, with the villain dead, it felt like Jackson's
world had collapsed.

That night, in a fit of total despair, Jackson toured the
pubs of Leeds, getting more and more drunk as he tried to
blot out the terrible events of the day. But the alcohol
refused to do its job. Jackson wasn't numbed, he simply
became even more morose and miserable. By the following
morning he had had enough. Feeling unable to return to his
old life in Bradford, he decided on a drastic change of
career. He went off to join the Army.

It was a momentous decision. Not, however, because he
was to shine in his new occupation. On the contrary. It was

now that John Jackson's criminal life began and he took his first tentative steps towards ending his days like his hero, dangling helplessly from the end of a rope.

Army life didn't suit Jackson. He soon had a reputation for being a rogue and a ruffian. The Army tolerated this to a certain extent but when, in 1883, he was convicted of stealing a mare and a horse, they would tolerate it no more. Jackson's army career came to an abrupt halt and he was sentenced to six months in Wakefield Prison, Yorkshire.

Charlie Peace had been well known for his daring escapes from confinement. Indeed, legend had it that he had once leapt from a speeding train to avoid arrest. Thus Jackson too had thoughts of escape even before he was sentenced.

The opportunity came soon enough. He was working in the reception cells of the prison and this gave him the opportunity to steal a suit of clothes. This he did and then, in the dead of night, he made his escape. Unhappily, however, his freedom did not last long. On January 5th, 1885, he was rearrested in Barnsley, Yorkshire. He was subsequently sentenced to a further term of six months, this time in Armley Prison.

He was released in the summer of 1885 and left Bradford to travel to Hull and then Oldham. On route he would stop off at likely-looking houses, break into them and steal what he could. The homes of Salvation Army officers were his favourite target. At one such house in Bradford he ransacked the entire place before stealing £3 in money and clothes worth £5.

Early in 1888, Jackson arrived in Manchester and again lived by house-breaking. On March 29th, he broke into a house in Eccles belonging to Salvation Army Captain Alfred Poynter and stole a signature stamp, a money box and twopence. Foolishly, however, he had asked too many questions amongst the locals about Poynter's home and suspicions had been raised. As a consequence, the police were expecting him.

Constable Crowther was waiting outside when he saw

Jackson scale the back garden wall and smash the kitchen window. He stood there patiently whilst the villain went about his work.

When Jackson emerged from the house with his booty, Crowther was ready to arrest him. He grabbed hold of the thief by the scruff of his neck and marched him down to the station. Subsequently Jackson appeared in court and, on April 9th, he was sentenced to six months hard labour and sent to Strangeways Prison.

For the first month of his imprisonment Jackson was kept in severe confinement. Then, as was the custom, he was allowed to follow his trade. Since he was trained as a plumber and gasfitter, John Jackson was sent to work in the blacksmith's shop which was attached to the prison.

One day Miss Little, matron of Strangeways, complained of a gas leak in the bedroom of her house, which was within the precincts of the prison. On Saturday, May 19th, Jackson was sent from the blacksmith's shop, in the charge of a warder named Platt, to deal with the problem. It took him an hour.

The following Monday, when it was discovered that the escape of gas still continued, Jackson was again sent over in the charge of a warder. Once again he was occupied for an hour, but despite all his efforts the gas still continued to escape.

The next day, Tuesday, May 22nd, he returned to Miss Little's house with a warder named Webb. A powerfully built man of 45, Webb had a kindly disposition which made him one of the most popular warders in the prison. Under his watchful eye, Jackson worked through the morning and then returned after lunch to finish the job. He was again accompanied by Webb.

Going away to get some tools, Jackson returned at approximately 3.00 p.m. and hammered away until 3.40 p.m. He then worked for a short time on the meter and, after returning to the blacksmith's shop with the warder, he went upstairs to the bedroom at 4.45 p.m.

Miss Little, at this time, was in the kitchen where she

remained for several minutes with the door closed. She then went into the parlour, which was beneath the bedroom. It was whilst she was in here that she heard strange rumbling sounds overhead, as if the furniture was being dragged across the floor.

She was immediately suspicious and went upstairs to try the door. It was locked. She called out, "What's the matter?" As she did a voice from within shouted back, "It's all right."

The matron was concerned. She felt that there was something wrong. Miss Little went downstairs and found the warder who was due to relieve Webb. She told him what had happened and he raced up the stairs. The door was still locked but, with the help of other warders who were now on the scene, they forced it open.

As the door gave way the warders saw their colleague on the floor. His head was covered in blood and the gaping wound in his skull was clearly visible. Webb's own boots were missing and a pair of prison issue boots lay in the middle of the room. Needless to say, Jackson had gone.

It was easy to see how he had escaped. There was a large hole in the ceiling and plaster all over the floor. Evidently he had used a chair to climb on to the mantlepiece and, from there, he had lifted himself into the roof void. He had dislodged enough slates to allow him to clamber up to the roof itself and, from there, he had fled. The house backed on to Southall Street, and it was down this wall, a drop of approximately 10 feet, that Jackson must have jumped.

Dr Braddon, the prison surgeon, came at once to attend to the injured warder. "Where are my boots?" whispered Webb in a feeble voice. "You have a cut on your head, how did it happen?" asked Braddon hurriedly. Webb thought for a moment, then said, "I fell."

"Where is the plumber?" asked Dr Braddon, referring to Jackson. "He is here," said Webb. These were the last words the warder would ever utter for he then lost consciousness and died a few moments later.

It was supposed, because there was no sign of a struggle,

that Jackson had persuaded Webb to put his nose to the pipe in order to discover where gas was still escaping. When he did so, Jackson seized the hammer and dealt him the fatal blow.

A post-mortem later revealed that Webb received a blow to the back of the head which was delivered with terrible violence. He had only been struck once, but it fractured his skull.

On the roof of the house the hammer Jackson used to break through the slates was retrieved. This hammer, said Dr Braddon, was also the murder weapon. The head fitted perfectly into the hole in the warder's skull.

"So why did he say he fell?" asked one of the warders. Braddon explained that it was quite possible that a man struck with such force from behind would have no notion what had happened to him. It was quite likely that he would have thought he had fallen or slipped.

Meanwhile, Jackson was putting as much distance between himself and the prison as he could manage. After his escape, which had taken no more than five minutes, he had run down Southall Street and then turned about for half a mile. Eventually, he crossed Cheetham Hill Road and got into Red Bank and thence to Oldham. Here he managed to beg some clothes, throwing his prison ones into a ditch. Later, his talent for house-breaking would get him more clothes and money.

In their search for Jackson, the Manchester police mounted an intense publicity campaign. A reproduction of his photograph appeared in the newspapers and posters were put up throughout the city. But it achieved nothing, other than to spread a sense of fear through the population.

Many people thought they had seen him. When a large cistern fell in the yard behind the Liberal Club Mr Hooley, who occupied the ground floor, and Mr Smith his next door neighbour, were both so certain that it was Jackson attempting a burglary that they mounted an all-night vigil to catch the villain at his crime. Smith got himself a pistol and sat with his bulldog by his side. Hooley armed himself with a poker and sat with his retriever. And each spent the night glaring at the other through the window. There was much mirth in the morning when they realised their foolishness. The story even made the local papers. But whilst this comedy was cause for some laughter, it did nothing to help the police in their efforts to catch the killer.

Jackson was finally apprehended in Bradford on June 2nd. He had evidently had a bad time of it, and appeared in a depressed condition, sighing and groaning constantly in a most dejected way.

Jackson immediately admitted who he was. "I am the man that done it, but I don't know what possessed me to do it." He declared that he only knew Warder Webb was dead when he read about it the next day in the newspapers. He added that he had no intention of killing him. "If I had to answer to my Maker at this moment, I would tell Him I had no intention of killing that man," he declared.

Asked how he survived whilst on the run, Jackson concocted a story about various benefactors who had helped him. "I met a man in Halifax who knew me," he said "and he gave me money. Afterwards I met a man I knew in Leeds who gave me something, then you know, I had the money I got from the house at Oldham."

John Jackson was brought to trial and promptly found guilty. Before his execution, which was carried out by James Berry, Jackson confessed to the crime. He was then led to the scaffold at Strangeways Prison and, on Tuesday, 7th August, 1888, he met his death. His body was later interred in the prison yard.

For a few weeks John Jackson's dream of being as notorious as his hero Charlie Peace had come true when he was known, as one newspaper of the time put it, as "a daring and adroit criminal, the recital of whose exploits caused wonder and consternation throughout the land."

Unfortunately, unlike Peace, it was Jackson's fate to be quickly forgotten.

19

THE LANCASHIRE POISONER

Mary Ann Britland had a problem with mice. At least that is what everyone thought when she went to the chemist to buy the arsenic.

Thirty-eight-year-old Mary Ann Britland was delighted with the new house at 92 Turner Lane, Ashton-under-Lyne, Lancashire. It was much roomier than her last home and had a nice big back yard. She, her husband Thomas and their two daughters, Elizabeth, 19, and Suzannah, 18, would surely be happy here and, as they moved in the last of their possessions in the winter of 1885 they were filled with excitement.

There was, however, one problem with their new home: mice. The house was overrun with them. They got into cupboards and drawers, ate the Britlands' food and destroyed their clothes. It was enough to drive anyone to distraction and for Mrs Britland, who was a woman who prided herself on keeping a clean and tidy house, it was nothing short of a disaster. She was soon at her wits' end.

She complained about the mice problem to her landlord, Mr Fielding-Oldfield, but he gruffly denied the accusation. He said that the mice were nothing to do with him and suggested that she get herself a cat. Mrs Britland told him this was impossible as the family kept a pet canary. Moreover, she was not in the least partial to cats and didn't want one in her house. Mr Fielding-Oldfield then suggested poison to solve the problem. Mrs Britland considered this to be an excellent idea and told him she would attend to it straight away.

As a consequence, the following day Mrs Britland walked to Hirst's chemist's shop in Old Street and purchased three packets of *Harrison's Vermin Killer*. This was a lethal concoction of strychnine and arsenic mixed with rice and Mrs Britland had to sign the poisons book before she could have it. As was customary, her signature also had to be witnessed by a third person. Usually it was the chemist's assistant who fulfilled this duty, but he was away that day so fellow customer William Waterhouse, a retired watchmaker, obliged.

Joking as he appended his name, he said, "Now mind, Missus, you administer them scientifically and not in too large doses, or you will not get the insurance money."

Mrs Britland was not amused. "Oh! If you think I could do anything of that sort, may God forgive you," she snapped curtly, and gathering up the packets of poison, flounced out of the shop.

To their neighbours in Turner Lane, the Britlands seemed to be a happy, hard-working family. Thomas, who was 44, worked as a carter and occasional barman at a pub called Heap's Vaults. He was a cheerful, friendly soul with no obvious faults or vices. He was fond of his beer, of course, but drank no more than most other working men. For the most part he carried himself with perfect decorum and dignity.

Thomas's wife and children were equally respectable. Mary Ann worked at Fisher's Mill in Turner Lane, as did their eldest daughter, Elizabeth. Suzannah, their youngest child, was in service in Oldham. There was no controversy attached to them and no hint that anything was wrong. To everyone who encountered them the Britlands appeared an entirely normal family. Soon, however, that was all to change.

On the evening of Monday, March 8th, 1886, Elizabeth returned home having spent a happy day out with her young man, William Davies. She had a light supper then went to bed. A short time later, however, she was woken by the most agonizing cramps in her stomach. She cried out in pain.

Her mother came rushing to her aid and did what she could to help. But it was impossible to soothe the girl. Elizabeth was writhing about in pain and obviously in agony. The dreadful discomfort went on all through the night until finally the day dawned and Mrs Britland was able to go for the doctor.

Dr Thompson arrived at 10 a.m. and hurried upstairs to see the patient. He had been told that Elizabeth was at death's door. Soon enough, however, he decided that her mother had been exaggerating. The girl was clearly ill but, after examining her he declared there was no great cause for alarm. Her symptoms, he said, were common enough. In his opinion she was suffering from nothing more than an upset stomach, and he prescribed accordingly.

The following morning Mrs Britland, still bothered by the mice, put on her shawl and slipped round to Hirst's again to buy another packet of *Harrison's Vermin Killer*. This errand done, she spent the rest of the day nursing Elizabeth. For all the doctor's reassurance, her daughter was still very ill.

Mrs Britland called for Dr Thompson again that afternoon and, once more, he came to the house. Thompson found little improvement in his patient, who was now complaining of a choking feeling in her throat. But he still did not consider her condition to be serious. If anything, he was even more dismissive than he had been before. He put most of the girl's symptoms down to hysteria and told her mother that rest, peace and quiet would probably see her right. But he also gave Mrs Britland another bottle of stomach medicine to give to her daughter if the pains continued.

Thompson had scarcely gone when Elizabeth's condition took a dramatic turn for the worse. She began to shiver and twitch in the most alarming fashion. Her mother administered more stomach medicine but it made no difference at all. Elizabeth continued to shake and shudder.

Mrs Britland was powerless.

Normally, with her husband out at work, Mary Britland would have had to cope alone, but fortunately she had found some wonderfully caring neighbours in Thomas and Mary Ann Dixon, who lived only a few doors away. She rushed round to fetch them.

While she held on to Elizabeth's arms, the Dixons held down the girl's legs and, between them, they calmed her through one frenzied fit after another. Mrs Dixon suggested that they should call for the doctor again but, as he had already called twice and had been of little use, Mary Britland decided against it. Instead they tried to manage by themselves. The fits went on for hour after hour, with hardly a moment of peace. But finally, towards evening, the patient became calmer. Then, at 9 o'clock, she died.

When Dr Thompson attended again, it was too late for him to reconsider his original diagnosis. But in any case he doubted what he would have said. He was at a loss to know what the girl had suffered and wrote out the death certificate stating simply that death was due to bilious vomiting and convulsions and spasms of the heart. He saw nothing suspicious and had no reason to call for an investigation. But he was perplexed all the same.

That morning, March 10th, Mrs Sarah Lord, an elderly widow who was well known to the family, came to wash Elizabeth's body prior to burial. She had been as shocked as anyone to hear of the girl's death. Mrs Lord had seen Elizabeth just two days before and she had seemed in perfectly good health. "What on earth happened to the poor dear?" she kept asking.

Understandably, Mary Britland was far too upset to talk about it and she gave the woman only the barest details. Breaking into tears she asked Mrs Lord to stop asking questions and begged her to hurry up and wash the body quickly before it went stiff.

As Mrs Lord complied, she was struck by how tightly clenched the girl's hands were, a disturbing indication of the agony she must have been in. She tried several times to open the fingers, but rigor mortis had already set in.

On Thursday, March 11th, Mrs Britland went to see Mr Richard Mortimer, the agent for the Prudential Insurance Society who, because of her daughter's death, paid her £10.00 "club money" out of a life insurance fund to which she regularly subscribed. It was not the last time Mrs Britland would visit him.

On Friday, April 30th, Mrs Britland called at Mortimer's house and paid him one shilling and eight pence, the club money due on the life of her husband. It was not the usual day for the insurance money to be paid in; it should have been Saturday and as a rule Mortimer called on subscribers to collect it. But Mrs Britland explained that as she would be away on Saturday she thought she should pay the money now – just in case.

Later that afternoon, Mrs Britland bumped into a friend, Mary Hadfield, and asked her if she would go with her to Kilvington's, a chemist shop in Wellington Road. She needed to buy some more mouse powder, she said, as the damn creatures were still eating her flannels, and would need a witness to sign the poison register.

The women went into Kilvington's together and Mrs Britland purchased three packets of *Hunter's Infallible Vermin and Insect Destroyer*.

Thomas Britland arrived home late that evening. He ate his supper as usual and went straight to bed. He woke up feeling dizzy and unwell, so at 10 o'clock the next morning Mrs Britland went to fetch Dr Charles Tucker.

The doctor was perplexed by Mr Britland's condition. He noticed that, throughout the examination, Britland was glancing nervously about the room. He queried this with him and Britland, in a shaking voice, answered, "I don't know: there are queer things about." He then went on to whisper that he could often see and hear people moving about. Whenever he went to investigate these strange occurrences, however, he found nothing. He added that he had not slept well for weeks.

None of this information made much sense to Dr

Tucker, but when Birtland also mentioned that he had recently drunk more beer in an evening "than I have in my entire life" the doctor immediately grasped the true nature of the man's condition. Dr Tucker decided that his patient was suffering from incipient *delirium tremens* and treated him accordingly.

All that weekend, Thomas Britland suffered, but it did nothing to distract his wife from the mice problem. At half-past nine on the morning of Monday, May 3rd, Mary again paid a visit to Hirst's to buy a further three packets of *Harrison's Vermin Killer*. She returned later with the poison in her bag and found her husband's condition had deteriorated seriously.

At 12 noon, Britland had a particularly bad attack of pain and vomiting and Mrs Britland sent for the Dixons to come and help. By the time they arrived, all sensation had left her husband's legs and Mr Dixon and Mrs Britland set about rubbing him to try and restore the circulation. But it did no good. Then Mary Britland prepared a bowl of mustard and hot water into which her husband might dip his feet. Alas, just as he set his limbs into the steaming mixture, Thomas Britland fell back and gasped: "Mary Ann, I must leave thee!" He then rolled over and died.

When Dr Tucker arrived, he certified that Britland had died from epilepsy and that same afternoon Mrs Britland, accompanied by Thomas Dixon, went to Mossley to collect eight pounds club money from James Nield, the treasurer of the Mossley District of the Independent Order of Oddfellows, of which Thomas Britland had been a member.

Unfortunately in their haste to get there, they failed to take the proper death certificate with them and so they had to go back to fetch it. In fact, they were unable to collect the money until the following day when they returned to Mr Mortimer with the correct documentation and received the eight pounds that was Mrs Britland's due. She also received a further £11. 7s. insurance payment from the Prudential. But, as Mrs Britland would later say, "money is no exchange for a husband."

After Thomas's funeral Mary was still understandably distraught and Mrs Dixon generously invited the widow to spend as much time as she liked at their house rather than at number 82. She realised that, with Suzannah still away in service, Mrs Britland would be alone in her grief and might be in need of company and friendship. From Mary Britland's point of view the invitation was a mixed blessing. She welcomed her neighbour's kindness, but she was concerned about the gossip that was going about the town.

Rumours of an affair between Mr Dixon and Mrs Britland had been doing the rounds after they had been seen boarding the Oldham train together some weeks before. Some of the more mischievous gossips had even suggested that Thomas Britland's "noises around the house at night" were not entirely the product of his fevered brain. And now, with Thomas dead, she wouldn't dare guess what was being said. But she reflected that, moving in to the Dixons' home at the invitation of Mr Dixon's wife might actually take some of the steam out of the gossip. Mrs Britland thus consented.

For a brief while it worked. Suspicions were abated and the gossip died down. But then a neighbour spotted Thomas Dixon accompanying Mrs Britland into an Ashton hat shop, where a hat her husband had bought a couple of months before his death, and never worn, was exchanged for a nice new Sunday hat for Dixon. This was all that was needed to start the tongues wagging again.

On Thursday, May 13th, Mr and Mrs Dixon went into Ashton together to do some afternoon shopping. Mrs Dixon returned home alone at 10 o'clock that evening because her husband had been detained on an errand in the town. As the supper was already prepared, she went and invited "poor Mary Ann" to eat with them and stay the night. Dixon arrived home at around 10.30 and the gathering, Mr and Mrs Dixon, Selina Wolfenden (Mrs Dixon's unmarried sister, who lived with them) and Mrs Britland sat down to enjoy supper. The meal was quickly consumed and at 11 p.m. the Dixons and the rest of the party, including Mrs Britland, retired to bed.

Fifteen minutes later, Mrs Dixon began complaining of pains in her stomach. Dixon got up to make her some tea. Mrs Britland, who was in Miss Wolfenden's room, heard the commotion.

"Tom, is that you?" she called out. "What's to do?"

"Mary's ill," he replied on his way downstairs.

Mrs Dixon was crying out with pain and thrashing about in bed. She was making a frightful noise and soon the entire household was roused, including Mrs Dixon's father, who liked to keep himself to himself in an attic room. With every appearance of distress at her friend's suffering, Mrs Britland quickly warmed some flannels to apply to Mary Dixon's stomach. Mary's husband went out to fetch Dr Thompson, the physician who had unsuccessfully treated Elizabeth Britland.

On arriving at the house Thompson administered a drug to relieve the pain and this seemed to work. By the time the doctor left, Mrs Dixon had become quieter and the pain had given way to shivering and twitching. She was very thirsty, however, and neither the tea nor the medicine did anything to relieve this. Then, to the horror of those present, Mary Dixon began grinding her teeth and her eyes became fixed, almost popping from her head. At 5.50. a.m. she died.

Again, as had been the case with Elizabeth Britland, Dr Thompson was not present at the time of death so he had to rely on Mr Dixon's description of the symptoms in order to complete the certificate. He declared that Mary Britland's death had been due to abdominal spasms.

Mrs Lord arrived later that morning to lay out Mrs Dixon's body. Mrs Britland again tersely instructed her to wash the body quickly before it went stiff.

Mrs Lord was shocked to find the dead woman beaded with perspiration, her hands clenched tightly. It was a grotesque sight, similar to that she had encountered when laying out both Elizabeth and Thomas Britland.

"I have laid out many bodies," she told the neighbours afterwards, "but I never saw any like these 'afore."

As a consequence of her remarks, suspicion at these sudden deaths began to mount and resulted in a letter being sent anonymously to the police.

Thomas Dixon had been to visit Amos Perry of the Union Friendly Insurance Society to inform him of Mrs Dixon's death. Perry offered his condolences and agreed to return home with him in order to sign the necessary documents. The two men entered the house to find Mary Ann Britland close to hysterics.

"Who dost think has been here?" she shrieked. "Chief Inspector Dalgliesh and Inspector Snell! And they wanted to know about Mary! They wanted to see the medicine and they went into the backyard and looked about."

"I don't care if one hundred and fifty Dalglieshes have been here," retorted Dixon, angrily thumping his fist on the table. "I would rather have my Mary than the club money any time."

"No doubt," agreed Perry, whose presence had been overlooked during this dramatic exchange. "Still, there have been three deaths in Turner Lane, all of a similar character, and Dalgliesh might well want to know about it."

"What's it got to do with them?" cried Mrs Britland hotly. "Do they think we poisoned her?"

Perry, rather embarrassed by the scene he had unwittingly stepped into, attempted to avoid the subject. He valiantly turned the conversation back to the reason for his visit, signing the papers which would release the club money. Mrs Britland agreed to act as witness, but her hands shook so badly that she had to be soothed before she could sign her name.

The following morning, May 15th, Perry paid out £19.17s.6d to Thomas Dixon.

Later that day John Law, the owner of a café in Warrington Street, called at Dixon's house to discuss supplying refreshments for Mrs Dixon's funeral. Mrs Britland opened the door to him, and was shaking visibly. Unprompted, she began telling about the visit of the two policemen and that a post-mortem was going to be performed on Mrs Dixon that afternoon.

She ushered John Law up to the front bedroom, where Mrs Dixon was laid out. "Do you think she has been poisoned?" Mrs Britland whispered, inviting him with a gesture to survey the body.

With an uncomfortable glance at the corpse, Law told her that he did not know about poison, but Mrs Britland continued to press him for an opinion, as if his answer was of the utmost importance.

"Have you ever seen anyone poisoned?"

"I have seen one man," Law admitted, "but he'd had a mouse powder. That man swelled and went black."

Mrs Britland, looking over at the corpse, said with some relief, "Mary is not swelled."

"Perhaps she didn't have a full dose," suggested Law.

"Why? Can they tell?" Mrs Britland asked anxiously.

"Yes, if they open her up," replied Law, airily. "Many things can be told from a dead body."

Mrs Britland, conspiratorially drawing him closer, as if the corpse of Mrs Dixon might overhear, asked: "Could they tell if she had had it in her tea?"

Law nodded. "They could tell whichever way she'd had it."

Mrs Britland fell silent for a moment then, fidgeting with her brooch, she confided that she had bought some mouse powder the week before. Law suddenly realised the true nature of their conversation.

"Does Mr Dixon know about this?" he asked.

"No, no, he doesn't," Mrs Britland replied.

Law advised her to tell him immediately. He called him upstairs, but Mrs Britland was unwilling to say anything more. Law, therefore, rather bluntly told Dixon about the mouse powder. Dixon was horrified.

"What! Bought a mouse powder? I would rather have given you ten pounds than you should have bought any such stuff!" and he threw his arms around his dead wife and sobbed, "If anyone has given you poison, do tell me!"

Mrs Britland turned to Law, who stood looking on in some bewilderment, and begged him not to say anything to anyone about the mouse powder. Law, who certainly didn't want to be called as a murder trial witness, gladly promised her he wouldn't.

At 2.00 p.m. that afternoon Dr Alexander Hamilton, watched carefully by Dalgliesh and Snell, performed a post-mortem examination on Mrs Dixon in the tiny front bedroom of the house in Turner Lane.

Mrs Mary Dixon Snr., Thomas Dixon's step-mother, called to pay her respects and offer her help. As she was washing up some pots at the sink she noticed two empty glass jars on the mantlepiece and Mrs Britland, who had just come up behind her, said, "I wonder what those jars are for."

"To take away the stomach and contents to see if there is anything awry. Maybe there is something there that shouldn't be there" said Mrs Dixon.

Mrs Britland's jaw dropped.

It was at the inquest that the truth came out. Lethal amounts of strychnine and arsenic had been found in Mrs Dixon's stomach. Even before the proceedings had concluded, Mrs Britland was arrested. She was charged, not only with the wilful murder of Mary Ann Dixon, but also on the suspicion of having caused the deaths of her own husband and daughter.

Thomas Dixon was also arrested and charged with being an accessory. Subsequently, however, he was released.

"He ought to have been locked up all the same with me. It was him that led me into it, and he wanted to go away before I was locked up," complained Mary Britland to the guard who accompanied her on the train to Strangeways Prison. "He told me he would go with me when the bother was over, but I had nothing to go away for, and if I went away people would only think I was guilty whether I am or not."

Mrs Britland's trial took place on Thursday, July 22nd, 1886, before Mr Justice Cave. Mr Addison appeared for the prosecution and Mr Blair for the defence. She pleaded not guilty.

During the case, the court heard of the supposed affair between the prisoner and Mary Dixon's husband. Suzannah Britland, Mr Britland's surviving daughter, told the court that she had often heard her father complain of the frequency of Thomas Dixon's visits to his house, although she had never witnessed any impropriety. Other witnesses also testified to having frequently seen the couple in each other's company.

Evidence was also presented to show that Thomas Dixon was not happy with his wife. William Davies, Elizabeth Britland's sweetheart, testified that he had often heard Dixon making disparaging remarks about his wife, saying that she wasn't "up to much" and that she could "hardly sew a button on." Other neighbours told the court how unkempt and disorganised Mrs Dixon had been, and how entirely unlike the efficient and capable Mrs Britland she was.

Dr Harris was then called to the stand and gave details of the findings he and Dr Alexander Hamilton had made on Thursday, June 10th, 1886, having examined the exhumed bodies of Thomas and Elizabeth Britland. In Thomas's body the pathologist had found one-tenth of a grain of arsenic; in Elizabeth's one-twentieth of a grain. No strychnine was found in either of their bodies, but this was only to be expected because by the time of the exhumations the poison would have been fully absorbed into the tissues.

The mouse powders had already been taken from Mrs Britland's house and had been sent for analysis. The conclusions were read out in court. *Hunter's Infallible Vermin and Insect Destroyer* contained 2.2 grains of strychnine, while *Harrison's Vermin Killer* contained 2.2 grains of strychnine and 3.52 grains of arsenic. The latter, with its mixture of poisons, was by far the more lethal of the two. Indeed, the difference in potency was borne out (so maintained Addison for the prosecution) by their differing effects on Elizabeth and Thomas Britland.

According to the chemist's poisons book, Mrs Britland had purchased *Harrison's Vermin Killer* before her daughter became ill, and again on the day she died. She had then changed chemists because, Addison claimed, she feared rousing too much suspicion. On April 30th, Mrs Britland had gone to Kilvington's in Wellington Road, where, according to Mr Kilvington's poisons book, she had bought three packets of *Hunter's Infallible Vermin and Insect Destroyer*. That was the evening when, after supper, Thomas Britland became ill.

"Because this mouse powder was of a less lethal nature," the prosecution insisted, "it failed to kill Mr Britland outright. It was a very desperate and determined woman who went back to Hirst's chemist's shop on May 3rd to buy three more packets of the more effective poison; the proven brand."

Addison then cited the evidence of Dr Julius Dreschfeld, physician to the Manchester Royal Infirmary, who had testified that the symptoms described in the deaths of Elizabeth Britland, her father Thomas and Mrs Dixon – spasms of the lower limbs and trunk, vomiting and diarrhoea – were all consistent with strychnine poisoning. However, if arsenic was mixed with strychnine (*Harrison's Vermin Killer*) the spasms would not be as great, but death would be much quicker.

Another effect of strychnine poisoning is that rigor mortis sets in very soon after death. This was why, declared Addison, Mrs Britland had been insistent that the corpses be laid out without delay. The prisoner, he claimed, knew that certain poisons had this effect on the body.

Mr Blair, for the defence, said that at no time during the trial had a motive for the alleged crimes been given. The insurance money was no compensation for the loss of her husband's regular income and there was no real evidence of an affair between the accused and Thomas Dixon.

Blair declared that the reason Mrs Britland had bought

mouse powder was entirely innocent. The house was over-run with mice, he stated. The court had already heard as much from Suzannah Britland and others. Perhaps, he conceded, the poison had been taken accidentally. But it was unthinkable that it had been administered on purpose. If Mrs Britland had meant mischief, then surely she would not have bought the mouse powder so openly?

"If the case for the prosecution is sure," concluded Blair passionately, "then this ordinary, simple woman at my back is the worst criminal that has been tried in twenty-two years of this court's existence."

Of course, he did not and never could believe this. But would the jury?

The judge certainly did not share his opinion. Turning to the jury Mr Justice Cave pointed out that there was no need to prove a motive in order to prove a case and that although it was true people could be careless and accidents with household poisons had occurred before, it was hard to believe this had happened three times. The questions the jury had to consider were: did Mary Ann Dixon die because mouse powder had been given to her in food, and if so, was Mrs Britland responsible?

It was no easy task. Opinion amongst the jury members was bitterly divided. The woman in the dock certainly didn't look like a killer and, as Mr Blair had pointed out, what motive did she have? But the circumstantial evidence seemed to be damning. Was she innocent or was she guilty?

After two hours the jury gave up and their foreman told the judge that they were unable to reach a verdict. The judge, however, refused to accept this and ordered them to retire again. The jurors diligently debated the case for several more hours but were still unable to agree. At 10 o'clock in the evening they had still not reached a verdict.

The judge reminded them of the salient points of the case. He told them that one person present that night at supper, Mrs Britland, Mr Dixon or Selina Wolfenden, was responsible for the death of Mrs Dixon. He also told them that only Mrs Britland was known to have bought mouse powder. The jurors agreed with these bald statements, but they also felt that Thomas Dixon must also have been in some way involved. The judge then reminded them of John Law's conversation with Mrs Britland on May 15th which indicated that Dixon was not aware she had purchased mouse powder and was indeed shocked by the news. "And if this is true," he said, "it is very difficult to see what part he had in the matter."

The jury retired for a further five minutes and then returned with a clear verdict of guilt against Mrs Britland, without any recommendation for mercy.

The judge told her sternly, "There is no kind of murder that is worse than that of administering poison, and especially when it is administered by one person in the household of another who had sheltered her and taken her in." He then pronounced the sentence of death.

After sentence had been passed Mrs Britland turned to address the court. In faltering speech she declared, "I am quite innocent, I am not guilty at all."

Except when Suzannah had given evidence, Mrs Britland had maintained a calm demeanour, but now she broke down weeping. Her cries of anguish could be heard long after she was taken to the cells below the court. "She cried for mercy, but had none for her victims," noted one cynical observer.

Mrs Britland's solicitor immediately started up a petition on her behalf, but collected few signatures. Those who had not been able to attend the trial had read all about her in the newspapers, and they had been less than kind to her.

At Strangeways Mrs Britland became very depressed. Her mother and Suzannah, who visited her daily, told the newspapers that she had confessed her guilt to them.

On the morning of the execution, Monday, August 9th, 1886, Mrs Britland was paralysed with fear and had to be half-carried screaming to the scaffold.

"Oh, forgive me, forgive me," she wailed as the bolt was drawn by executioner James Berry. She died instantly, becoming the first woman to be hanged at Strangeways.

20

MURDER IN BURY

George Gordon suspected that something was going on with the manager of his furniture store in Bolton but he never imagined that it would lead to his own death.

Promptly at 9 o'clock on Wednesday morning, September 25th, 1889, 19-year-old William Tootill unlocked the door of the Gordon Furnishing Company's shop at 39 Bolton Street, Bury, in Lancashire and looked around for the general manager. But 28-year-old William Dukes was nowhere to be seen. Tootill sighed and got on with his work. It was not unusual for his boss to be absent. Dukes was a skiver. He was often late and sometimes would not even bother to turn up at all. Tootill already had a good idea of where the man might be.

The Railway Inn stood directly opposite the shop, and the Lord Nelson was a few doors further down. Tootill was almost certain that Dukes could be found in one or other of these establishments, but he didn't go looking for him. After all, he considered himself capable enough to carry on the business of the shop, selling and hiring out furniture, without supervision. He relished the responsibility and only regretted that he didn't have Dukes's salary to go with it. Life, he reasoned, was simply not fair.

Why George Gordon had given him the job Tootill couldn't imagine. William Dukes had moved to Lancashire from Burton-upon-Trent some twelve years before and had begun his working career as an office boy with a firm of Bolton solicitors, a job which he had managed to hold down for four years. Thereafter, however, he changed jobs frequently and Tootill could guess why. In the boy's experience, Bill Dukes had never completed a full day's work. Moreover, he had a strong suspicion that the man was also dishonest. He was almost certain that Dukes was fiddling the books though he had no proof of the fact.

Tootill knew he should report his suspicions to Mr Gordon, but he never did so. Despite his misgivings, he still felt a sense of loyalty to Bill Dukes and had no desire to betray him. In truth he felt a little sorry for the man. Dukes was married to a sickly young woman and had not much of a homelife. She lived in Manchester, but they also had a home in Bury, above a little sweet-shop in Paradise Street – a gift from Mrs Dukes' brother – and that was squalid and dirty. If Mr Dukes had been embezzling money from the firm, he certainly hadn't spent it there. The place reeked of poverty and hardly had a stick of furniture in it. Tootill had visited him there once. It had been quite a shock.

As Tootill went about his morning chores, idly wondering if his boss might turn up before lunchtime, the train from Manchester chuffed gently into Bolton Street station. George Gordon, whose family owned the Bury shop, alighted. George's father, Samuel Gordon, had come to Manchester from Poland 25 years earlier, in 1864. A Jewish refugee fleeing persecution, he had settled in Cheetham Hill, a predominantly Jewish district of Manchester, and had opened his first furniture shop in Great Ducie Street shortly after. Over the years the business flourished and expanded and now it was a small empire with several branch shops, including the one in Bury. Samuel, however, had grown old and ill and his sons, George and Meyer, were increasingly taking over the running of the business. Or at least they had been until a bitter row divided them and Meyer went off to pursue his own interests. That left George to run it almost single-handed for his father.

George visited the Bury shop every week, usually on a Tuesday – it was the only day he was free to do this in his busy schedule. He checked the books and collected the takings. However, over the past five weeks he hadn't visited the shop at all. Instead he had been preoccupied with a rather peculiar series of requests by one of William Dukes's customers.

It had begun on August 19th, when he had received a letter from one C. Alstead at Lime Tree House, Prestwich.

Dear Sir,
Please call personally at my house tomorrow (Tuesday) morning
between 11 and one: not before 11 and not after one. I wish to
furnish, for cash, a drawing and dining room and being indis-
posed, cannot leave the house.

Mr Alstead was not known to George Gordon, but Dukes had assured him that the man was a valued customer. He was, said Dukes, ready to spend upwards of fifty or sixty pounds and contacted Mr Gordon only because the selection of stock at the main Manchester shop was more extensive than that held in the Bury branch.

George Gordon thus set off as requested to visit Mr Alstead and reasoned that, as Prestwich lies between Manchester and Bury, he would be able to call on Bolton Street later in the day. However, though he got to Prestwich in good time, he could not find Lime Tree House anywhere and none of the locals had heard of it. Eventually he gave up looking, but he had wasted so much time on the search that it was now too late to go on to Bury. His visit there would have to wait a week.

The following Monday, however, another missive arrived from Mr Alstead. This time it was a post-card saying that he would be calling in at the shop the next day and hoped to be able to speak to Mr Gordon about his proposed purchases. Once more, therefore, George Gordon was detained from travelling to Bury. And yet again it turned out to be a wasted day. Mr Alstead never turned up.

Over the coming weeks Mr Alstead continued to make appointments to see Mr Gordon – always on a Tuesday – but he failed to keep any of them. After he had missed the fifth appointment George Gordon finally began to get suspicious. He started to think that it might have all been a ruse designed to stop him visiting the Bury shop. He now doubted if Mr Alstead even existed.

Wednesday was the eve of the Jewish New Year and George Gordon didn't want any worries hanging over him during the festivities. He therefore resolved to go up to Bury without delay, to speak to William Dukes and find out what on earth was going on.

Mr Gordon arrived in the shop at 9.30 that morning, and as he had half-expected his general manager was not there. The boy Tootill was all on his own, busily engrossed in applying polish to a wooden table.

"Where's Dukes?" Gordon bellowed.

"He had to be out on business this morning sir," the boy nervously replied, putting down the polish and hastily trying to smooth his hair. "He should be back very shortly."

"In that case I'll wait for him here," Gordon said, seating himself in a large armchair close to the shop door. Uneasily, William Tootill tried to continue with his work, desperately hoping that his boss would be neither too late nor too drunk when he returned to the shop.

The hours ticked by and George Gordon became more and more impatient. But then, at 11.45 a.m., a telegram arrived. Dukes had sent it from Manchester where, so he claimed, he was currently attending to the needs of his Mr Alstead. George Gordon was dumbfounded, but he didn't believe a word of it. Dukes had written that he would be back in the Bury shop that afternoon. Gordon decided to wait for him.

Dukes walked through the door a few minutes after 1.00 p.m. and immediately encountered the angry proprietor. He tried to be apologetic about his absence and explained again that he had been with Mr Alstead. But Mr George would have none of it. He was clearly furious. The two men then retired into the small warehouse at the back of the shop to talk, leaving Tootill wondering if Dukes was to be seriously told off. After a while, however, he concluded that the problem had been resolved. Perhaps, after all, his boss had been telling the truth.

Indeed, an hour later, this seemed to be borne out. George Fowler, a fellow employee of the Gordon Furnishing Company, arrived from the Manchester shop saying that he had to transport a number of items of furniture to Mr Alstead's house in Prestwich. Tootill called to his boss to let him know that the boy had arrived, and both Dukes and Mr Gordon came out to supervise the loading of the cart. Then they went back inside the warehouse. They seemed in reasonably good humour.

A little while later, Dukes came out alone. He handed Fowler and Tootill a note of Mr Alstead's address, Lime Tree House, Prestwich, and told them to get moving. "Mr Gordon and Mr Alstead have gone to Prestwich by train," he warned, "so you have got to look sharp and get there before them." Neither of the boys had seen Gordon leave, but they gave the matter no thought. They both set off for Prestwich.

Alas, however, although the pair searched Prestwich for more than three-quarters of an hour, they could find neither Lime Tree House nor anyone named Alstead. Eventually they gave up and, at 5.00 p.m. they returned to the shop, the van still piled high with Alstead's purchases.

When Dukes learnt of their difficulties he looked at them with utter contempt. It was clear that he regarded them both as being unbelievably stupid. Hurriedly he began to sketch out directions, then suddenly changed his mind. Scrunching up his piece of paper, he threw it into a bin.

"I have no time to bother with it now," he declared, "Tell Mr Gordon I will deliver the suite tomorrow." Dukes then went out.

Going back into the shop for his smart jacket, Tootill was surprised to find the warehouse door, which was always kept open, had now been locked. This, he thought, was rather odd, especially when Dukes returned and unlocked it again a few minutes later. What was odder still, however, was the message his boss gave to Fowler, which he told him to deliver to the Gordons when he got back to Manchester:

"If old Samuel Gordon asks about his son, he has gone to Burnley."

Tootill knew that the Gordon family had a branch shop there, so the message made some sense. But Mr Dukes had already told him that George Gordon had gone ahead to Prestwich. So why should he now be going off to Burnley as well?

Tootill didn't linger on the puzzle for long, however, because just then Dukes came across and told him that he could go home for the rest of the day. Normally Tootill had to work until 8 o'clock so it was an extraordinarily early reprieve. He hastily put on his jacket and gleefully walked out of the door. It was only when he was walking down the road that Tootill began to think that this was rather odd too.

As Tootill was leaving, Dukes mentioned he was off to the theatre for the evening. Nevertheless, a light was seen burning late at the shop.

At 8.30 a.m. the following morning, Thursday, September 26th, William Dukes called at Tootill's lodgings to tell him that an important order had just come in from Rochdale and had to be sent out immediately. He would have to hire a cart from William Simpkin but first he wanted Tootill to come with him to the shop and help him put a lock on a wardrobe.

Tootill accompanied his boss back to Bolton Street and set to work. They got the lock fitted fairly quickly and moved the wardrobe downstairs to the kitchen where it was set upright near the cellar door. Dukes then told Tootill to go off and get the cart.

Half an hour later, Tootill returned with Simpkin and his cart. They went into the shop and Tootill walked over to the kitchen to get Dukes. The door to the kitchen was locked and the blinds drawn and Tootill had rattled the handle for a few moments before Dukes came out.

Dukes told Simpkin that he wanted a suite of furniture taken to a Mrs Shorrocks at the Golden Fleece pub in Rochdale. There was a very heavy wardrobe amongst the load, he said, the one that he had brought down with Tootill a little while earlier. He wondered if Simpkin's cart would bear the weight. Later, still fussing about the wardrobe, he told Simpkin that it was to be put on the tail-end of the cart and that he would travel with it himself. They then began loading up.

It was at 11 o'clock, when they were all busy at their work, that old Mr Samuel Gordon and his son, Meyer, arrived. The old man looked frail and agitated. Meyer, who had something of a reputation for violence, was red-faced and angry. They were both looking for George, whom they had not seen since the previous morning.

Dukes told them that as far as he knew, Mr Gordon had gone to the shop in Burnley but Meyer wouldn't believe it. George Gordon had told his family earlier that he felt all was not as it should be at the Bury store. He said that he was worried about Bill Dukes and believed that he was up to no good. Meyer thus already suspected that something untoward had happened and would not be fobbed off with any of Dukes's lame explanations. He told Dukes bluntly that he was talking nonsense. The previous evening had been the Jewish New Year and George would not have been absent from his family for anything. Besides, the Burnley shop had closed for the holiday.

Dukes persisted with his claim all the same. But Meyer refused to be convinced. He just got more and more annoyed. Eventually Meyer declared that the time for talk was over. He demanded that they should go to the police immediately. "You can explain George's disappearance there," he said.

Dukes hesitated but Meyer Gordon refused to take no for an answer. He grabbed the manager by his lapels and frogmarched him down the road.

At the station Superintendent Henderson did all he could to calm Meyer, but the man would not be placated. He was adamant that something terrible had happened to his brother and demanded that the police search the shop in Bolton Street. He went on to explain again that Wednesday had been the festival of the Jewish New Year and if George had been alive he would have been with his family. Nothing would have kept his brother away from the festivities.

Superintendent Henderson didn't know what to make of Meyer Gordon's allegation. He was tempted to think that the man was just being hysterical, but Meyer was so insistent that he felt bound to investigate. Summoning two junior policemen, Constables Bremner and M'Clellan, he instructed them to go to the shop and find out what they could.

Neither policeman had much enthusiasm for the task. They both felt that they had been sent on a wild goose chase and were reluctant to do anything but give the shop a cursory looking over. Meyer, however, insisted that they search the premises from top to bottom.

There was scant evidence of anything untoward having happened. But the shop was in something of a state. Chairs and tables were lying haphazardly about and the whole building was in considerable disarray. Bill Dukes followed the policemen around, clearly uneasy with what was going on. But he made no attempt to hinder them. Every now and again he tried to make light of the situation, claiming that the shop was always in a mess because his assistant was an oaf. At one point he whispered to PC Bremner that George Gordon had probably run off with a woman but for the rest of the time he stuck to his story about him being in Burnley.

The policemen continued with their search for a little while and were about to give up when Constable Bremner noticed a bloodstained screwdriver in the kitchen. It was next to the wardrobe that Tootill and Simpkin were going to take to Rochdale. He carefully picked it up and showed it to his colleague. This macabre discovery was the first indication that something really was wrong. They looked at Bill Dukes but he offered no explanation.

Then they discussed going down into the cellar. At this suggestion all the colour drained from Bill Dukes's face and he became decidedly anxious. "There's nothing down there," he said with forced airiness. The policemen now became intensely suspicious. Indeed, they were convinced that something was down there. So down they all went.

At the bottom, a couple of stone flags had been raised and there was a spade nearby. But the soil under the flags was hard and evidently untouched. Meyer looked at the stones carefully. Perhaps he was expecting them to be stained with blood or yield some other clue. If so, he was disappointed. They were covered only with dirt and dust. The policemen shone their lights into the corners of the room, evidently expecting that something would reveal itself. But there was nothing there. Eventually, after more fruitless examination, they all gave up and the party went back upstairs. But now the search became much more intensive. They went through all the rooms a second time, but still found nothing. And then they went outside.

They walked over to the small warehouse behind the shop, the one which Tootill had found locked the previous day. There, amongst all the stored items of furniture was a grate. It contained the ashes and unburnt remains of accounts books, papers and articles of clothing, including a hat that had evidently been burnt there. This, in itself, was curious. But on examining it, they found something more worrying still. On the ironwork around the grate were bloodstains.

Meyer turned on Dukes. "Now, what about my brother?" he demanded.

Dukes, as calm as ever, said nothing.

The group now returned to the main building and the kitchen where the policemen began rummaging around. Meyer walked over to the wardrobe and gave it a push.

"Who does this belong to?" he asked Dukes.

Dukes replied that a customer named Mrs Shorrocks was expecting it to be delivered, but there was something in his voice that made Meyer uneasy. He tried to push the wardrobe, and it was surprisingly heavy. Dukes quickly said that Mrs Shorrocks had filled it with things she had bought in Bury. Meyer stared at him.

The wardrobe was locked, so Meyer asked for the key.

Dukes said that Mrs Shorrocks had taken it with her. It was an implausible explanation which no one believed. Meyer flew into a rage.

Furious, he seized one of the gilt fittings and wrenched it open. Then he gave a cry.

Meyer had found his brother.

George Gordon lay doubled up in the wardrobe, his head wrapped tightly in a blood-saturated sack. He was unquestionably dead. Tucked beside him was a coal-hammer that was covered in blood. Meyer and his elderly father rounded on Dukes. Shouting that he was a demon and a murderer they both lunged at him and had to be held back by the police officers who feared even more blood being spilled.

Dukes, however, seemed unperturbed.

"I did not murder him," he calmly told them, "but I can tell you about it."

Old Samuel Gordon gazed down into the wardrobe that was his son's coffin, his tears dripping freely on to the body. Meyer too began weeping inconsolably.

Dukes was arrested and taken away.

At the police station, Bill Dukes was found to have the key to the wardrobe in his pocket. It was wrapped up in a bloodstained handkerchief.

Although he had said at the time of his arrest that he could explain everything, he never did. The police had to work out the story for themselves.

They came to the conclusion that George Gordon had been struck from behind while he was looking over the shop's accounts. Dukes had then wrapped his head in rags and beaten it with the hammer to make it unrecognisable. He had originally intended to bury the body in the cellar. but the soil there was too compacted to dig so, rather than waste time, he had brought the wardrobe down and put the body in that.

Nobody thought the murder had been premeditated. Instead it was regarded to have been the desperate act of a very desperate man. Gordon had evidently found out that

Dukes was defrauding the company and Dukes had killed him in a moment of panic.

The funeral of George Gordon took place on Sunday, September 29th, at the Hebrew cemetery in Crumpsall. The press reported on that day that Madame Tussaud's wax works in London was negotiating for the wardrobe in which Gordon's body had been found. However, the family was asking a high price because they needed the money to ensure the future of the dead man's three children.

On Wednesday, December 4th, 1889, William Dukes went on trial at Manchester Assizes before Mr Justice Charles. He pleaded not guilty to the wilful murder of George Gordon.

Mr Blair led for the prosecution and Mr Cottingham for the defence.

Mr Robert Mitchell, the Bury surgeon who had carried out the post-mortem examination on George Gordon, told the court the extent of the deceased's injuries. There were large wounds to the back of the skull, which indicated that he had been attacked from behind, and which was consistent with the police theory of what had happened. There were also other wounds on the right eyebrow, temple and upper part of the forehead. All these injuries were, in the surgeon's opinion, sufficient to have caused death. However, he was certain that death had occurred almost immediately from the blows to the back of the head.

In his opinion the hammer, which had been found in the wardrobe, could have produced these wounds though any similar heavy object could have served as well. It was also obvious from the way in which the skull had been driven through that some of the blows had been made with the screwdriver. He had also found that the skin on the throat had been torn away as though a blunt and jagged knife had been drawn across it.

Cross-examined for the defence, Mr Mitchell claimed that it would not have been possible for the injuries to have occurred by accident. The surgeon agreed that if two angry men had been fighting and one fell with the back of his head on a fender, it might possibly cause a fracture. But he added that this would not have been such a fracture as the one Gordon had sustained.

Mr Isaiah Jones, house surgeon at Bury Infirmary, affirmed that Gordon's skull wounds certainly could not have been caused by a fall against the fender. He did not think any of the fractures could have been caused by such a fall.

During the trial the jury also learned about the mysterious Mr Alstead. A close friend of William Dukes, Miss Lucy Hawkins, a hat-trimmer who lived close to his home at 24 Butcher Lane, Bury, was summoned by the prosecution and told the court that on August 19th, 1889, Dukes had asked her to write a letter for him, signed in the name C. Alstead and addressed to the Gordon Furnishing Company in Great Ducie Street, Manchester. Miss Hawkins claimed that Dukes had asked her to write it because he wanted half a day off in Manchester. Gordon, so he told her, would not allow him even an hour.

Miss Hawkins also admitted writing the second postcard. The subsequent letters and telegrams, however, were evidently written by Dukes himself.

The police informed the court that neither Lime Tree House nor any person named C. Alstead existed in Prestwich. They also said that Mrs Shorrocks of the Golden Fleece pub in Rochdale to whom the wardrobe had supposedly been sold was a similarly fictitious character.

William Tootill told the court that on the day of the murder, Dukes had asked him to burn a large quantity of old advertising bills. When police went through the ashes afterwards, they found part of the binding of a ledger, and a further search of the shop failed to turn up any account books. Had Dukes burned them on the fire?

Richard Ainsworth, son of the landlord of the Lord Nelson in Bolton Street, told the court that Dukes had been in his pub on the morning of Wednesday, September 25th, the day of the murder. He recalled that Dukes seemed anxious, and had asked: "Can anyone see me from outside?" His explanation for this unease was that he was hiding from some people whose order he had mislaid.

Ainsworth then testified that Dukes had left the pub at 11.45 a.m. although he came back briefly at around nine that evening. Ainsworth had not been there when Dukes and Brooks called in again at three, but a servant remembered seeing them.

Others also gave evidence of seeing Dukes in the pub. None of them claimed that he was drunk, but many said that he seemed nervous. Frederick Brooks, who often did casual work for him, said that Dukes had seemed very tense and silent when he drank with him at 3 o'clock that day. "He was like a man who has just had a shock," he said.

Charles James, a clerk at Bury Post Office was next to the stand. He said that shortly after 5 o'clock on that Wednesday afternoon, Mr Dukes had come into the post office and written two telegrams. One was to the Gordon Furnishing Company in Manchester. "Gone Burnley, return tomorrow, all right – George." The other was to Mrs Dukes, William Dukes's wife, in Elizabeth Street, Cheetham Hill, Manchester. It read: "All right. Will meet last train. William."

Fabian Goldstone, general manager of the Gordon Furnishing Company in Burnley (and George Gordon's brother-in-law), told the court that he had gone to Manchester on the afternoon in question to spend the Jewish New Year with his family. He had made no arrangements at all for George to visit him and he couldn't imagine why his brother-in-law would have said such a thing. He said that George would have known that he would be closing up the Burnley shop on Wednesday. It had been arranged weeks before and, in any case, it was what he did every year. He always spent New Year with the Gordons in Manchester.

Mr Goldstone had already arrived at the Manchester store when the telegram, supposedly sent by George Gordon, had arrived. He was utterly perplexed by what it said. So too was everyone else. "Nobody could understand it," he claimed, "it made no sense."

Elderly Samuel Gordon, George's father, was particularly worried. He felt sure that it meant something very serious had happened, and it was as much to put the old man's mind at rest as it was to solve the mystery that Goldstone had then decided to travel to Bury and find out what was really going on.

Goldstone said he arrived in the town shortly after 11 o'clock that night and the first person he saw as he alighted from the train was Dukes. He said he was there to meet his wife.

Goldstone asked him about George and Dukes confirmed that, as far as he knew, he had indeed gone to Burnley. Dukes did not know why George Gordon had gone there, he said, but he thought it was because of something more than mere business. He also said that he knew about the telegram. In fact he had sent it himself, on George Gordon's request.

According to Fabian Goldstone, Bill Dukes then went on to relate an extraordinary story about what had been happening that day. He said that Mr Gordon had spent most of the afternoon in the Bury shop, looking over the books and checking the stock and had been happy with it. He had then left, together with Dukes himself, and walked to the station. It was there, Dukes claimed, that George had met up with a Jewish-looking couple and Dukes had bid him goodbye.

According to Goldstone, Dukes went on to say that George Gordon had spent a few minutes chatting to the couple and then ran up to speak to him again. He asked Dukes to do him a favour. He told him to send a telegram to his father saying he had gone to Burnley on business and planned to be back in the morning. Dukes agreed to the request and sent the telegram exactly as he was told.

Goldstone told the court that he was troubled by Dukes's story and didn't believe that he was telling the truth. But there was little he could do about it. He decided to travel back to Manchester but, as the last train had already left, he was forced to spend the night in a hotel and catch the first one in the morning. When he arrived back in Manchester on Thursday George was still not home.

Meyer Gordon then told the court that he and his father had received the mystifying telegram at 5.10 p.m. that Wednesday. Meyer couldn't believe it, because apart from the fact that the Burnley shop was closed, something George would have been aware of, it was also the beginning of the Jewish New Year. George wouldn't have dreamt of being away from his family at such a time. "It was unthinkable that George would have been away," he said.

Meyer telegraphed the shop in Bury the following day but got no reply. He then decided to go there in person and took his father with him. Already nervous as to what they might find, their alarm greatly increased when they arrived at the shop and found all blinds were drawn. This, coupled with Dukes's unsatisfactory answers to their questions, made them decide to call in the police.

Under cross-examination by Mr Cottingham, Meyer told the court that he had left the business in June that year after quarrelling with George. He and George often had what he termed "brotherly quarrels", and he broke down and wept when reminded that he had once summonsed his brother before the magistrates.

"Do not throw that in my face any more," he begged. "I do not wish my feelings to be hurt."

It was now William Dukes's turn to give evidence. Pale and haggard, he walked up to the stand.

Dukes read out his statement to the court. It followed none of his earlier claims. Now he was admitting his guilt, but he claimed it was all accidental and entirely in self-defence.

"On the day in question," he began, "Mr Gordon came to the shop. Having seen him, and knowing that I was in drink, I tried to avoid him. In the afternoon, he was very angry because he'd missed me that morning. I told him I was sorry and with that he said, 'Well, the Jewish New Year commences at six o'clock. I have five weeks' business to look at today, so I will take the books to examine at home.'

"He then went out," continued Dukes, "apparently to go to the station. But he returned again in a short space of time. He took off his coat and said he would see to the order that was to go to Prestwich, to C. Alstead. He asked me what had to go, so I told him that amongst the articles was a mirror – a large mirror with a gilt frame – and he assisted me in getting it off the wall. We took it into the kitchen. When we were putting it on the table, it slipped out of my hands. The glass came out of the frame. Well, of course, on top of what I had done, he was even more angry, and asked if I had any tools to repair it with. I said I had, and got some wood to make wedges. I got an old table knife and the hammer. He was just chopping a wedge when he said, 'I have a good mind to throw you out of the bloody shop.'

"I said, 'You can discharge me, but you must not hit me.' He said, 'Who the hell are you talking to?' and rushed at me with the hammer. I dodged out of his way. Then he turned round and ran at me again. I put my heels behind his and threw him. He came down on the fender with the back of his head.

"In my passion, and having drink in me, I really do not know what took place after that, but I believe I struck him on the forehead with the hammer. It might equally have been my life if I had not defended myself."

Dukes, who was very overcome as he concluded his speech, looked intently at the jury to see what impression it had made on them. Then he sat down.

Mr Blair, prosecuting, argued that what Dukes was trying to say in his statement was that the drink had made him do it. However, he pointed out that no one who had seen Dukes that day thought he was the worse for drink. Besides, Gordon's body was hideously mutilated, whereas Dukes had hardly a scratch on him.

Mr Cottingham then spoke up for Dukes. He agreed that his client was guilty of fiddling the books. He also admitted that he was guilty of sending out false contracts to deceive George Gordon and stop him coming to the shop. But William Dukes was not the sort of man who would think he could solve these problems by killing his boss. Cottingham reminded the court of the ample testimony they had heard of Dukes spending much of the day drinking in the pub. This was not, he claimed, the action of a man intent on murder. It was more the action of a frightened coward desperately trying to avoid a confrontation.

Cottingham then instructed the jurors to ask themselves if they thought that the fall on the fender might have caused the fatal fracture to Gordon's skull. After all, there was nothing to refute this suggestion other than the evidence of surgeons Mr Mitchell and Mr Jones. This, he stressed, was expert opinion but it was not fact. They could easily be mistaken.

Cottingham argued that Gordon had attacked Dukes after he'd let the mirror fall. Dukes had naturally resisted, taken the hammer from him, and in his terror, used it.

In summing up, Mr Justice Charles said: "It is not denied that Dukes actually dealt the blows which caused the death of George Gordon, but the question at issue is, did he do it under such provocation as led him to suppose that his own life was in danger? Is he, therefore, guilty of murder or manslaughter?"

The judge reminded the jury that angry words alone were not enough. Only if the words are followed by an act to injure the other person can provocation be claimed. Both George Fowler the carter, and William Tootill the general assistant, had heard an angry exchange between Gordon and Dukes. But both quarrelling men had afterwards helped load the cart. It was when Duke and Gordon went back inside that no more angry words were heard. There had, therefore, been no witness that an argument had taken place between them immediately prior to the murder.

"This is a case," concluded the judge, "where there is a motive – defrauding the books. After all, if it was self-defence, why didn't Dukes say so earlier?"

The jury took only 12 minutes to reach a verdict. Dukes clung to the dock rail as the foreman said "guilty," but he did not speak. Sentence of death was passed and he was taken back to Strangeways Prison, shaking uncontrollably.

While in prison Dukes had written many letters. One was to a close friend named Wicksted and was published in a newspaper.

Monday,
December 23rd

Dear Wicksted,
I trust that this will be a lesson to all young men to look before they leap. I remember saying last Christmas, 'I wonder where we shall be next Christmas.' Ah! my friend, we know not what is before us, but like others have said, my troubles end tomorrow. God knows when drink is in a man he cannot have any control of himself, for what he does is not to his knowledge, and therefore my friend, be moderate.

On the day before he was due to hang, Dukes's cheerful manner broke down when he heard that his appeal had failed. That night he slept very badly.

Dukes was hanged at Strangeways Prison, Manchester, on Christmas Eve, Tuesday, December 24th, 1889, by James Berry. As the cap was pulled over his face, Dukes shouted to the reporters, "Tell my wife that I die happy!"

Death was instantaneous. Berry later told reporters that it was one of the quickest executions he had ever conducted. Outside, the black flag was hoisted as usual, as a sign to the few people – mostly Jews – who had gathered round the main entrance of the prison that justice had been done.

21

A WEEK AFTER HALLOWEEN

*Everyone thought it was a joke when Fred
Fielding bought a knife. Then he used it to
murder his sweetheart.*

"I've a murder to do and have come to buy a knife."

Assuming he was joking, the staff and customers in the
small ironmonger's shop on Rishton's High Street laughed
along with the young man who was waiting to be served.
Handing over the money, he slipped the knife into his
pocket and left. A week later, newspapers reported the
murder.

The sound of fireworks and the smell of burning wood
filled the air as 23-year-old weaver Eleanor Pilkington left
her home in Spring Street, Rishton, a Lancashire village
near Blackburn, and met two sisters, Evelyn and Doris
Walker. Their destination was Mercer Hall in nearby Great
Harwood, which was holding a special dance. It was bonfire
night, Saturday, November 5th, 1927.

During the evening, Eleanor, who had recently split up
with her fiancé, danced with the two girls, politely declining
several young men's offers for a dance. She'd had enough
of men for the time being, she told Doris. When the dance
ended the three caught the bus home and alighted at the
junction of Harwood Road and High Street, barely 100
yards from Spring Street. As they walked along the pavement they spotted Eleanor's former boyfriend approaching
on the opposite side.

Twenty-four-year-old Fred Fielding had been courting
Eleanor for four years, up until the summer. Then, after
applying to join the Metropolitan Police Force, he moved

to London. After three months' probation he decided against this career and returned to his home town of Clayton-le-Moors in September.

A week after his return Eleanor broke off their engagement, and Fielding was devastated. He took to drink, changing from a hard worker into little more than a drunken layabout. He lost his new job as an iron-moulder at the local foundry, and then he lost his home.

Eleanor saw Fred approaching and whispered to the sisters to keep walking. The two old lovers exchanged a greeting. "I want to speak to you, Ellie," said Fielding, shepherding her into a shop doorway. They talked for a moment, until Doris called out, asking if Eleanor was coming home with them.

"I'll be right with you," Eleanor replied, slipping past Fred Fielding and heading towards her friends. Fielding followed and as the four walked down the street, he turned and asked: "Am I taking you home tonight then?"

"No, they are," said Eleanor, pointing to Evelyn and Doris. As they entered Spring Street, Fielding slipped his hand into his pocket and silently withdrew a knife. Putting his arm around Eleanor's shoulders, he stabbed her twice in the neck. She cried out in pain and, seeing blood spurting, Doris quickly ushered her into her home, which was just a few doors away. Evelyn summoned help while Doris rushed out to fetch Eleanor's parents from further up the street. Tom Walker, Doris and Evelyn's father, seated Eleanor in a chair and tried to stem the flow of blood, but no sooner had she sat down than she collapsed to the floor. She was dead before her parents could reach the house – and Fielding was nowhere to be seen. He would soon turn up, however.

An hour later Fielding was walking down Furthergate, near Blackburn town centre. He approached Police Constable Ben Greatorex. "I have just stabbed a girl at Rishton and wish to be taken to the nearest police station," he told the startled officer. The man had obviously been drinking, but on seeing blood on his hands Greatorex questioned him, and escorted him to nearby Copy Nook police station. There Fielding produced the bloodstained knife.

Word had just been received there of the incident at Rishton, and Fielding was placed in a cell pending inquiries.

"Is she dead?" he asked, and when told that she was, he replied coldly, "Good."

On November 22nd, 1927, Fred Fielding was tried at Manchester Assizes before Mr Justice Finlay. The packed court was still buzzing with the passing of the death sentence, moments earlier, on a young Liverpool wife-murderer, as the accused was ushered into the dock, looking pale and nervous. Neatly dressed in a brown suit, he was tall, well-built and athletic in appearance

Mr A. Leslie, prosecuting, said that there was exceptional evidence of premeditation. Fielding, he said, had expressed a deliberate intention to commit the murder.

The prisoner had been regarded by Eleanor's father as a potential son-in-law until relations between the couple deteriorated and she "threw him over." Then his feelings changed. A week before the murder Fielding had turned up at Eleanor's house late at night. He was drunk and shouted for her to speak to him. Receiving no reply, he threw a stone through her window, and when her father told him to clear off, Fielding replied, "If you don't fetch Eleanor you will be without a daughter before the week's out."

Mr Pilkington said that he would fetch the police. Fielding replied that he would save him the trouble and walked away, returning minutes later with Police Constable Stimson to whom he admitted breaking the window and asking if he would be arrested. Assuming that Fielding only wanted a bed for the night, and advised by Eleanor's father that he didn't wish to press charges, the officer told Fielding to be on his way and escorted him from the scene.

The court was told of Fielding's statement in the iron-monger's shop. This, the defence maintained, was merely a joke. But nobody was laughing now.

A witness testified that Fielding had spoken to him as he

alighted from a bus after returning from the bonfire night dance. The girls had already walked ahead as Fielding approached him, and demanded to know who Eleanor had been dancing with. Told that she had only danced with the Walker sisters, he strode off in pursuit.

Faced with Fielding's confession to the murder at the time he was arrested, and which he never denied, the defence sought to save his neck by persuading the jury to find him guilty of manslaughter. The reason they should accept this plea, said his counsel, Mr B. I. Ormerod, was that at the time of the murder Fielding was so drunk as to be unable to form the necessary intent to commit murder.

The landlord of the Petre Arms said that on bonfire night the accused had consumed between eight and 10 pints of beer, and he was very drunk when he staggered outside at closing time.

This defence failed, and nobody was surprised when after 15 minutes the jury returned and found Fielding guilty. Mr Justice Finlay donned the black cap and for the second time that day sentenced a man to be hanged.

Fielding's appeal was dismissed on December 19th, the appeal judges headed by the Lord Chief Justice ruling that drink was no excuse for murder.

Fred Fielding spent his last Christmas in the condemned cell at Strangeways Prison, his counsel's plea for clemency having failed. At 8 a.m. on January 3rd, 1928, he was hanged by Tom Pierrepoint as a small crowd gathered outside. Pointing out the location of the scaffold behind the prison walls, one man told his companions that this was the eleventh successive execution he had attended outside Strangeways.

22

THE MURDER OF LIZZIE HOLT

*In November 1890 a schoolteacher was found
murdered in Bolton's woodlands. The woman
had been neither raped nor robbed. So what was
the reason for the attack?*

Motiveless killings are often thought to be a modern
phenomenon, stemming from overcrowding, unemployment, alienation and other ills particular to our "high-tech"
society. But Victorian England also had its fair share of
motiveless murders. Then too there were brutal and hor-
rific killings carried out without rhyme or reason.

One such case occurred in the pretty rural village of
Belmont, near Bolton in Lancashire in the late autumn of
1890. Such was the violence of the crime that at first many
people thought that a wild animal had been responsible
whilst others speculated on the dark forces of the super-
natural. In the end, however, it was established that it was
a work of evil of a more mundane kind.

It began on the morning of Saturday, November 15th,
1890, when young Clement Talbot was out playing with his
dog in a lonely wooded spot called Longworth Clough, a
few miles outside Belmont. It was a bright, crisp day and the
two were happily scampering through the trees when the
dog suddenly began to paw at some bracken. The boy went
over to see what his pet had found, little knowing what it
would be. And then he saw it. It was the mangled corpse of
his schoolteacher, Elizabeth Ann Holt.

In death, she was ghastly to behold. Her head had been
kicked in, her throat slashed, and her clothes had been torn
from her body as if, to quote one contemporary newspaper

report on the crime, "she had been the victim of a ferocious attack by some wild animal."

The body was taken to her mother's cottage in the village of Egerton, where Dr Robinson performed an immediate post-mortem examination. It was his opinion that she had been dead for about a week and he had no doubts at all about what had caused her demise. She had suffered appalling wounds to her head and throat. The doctor, however, could not establish a reason for the attack. Although her clothes, particularly her underwear, had been ripped to shreds, there had been no sexual assault nor a discernible attempt at rape. Neither had she been robbed. Her parcels and purse were found intact by her body. Elizabeth Holt had evidently been killed for no other reason than someone had wished her death.

Miss Holt, 21, had lived with her mother and younger sister, Sarah, in Egerton. She worked as a teacher at Belmont village school, a few miles away from her home.

Because of the distance involved in travelling, it had been her habit to stay in Belmont at the house of the schoolmaster, Henry Swayles, and his family. But she would invariably return to her mother's home for the weekends. Every Monday she would set off early on her walk to Belmont and then return to Egerton on Friday night.

Her sister, Sarah Holt, tearfully told the police that on Monday, November 10th, Lizzie had left home as usual at 7.30. She had with her some parcels of food and clothing. Neither Sarah nor her mother had known until the following Saturday, when Lizzie was found dead, that she had not been at school all week. The police asked Sarah if Lizzie had had any enemies and if she could think of anyone who would want to see her sister dead. The girl replied firmly that Lizzie had been very popular and well liked by everyone.

Henry Swayles, a schoolmaster at the National School in Belmont, told the police that although Miss Holt had not arrived at the school on November 10th, he hadn't thought there was anything worrying in her staying away. It had happened twice before, he explained, though on both those occasions she had given him notice. This time he had not heard from her at all during that week, but he had still not thought it necessary to contact her home.

A farmer, Robert Scholes, told the police that on the morning of November 10th, he had been driving his milk cart along Longworth Lane when he saw Lizzie Holt, whom he knew well, walking towards Belmont. A moment later, he said, he spotted a local ruffian by the name of Thomas Macdonald, walking about 150 yards behind the pretty teacher, and going in the same direction. Rowland Heaton, another farmer, also remembered having seen the pair walking along Longworth Lane, some distance apart, but going towards Belmont. It had been raining, he recalled, and Miss Holt had had her umbrella up.

Thomas Macdonald, 32, was well known to the local police as a nasty piece of work. Twelve years earlier he had waylaid a girl on the moors and raped her, a crime for which he was sentenced to 10 years' penal servitude. After serving only eight, he was released for good behaviour and had gone to live in Egerton, supported mainly by his long-suffering aunt, Mrs Honor Bann. Except for some casual work at Longworth Collieries, he spent most of his time idling around the village, drinking and getting into fights. It was a pastime for which he periodically ended up in the cells.

The police already had reason to suspect Macdonald of having blood on his hands. A few weeks earlier he had been drinking in Bolton with a young navvy named Mather. The following day Mather was found dead, floating in Belmont reservoir. Macdonald was arrested on a charge of manslaughter. The police were firmly convinced that he was the culprit, but he denied everything and there was little material evidence to incriminate him. Eventually they were forced to let him go, but no one else was apprehended for the crime.

Now, with Macdonald's name emerging again as a possible suspect in a new murder case, the police were quick to act. That same evening, PC Hargreaves and Sergeant Hayward went to his aunt's house to arrest him. "Tom," said Hayward, when Thomas Macdonald opened the door. "You are going to be taken into custody on suspicion of having caused the death of Elizabeth Ann Holt at Longworth Clough."

Macdonald stared at them blankly. Then he shrugged his shoulders. "Yes, I was there," he admitted, "but I did her no harm. You will have to find another for this."

At Bolton Police station Macdonald was closely interrogated about his movements on November 10th. He admitted he had been to Belmont in the morning, and that he had seen Miss Holt – whom he knew by sight – walking along Longworth Lane in front of him. But, he claimed, he had overtaken her and gone on to Belmont, where he had worked that day at the Longworth Collieries. Later that evening, after being paid, he had got drunk, for which he had been arrested. He had spent the night in the cells of the local police station.

John Brierley, the underground manager at Longworth Collieries, could not back up this story. He told the police that he knew Macdonald well, but said he had certainly not employed him on November 10th. PC Golightly, however, verified that he had arrested the suspect for being drunk and disorderly on the evening of November 10th. He remembered that Macdonald had been in quite a state, with blood on his clothes, a scar over his left eyebrow, a scratch on his left cheek and a bleeding lip. When questioned about his wounds, he had said that he had been in a fight earlier in the day which, at the time, seemed plausible enough. Now, though, it was deeply suspicious.

As the investigation continued, Macdonald's clothes were sent to Frank Paul, the professor of medical jurisprudence at University College, Liverpool, for examination. He found blood marks on the man's clogs, pen-knife and the sleeves and cuffs of his jacket.

If the police needed any more proof in order to charge Macdonald, it came when his Aunt Honor told them that her nephew had in fact confessed to her that he had murdered Miss Holt.

On November 19th, Macdonald was formally charged with her murder, and replied, "I will say nothing here." A week later, however, he did begin to speak.

Thomas Macdonald's trial took place at Liverpool Assizes on December 13th, 1890, before Mr Justice Cave. Mr Cottingham was elected to defend him.

The newspapers reported that there was a great deal of interest in the case, adding intriguingly that, "in marked contrast to previous murder trials in the same building, not a single woman was permitted to enter the court." Such was the horror of the crime it was supposed that it would be too much for their delicate sensibilities.

The prosecution had a strong case against Macdonald, and as witness after witness took the stand it grew stronger. Dr Robinson, who had performed the post-mortem, told the court that besides severe head wounds, Miss Holt's throat had been cut by a small sharp cutting instrument similar to the pen-knife belonging to Macdonald.

Jane Marsden, a neighbour of Macdonald's, told the court that at about 9.30 on the morning of November 10th, she had seen him come up the road from the direction of Belmont and go into his aunt's house. As he passed by her window, she said, she had noticed how dirty and sullied he appeared, as if he had been working all night.

Thomas Maclean, an overlooker at Ashton Mill where Mrs Bann, Macdonald's aunt, was employed, recalled how Macdonald had come to the mill on the morning of November 10th looking rather excited. He had his right hand up to his face, but there was no sign of any blood.

"What does thee want here, Tom?" Maclean had asked, "surely, thee's not looking for work?"

Macdonald hadn't been amused. "Go and tell my auntie she's wanted up yonder straight away," he'd said sharply. After Maclean had fetched Mrs Bann, she put on her shawl and hurried away with her nephew. Maclean assumed they were going home.

Honor Bann was next to give evidence. She told the court that when she'd left for work on the morning of the murder, her nephew was still in the house. Later in the day she had been very surprised when Maclean came up and said he was outside asking for her. At first, Macdonald explained his visit by telling her that she was needed at home immediately. He told her that someone had arrived at the house from America to see her. However, when they had got some distance from the mill, he suddenly confessed to her that he had committed a murder.

Stunned, Mrs Bann had asked him who he'd murdered, for it never occurred to her to doubt him. He told her it was Lizzie Holt.

Mr Cottingham, defending, butted in at this point: "Did your nephew actually say he had murdered Lizzie Holt?"

Mrs Bann thought for a moment, then nodded: "I have told the truth and cannot get over it."

"What was your reaction to the confession?" asked Cottingham. Mrs Bann, wiping tears from her cheeks, said, "I told him to go drown his self afore he brought more disgrace on the family."

To this, Macdonald had replied that he was going to give himself up. Then he turned from her and walked away.

Mrs Bann had then gone back to work and told no one about what he had said. At 5 o'clock, she said she went home but her nephew wasn't there. He didn't return until the following day, when he told her he had spent the night at the police station after being arrested for drunkenness.

She'd heard nothing more about the murder until he was arrested at her house on the following Saturday evening. During that week, however, she had asked him if she could wash his shirt, and he told her he had already done it himself.

"Was this usual?" asked the prosecutor. "Had he on other occasions washed his shirt?"

"No, never," admitted Mrs Bann.

During their investigation, the police had tried to find evidence of any past quarrel between Lizzie Holt and

Macdonald, but though the two had lived in the same village it seemed they had never even spoken to one another. However, the police did find some witnesses who were willing to testify to the hostile feelings Macdonald harboured for the dead girl.

John Henry, a friend of Macdonald, told the court that Tom had once boasted to him that many people in Egerton were scared of him, and that Lizzie Holt in particular feared him to the extent that whenever she saw him coming she always rushed away. He had told this story with some glee, the witness said.

Richard Radcliffe told the court that once, on November 3rd, while he and Macdonald were talking together in Longworth Lane, Miss Holt had suddenly passed them by on her way to Belmont. Macdonald, looking up, had said lewdly, referring very pointedly to the girl, "What's think about yon tockus [backside]? I should like to take the pride out o' yon." Another witness, John Lee, said that he had also overheard this conversation, but he thought it had been made jokingly and did not think much more about it.

There was a sensation in the court when two confessions Macdonald had made to officers at Bolton Road police station on November 25th and 26th were read out:

"At eight o'clock on the morning of November 10th, I started from home to go over to Belmont to see the manager at Longworth Collieries about work. On Longworth Lane I overtook the deceased. As soon as I overtook her, I got hold of her shoulder. I asked her what she had been telling lies about me for. I told her that she had set it out that I'd followed her a few weeks ago for the purpose of doing her harm. She told me to let go of her shoulder. I told her I would not do so until she had retracted what she had said. She jerked her shoulder away out of my hand, shut her umbrella, took hold of the small end of it and struck me with it. I became enraged, threw her down and beat her about the head and cut her throat.

"Then I dragged her across the lane and down into Longworth Clough. I cut open her clothes to see if her heart was beating. I found it did not beat. I then went home."

He denied that he had tried to rape her.

"A great many people think this girl was simply got hold of for the purpose of ravishing her, but I can swear on my dying oath such is not the case."

The day after making that statement, November 26th, Macdonald had made another, in which he added more details: "Man, I had a job with her. When she struck me with the umbrella on the head, she might have got away, for I was quiet for a few minutes. The first time I knocked her down she got up and I had to put my leg behind hers before I got her down the second time. I soon finished her off then with my clogs and the knife. When I took her to the bottom of the clough I was nearly making a mess of myself. When I was half-way home I was looking for my knife to cut some tobacco. I had to go back for it, and when I went back for it I found it underneath the body."

The reading out of these two statements caused an understandable uproar in the courtroom. Clearly there was little hope left for the accused. Mr Cottingham now pleaded for Macdonald's life.

"There is no doubt he is guilty of a cruel and violent homicide," he said. "But I plead not for an acquittal, not for the establishment of innocence, I plead for life alone."

Pale and haggard, Macdonald, who had harangued witnesses and counsel alike throughout the proceedings, suddenly got to his feet and shouted out, "I don't want it. I am guilty straight off. Let it drop."

The jury retired, and half an hour later found Macdonald guilty of wilful murder. He heard the verdict and subsequent sentence of death without showing any emotion.

In prison Macdonald was visited by his aunt, Mrs Honor Bann. She found him very depressed and he refused to talk about the murder except to say that he was glad he had not taken Miss Holt's purse. He evidently believed that this proved he was really a good and honest person.

Mrs Bann looked at him pityingly and wanted to give him comfort. But though she could offer soothing words, she was unable to touch him. Between them was a thick iron grating, designed to separate relatives from condemned men and make it impossible for them to kiss or embrace. Macdonald stood all the time, pressing himself as close to the bars as possible. When it was time for her to leave, he collapsed. Mrs Bann was led away in tears.

Macdonald's execution was set for the last day of the year, December 31st, 1890.

Minutes before the hanging, Berry, the executioner, suddenly realised he had forgotten to bring the white cap which is traditionally put over the condemned man's head. In something of a dilemma, he asked two reporters who were there to witness the execution, if he could borrow their handkerchiefs. The reporters, somewhat taken aback by this macabre request, obliged, and Berry tied the two handkerchiefs together. This, he thought, would be an adequate makeshift hood. But when Berry tried it out on one of the reporters he realised it would be far too tight.

"Well," sighed Berry. "I shall have to do without. I have hanged them without a cap before and I must do it again."

However, in the end an alternative was found. When the time came for the hanging, the reporters noticed that Berry had manufactured a white cap apparently made from an old towel. As he slipped it over Macdonald's head the condemned man was heard to murmur: "Lord Jesus, receive my soul." The lever was then drawn.

When the doctor got down into the pit beneath the gallows to feel for Macdonald's pulse, he noted that it took just sixty seconds for it to stop beating. Usually it takes between three and 15 minutes. It had been a speedy death for the villain.

Thomas Macdonald was buried under the footpath close to the coach-house where his execution had taken place.

How did a minor disagreement between two people who hardly knew each other come to end in brutal, sadistic murder?

Perhaps a clue can be found in the personalities of killer and victim. Macdonald was a violent man with very little self-control, and like many such people, had a deep resentment of authority. In her position as a schoolteacher, Miss Holt would certainly have represented authority to him, and was also, in his opinion, haughty and proud. This enraged him to such a pitch that he wanted to "take the pride out o' yon." When he grabbed her shoulder in Longworth Lane, it was probably to do just that. It is unlikely he had really intended to murder her. However, when she resisted, probably telling him exactly what she thought of him in the process, he must have completely lost control of himself. Murder was the only possible outcome.

23

THE SOUTHPORT LANDLADY

This was one murder for which the hangman's noose was not required. The villain performed the executioner's task himself.

The last evening in the life of Mrs Dorothy Allen, a wealthy Southport landlady, was spent with her two closest friends, Mr and Mrs Foster, at their home in the Lancashire seaside resort's Avondale Road. As that evening of Sunday, November 22nd, 1908, was cold and blustery, Mrs Foster tried to persuade Mrs Allen to stay overnight at her house. But the 59-year-old widow wouldn't hear of it – she liked to sleep in her own bed. Besides, it was only a short walk back to her own home in nearby Alexandra Road. Before she left, it was arranged that Mrs Foster would have tea with her the following Tuesday afternoon.

But when Mrs. Foster called at 6 Alexandra Road at the appointed time she could not get any response, no matter how long she rang the bell or how hard she knocked on the door. As her friend lived alone and had recently suffered a stroke, Mrs Foster was very concerned about her welfare and hurried to fetch her husband. When he too failed to get any reply, they called the police.

Forcing open the front door and going inside, they found Mrs Allen lying dead in a pool of blood in the hall. She had been shot in the face and in the back. In the dining room, crockery and a cooked breakfast of bacon and egg was scattered over the floor. There was also a smear of blood on a whisky bottle and bloody fingerprints on the door.

At first the police suspected that a burglar had broken into the house on either Sunday night or early on Monday

225

morning by smashing a window at the back of the premises and gaining access to the cellar. He had then unbolted the door leading from the cellar into the house by cutting out part of the door panel. (The manner in which he had done this led police to believe he might be left-handed.) After hiding for some time in the house, he had shot Mrs Allen as she was carrying the breakfast things from the kitchen to the dining room. It seemed she had been stooping to place the tray on a table when she received the shot in the back, causing the tray to capsize into an armchair.

Attempting to escape her attacker, she had staggered into the hall and along the passage to the kitchen where, from the amount of blood on the floor, she appeared to have stood for some time trying to hold the door closed against him. Weak through loss of blood, however, she would not have been unable to do this for long. She had then probably grappled with her attacker and in doing so was forced into the passage again, where she was shot in the head and sent reeling against the staircase and on to the floor. After robbing the place, the killer had left via the cellar.

Another theory was that the murderer had entered the house as a visitor by the front door and had later smashed the cellar window to mislead the police. The bottle of whisky (found with a smear of blood on it) had been put out for someone else because Mrs Allen, or so her friends insisted, drank little or no whisky and only kept a bottle for guests. This theory of a visitor was strengthened when a next-door neighbour told the police that at 10.20 p.m. on Sunday night she had distinctly heard the footsteps of "more than one person" coming from the passage dividing her house from Mrs Allen's.

Police suspected Mrs Allen had been killed on Monday morning. She had been seen drawing her blinds at about 8.55 a.m. on that day, but when a greengrocer's delivery man called 35 minutes later there was no response to the ringing of the door bell.

The motive for the murder was assumed to be robbery. Mrs Foster told the police her friend had been wearing two diamond rings, a wedding ring and a gold bracelet when she last saw her, and these were now missing together with the rest of her jewellery. It also emerged that the dead woman's real name was Mrs Olliver. Allen had been the name of her first husband, who had died 30 years earlier. She had then married soldier's clerk, William Olliver, but they had separated a few months after the wedding, Dorothy moving to Southport under the name of her first husband a short time later. William Olliver, however, was not a suspect. He had died in 1901.

An independent, practical woman, Dorothy Allen frequently let her house to visitors and, rather than pay workmen or servants, she insisted on doing virtually everything for herself. A short time before her murder she had lime-washed the cellar, distempered the walls and ceiling of the dining room and cut down a tree in the garden. But she also had an artistic streak. In nearly every room in the house were pictures, many of which she had painted herself.

Insisting on living alone, she had bought a police whistle for use in emergencies. As one of her friends told reporters, "Mrs Allen had a horror of burglars, not because she was afraid of them personally, but for fear that her jewellery and silver plate would attract them."

Local jewellers and pawnbrokers were visited by police, and it wasn't long before this paid off. Joseph Thompson, a jeweller of East Bank Street in Southport, told officers that a man he knew quite well named Henry Jackson had come into his shop at about 9.45 a.m. on Monday, November 23rd. Jackson had sold him two rings and a pair of earrings in a box.

During the transaction Jackson had asked Thompson if he remembered the earrings which he had apparently bought at his shop. Jackson then explained that the reason he was now selling them back to him was because he was hard up, and he asked £18 for them. As the price was low, Thompson had bought them. The jeweller told the police he had noticed that Jackson looked unwell and was very pale. When he commented upon it Jackson told him he had

had a long illness. The rings and earrings were identified by Mrs Foster as having belonged to Mrs Allen.

This was the second time that Henry Jackson's name had come up in connection with the case. Friends of Mrs Allen had already told them that a few years earlier he had been on very close terms with her. However, their friendship had been fractured, so gossip had it, because Jackson had sold a pony and trap belonging to Mrs Allen without her consent and then pocketed the money. They had not spoken to one another since.

Police enquiries about 54-year-old Jackson revealed that he was a commission agent, buying and selling on behalf of others for a commission. He had lately fallen on hard times and owed money in various places. The police also discovered that due to an injury he had not been able to use his right hand for the last 12 months.

On November 27th, Jackson was interviewed at his lodgings in Stanley Street, behind the Bold Arms Hotel on Lord Street. In contrast to Mrs Allen's villa, Jackson's lodgings were in a tiny run-down cottage into which the landlady, Mrs Rimmer, and her family squeezed as many paying lodgers as they could. Jackson, a widower, said he had known Mrs Allen for about 12 years. They had first met at a sale in Southport, and the friendship flourished with drives in Mrs Allen's pony and trap – the one Jackson later supposedly sold without her knowledge. He used to go to her as often as twice a week to do odd jobs.

"There was no question of love or marriage between us," he emphasised. "But she did tell me that she could not get married – though she did not tell me the reason. I was not aware she had a husband living at the time. I did not know it till I read it in the papers."

Jackson's friendship with Mrs Allen had ceased six or seven years ago. "Her mother persuaded me to break it off. She came to see me and explained that she had noticed how fond I was of her daughter, but that she could not get married. She thought it better that we parted and I agreed."

Asked where he was on the night of November 22nd and

the following morning, Jackson said: "I slept here on Sunday and every night since. I went to bed on Sunday night between nine and ten o'clock and I did not get up till about ten o'clock on Monday morning. I do not have a latch-key to this door. If I went out during the night I would have to knock someone up to let me in. I believe I remained in the house the whole day. I did not go round to Mrs Allen's house at all that day."

When asked if he had sold any jewellery that week Jackson at first denied that he had. Detectives then asked him to explain the fact that they had learnt he had sold some jewellery on the morning of November 23rd.

"Oh, I forgot about that," said Jackson. "But I remember now. A gentleman brought me some to sell for him."

"Who was the gentleman?"

"I cannot tell you," said Jackson, shaking his head. "Many people call here to ask me to sell things for them."

Asked if he would be surprised to learn the jewellery he sold was Mrs Allen's, he replied, "I would," his eyes widening in apparent astonishment. Shown the two rings and the earrings, he admitted they were those he had sold. "If that is Mrs Allen's jewellery I agree it is a most extraordinary thing that I should sell it," he said, adding, "Oh, yes, it is true I told Mr Thompson I was hard up and that I have not more than 25 shillings in the world at the present time, but I categorically deny murdering and robbing Mrs Allen."

Jackson still refused to name the man on whose behalf he said he had sold Mrs Allen's jewellery, but he did give the police a description of him. "He was tall, middle-aged, with a slight Scottish accent. He did not call at the house as far as I know," Jackson went on, "but met me in the passage between this house and Lord Street. He said, 'Is your name Jackson, commission agent?' and I replied, 'Yes' and he said, 'Will you sell some jewellery for me?' He then produced the articles you have shown to me... I got £18 for the jewellery, £2 of which I kept as my commission for selling it."

While Jackson was being interviewed, another detective went to speak to his landlady, Mrs Rimmer, who confirmed her lodger's story. She assured the policeman that Jackson had not gone out at all on the night of November 22nd, and that he did not rise until 10 o'clock the next morning. As Mrs Rimmer, a seemingly respectable woman, had backed up Jackson's alibi, and as nothing incriminating had been found in a search of his room, he was not arrested. It was 2.00 a.m. on the Saturday morning when police left the house at the end of their seven-hour interview with the suspect.

On Saturday afternoon a detective returned to Stanley Street and asked to speak to Jackson. Another lodger ran up to his room to get him, but a second later rushed down again, white-faced and shaking. He informed the policeman that Jackson was dead. The officer rushed upstairs to find Jackson lying stiff and fully clothed on his bed. On the table beside him was a bottle containing a white liquid which smelled suspiciously like strychnine. There was also a suicide note. "I am innocent of Mrs Allen's murder," Jackson had written, "and I hope whoever it was will be found I cannot bear such a disgrace being brought before the public scoff. God knows I have always respected Mrs Allen – signed Henry T. Jackson."

As a postscript he had added: "The police worried me with such questions about the deceased, asking me if she was a moral woman, or did she give one any chance for immorality. I distinctly say she was a perfect lady as to morals and I cannot do for anyone to state against her as long as I live. God knows I never had anything against her." Later, Jackson's body was formally identified by his son, a Manchester policeman. He told officers that when visiting Southport he had seen Mrs Allen with his father and they had seemed very fond of each other.

Police also learned that Jackson had been friendly with another woman named Alice Carr who worked in a cake shop on Lord Street, where he went daily to buy bread. She told them that two days after Mrs Allen's murder Jackson had come into the shop and given her a brooch. On the morning of his suicide he had come into the shop again and told her, "I'm in great trouble. I had detectives at my house until 2.00 a.m. this morning trying to make out that I murdered this woman. There is a brooch among the jewellery like that one I gave you, but it is not hers. It was my dear wife's."

The brooch was later identified as having belonged to Mrs Allen.

After leaving the cake shop, Jackson had gone to a chemist's where he bought strychnine, which he said was for his dogs. The subsequent post-mortem established that Jackson's body contained enough strychnine to have killed a score of people. It seemed to the police that Jackson, unable to stand the shame of being thought a killer, had taken his own life, and as a result Mrs Allen's murder might never be properly cleared up. Then the case took another unexpected twist.

A distressed Mrs Rimmer, Jackson's landlady, told the police she had lied about Jackson's whereabouts on Sunday, November 22nd. He had, in fact, been out all that night. "He went out about nine o'clock and did not come in again until the next morning," she said. After the detectives had begun questioning him, she revealed, "he said to me in the kitchen, 'If they ask you have I been out tell them no, except to the shops.'" Surprisingly, the police, during their questioning of Jackson, had allowed him to go alone into Mrs Rimmer's kitchen for a glass of lemonade. This had given him the chance to ask her to lie for him.

But Mrs Rimmer had more to say. "Since you left this afternoon," she told detectives, "I went to the sideboard in the parlour to get some pears. When I opened the door I saw a box there. It does not belong to me. I thought I had better send for you. I have not touched the box." She added that she thought it might have belonged to Jackson as she remembered seeing it once before in his room. As he had a complete run of the house he could easily have put it in her sideboard without her noticing.

It looked like a stationery box. But on opening it, police found not paper and envelopes inside, but a revolver with bloodstains on the barrel. There was also some jewellery, including two watches and several bracelets, one of which contained a portrait of Mrs Allen's first husband.

Mrs Rimmer said she had lied because she was frightened her house would become notorious, and she had no suspicion that Jackson was responsible for the murder. She had merely thought he was trying to avoid becoming involved as a witness.

At Jackson's inquest, Mrs Rimmer described how difficult it had been for her to get her lodging money from Jackson and how he had been in arrears for several weeks, always promising to pay. It was only after his death that she had learned that the arrears of the rent to her own landlord of £14 had been paid on her behalf by Jackson during the week of the murder.

She told how on the night of November 22nd he had told her he was going to his cousin's, but as it was a rough night he would be home by 9.45 or not at all that night. He did not return and she locked up the house as usual before going to bed. The next morning at about 10 o'clock, Jackson came through the back door carrying a parcel.

Asked why she had lied in support of his alibi, she said: "It was part of my duty as landlady to oblige my lodger."

In his summing up to the jury the coroner said, "There is no evidence to show that Jackson was in the murdered woman's house and no evidence to show how he got in or out, but if the police had known now what they would have known before if Mrs Rimmer had been a truthful woman and told them that there was a revolver and the murdered woman's jewellery at his lodging, then he would most certainly have been arrested... It is quite clear that Jackson had pressing financial obligations."

The jury brought in a verdict of wilful murder against Jackson and found that he had committed suicide.

Recalled to the witness box, Mrs Rimmer was told by the coroner: "If any person were to be blamed for Jackson not being here it is you. If your code of morals prevailed then crime would go undetected, and it is a question whether even now you have told all you know."

There seems little doubt that Jackson murdered Mrs Allen, but what was Mrs Rimmer's role in the affair? Was she as naïve as she seemed and thus willing to oblige a lodger – even a non-paying one – to the extent of lying to the police investigating a murder? Or could she, as the coroner suspected, have known more about the murder than she revealed at the inquest? After all, it does seem strange that both the murder weapon and Mrs Allen's jewellery should suddenly surface so conveniently immediately after Jackson's suicide.

The affair which had begun with the brutal murder of one Southport landlady had ended in the public disgrace of a second... and all because those two unfortunate women had fallen under the charming if ultimately fatal spell of Henry Theophilus Jackson.

24

THE MANCHESTER CAB
MYSTERY
PART I

*On February 27th, 1889, the body of John
Fletcher was found in the back of a hansom cab.
He had been murdered. Detective Caminada was
charged with solving the crime.*

It is a curious truth that very few English sons of Italian
parents join the police force in Britain. One of the notable
exceptions was Jerome Caminada – a man who enjoyed
phenomenal success as a detective. Yet today his name is
forgotten, except perhaps in Manchester. For it was in that
northern city that he earned an enviable reputation as a
policeman who had few equals.

Jerome Caminada was born in Manchester in the middle
of the last century. In the Caminada household money was
hard to come by and life was rough. The future did not hold
out many hopes and the boy could easily have been
swallowed into the lawless underworld that surrounded
him. But he never was. Instead, at the age of 24, Caminada
climbed into a new blue uniform and went out into the
streets of Manchester to pound a beat.

Although Caminada cannot be said to have gone out to
find trouble, or to invite it to find him, he seemed to have
an instinct for being where it occurred. Fortunately he had
the fists to deal with it. He also had the brains to match his
brawn. Men far better educated than this young Italian
from the slums were being outwitted by his clear thinking
and his sterling honesty.

Caminada put his trust in the old conman's adage, "you
can't get the better of an honest man," and it served him
well. It was not a great surprise when he was taken out of

uniform by his much impressed superiors and set to work in plain clothes. It was a promotion that was richly deserved and Caminada quickly proved himself worthy of it.

Those were the days when detectives were expected to employ frequent disguises in their attempts to penetrate the criminal underworld and Caminada became a veritable quick-change artiste. It was said that when he was disguised it was difficult even for someone who knew him intimately to discern the deception. The criminals of Manchester had finally met their match.

Jerome Caminada was the kind of cop who creates his own legend, and he was at the peak of his career when he tackled a case of murder in a four-wheeled hackney carriage. It occurred in the first part of 1889, a year when one of the fiction best-sellers of the day was Fergus Hume's *Mystery of a Hansom Cab*. Despite the conclusion that many people at that time jumped to, there was no sure connection between the real-life case and the popular mystery novel. But for a good many years afterwards, certainly in Manchester, there were stubborn adherents to the theory that the real-life killer had read Fergus Hume's popular thriller and been encouraged by its theme.

The Manchester mystery began in the afternoon of February 27th. A cold damp winter was waning away and there was a suggestion of fog in the air. Two men hailed a passing hackney carriage not far from the cathedral. The driver called out to them through the drifting mist, raised his whip in acknowledgement of their hail, and brought the four-wheeler to a halt.

As he did so, he turned in his seat and saw that one of the pair was rather elderly. The other was a good deal younger.

"Where to, gents?" he asked, lifting his chin up out of the depths of his turned-up collar.

It was the younger man who replied. He told the driver to take them to a pub in Deansgate, then opened the carriage door for his companion.

The older man did not speak, but he seemed ready enough to get into the carriage. His companion climbed in after him, the door slammed shut, and the cabby whipped up his horse. The cab rattled away.

Arriving at the public house, the driver was told to wait. Again it was the younger passenger who gave the instructions. The man sunk deep into his thick overcoat watched his two passengers step inside the lounge bar. He remained perched up on his seat, his face tilted to avoid the sting of the afternoon chill. In his usual way, when engaged to wait for a fare, he closed his eyes for a blissful forty winks, but was soon roused by the reappearance of the two men. He was told to take them this time to a house in Stretford Road.

After they seated themselves inside, he shook up the reins and started out for the address. Long before he reached the new destination, however, he was stopped by a passer-by on the pavement suddenly running after him, shouting and waving both arms excitedly.

The cabby hauled on the reins.

"What's up?" he shouted.

The words of the man waving his arms came clearly. "Your door's open. Someone just jumped out. I saw him run off."

Muttering a string of imprecations, the cabby, who knew all about being bilked, brought his horse to a stop and climbed down to the pavement. The door on that side was swinging open on its hinges. He looked inside and saw at once that the older of his two passengers was still reclining on the seat as though enjoying a quiet doze. The cabman breathed a sigh of relief. At least he still had a fare who would pay him.

Stretching across the interior of his cab, he shook the elderly man by the arm.

"You'd better wake up, sir," he said.

The elderly man did not open his eyes, but he replied somewhat testily: "Leave me alone. Go away and leave me alone."

The cabby closed the door and stood frowning through the window. He wondered what he could do in such an unusual situation. After all, the carriage had been hired by the missing man. Up to now the old man had said not a word.

He climbed back on to his seat, shook up his horse, and turned back for the centre of the city. When he saw a constable he stopped to tell him about the man inside the four-wheeler. The constable crossed over to the carriage, opened the door, and looked at the occupant, who was still reclining in one corner.

"You say he was with this other man in a pub?" the constable asked over his shoulder.

"That's right. In Deansgate."

"All right. You'd better drive him to the station. I'll come along with you."

The constable climbed into the cab and the driver went back to his seat. He was on the point of whipping up his horse when the constable suddenly put his head out of the window.

"Never mind going to the station," he called. "You'd better drive to the infirmary. He looks in a bad way to me."

Alarmed, the cabby made good time to this new destination. On their arrival, the old man was carried inside and someone went to fetch a doctor, who came hurrying when he heard that the police were already involved. The doctor undid the elderly man's collar and stooped close. When he straightened up, his face was grave.

"This man's dead," he informed the police constable.

The dead man was removed to where the doctor could examine the body. He found no signs of violence and no tell-tale signs that death had been induced by poisoning.

"As far as I can see," he told the hovering policeman, "he took a drink too many. After all, that's all it takes. Just the one."

The constable returned to where the cabby was waiting and gave him the news. When the unpaid cabby stopped swearing, he supplied the constable with a description of the young man who had disappeared.

"He wasn't very tall, but he was clean-shaven and wore a brown suit and a felt hat. He seemed to know his way about. And, oh, yes, he had a fresh complexion."

"How tall would you say?" asked the policeman, writing in his notebook.

"Only about 5 foot 3. Short, you might say."

"All right," said the constable snapping shut his book. "We'll go to the station this time. I don't doubt the sergeant will have some questions to put to you."

The report by the constable and the statement made by the driver seemed to settle the matter. It seemed a plain case of two men out drinking for the day. The elder of the pair had taken too much liquid stimulant on that cold day and his heart had given out.

The younger man, observing his companion's condition, had panicked, opening the door of the cab and flinging himself into the street with only one thought in mind. Not to get involved in any formal or official inquiry. It was simple as that. At least, it was until the result of the post-mortem was delivered. The findings of the surgeon who carried it out dramatically changed the official attitude towards the old man's death. He had not succumbed to alcoholic stimulants. He had been murdered. The analysis proved that he had been induced to drink a lethal amount of chloral hydrate.

It was not long after this discovery that Jerome Caminada was summoned to his chief's room. He was told of the finding of the old man's body and given a quick briefing on the case as it now appeared to the police.

"Murder," he was told, "explains something else. Why, when he arrived at the infirmary, the dead man was not wearing a watch and there was no money in his pockets. It was thought at first that he had used up his money in the last public house the pair called at – the one in Deansgate. But it now looks like murder with a motive – robbery."

The slim file of reports and statements was then passed to Caminada, who went straight to the address in Stretford Road that had been given to the cabman. He found himself at the home of a man who explained that he was a tailor. He was obviously surprised and mystified to receive a call from the police. When asked about the old man and his companion, the tailor shook his head and said that he had never seen either of them. It was a complete mystery to him.

"Then you've no idea why this address could have been given to the cab driver?" Caminada asked.

The man shook his head emphatically. "None at all."

The detective decided that the address must have been a blind one chosen at random to take the cab away from the centre of the city. And any other address in a similar district as far from Deansgate would have served the same purpose.

Caminada next began to investigate the dead man's past. This posed a problem. The old man, one John Fletcher, was a pillar of Free Trade respectability, and was a senior partner in a well established firm of Lancashire paper manufacturers, a member of the county council, and also a local Justice of the Peace. He was, to all appearances, most decidedly not a person to have consorted with a shady character such as his last companion appeared to be. Caminada had to don a pair of metaphorical kid gloves to conduct his inquiry. To begin with, he avoided contact with the dead man's family altogether.

Instead Caminada leaned over grubby bar counters and talked to known criminals. He backchatted with hard-faced women who never smiled with their eyes. He picked up scraps of information as a bird pecks at crumbs. Some were tall tales, some outright lies, a few held a flavour of truth. Among many things, he heard of a young man who had been spending money freely in pubs in one part of the city. He was a young man who sported a gold watch-chain with dangling seals. That watch sounded exactly like the one that the victim had been wearing.

Caminada sensed he was on the right track. He was convinced that the killer was a show-off, a man with a sense of being smarter than his fellows. Flaunting the watch-chain that he had stolen from the man he had killed was just the sort of behaviour Caminada had expected.

A hackney carriage driver recognised the description of the young man and remembered driving him to a public house which Caminada already knew too well. It was a meeting place for boxers and pugs, their manager, and the touts who hung on the fringes of that strange sporting world that moved around a four-cornered rope ring.

This, again, made sense. The chloral hydrate with which the victim had been drugged was best known to the underworld for its potency as "knock-out drops". But chloral hydrate was also known to the crooked fight fraternity. "Pig" Jack Parton for one had been known to make use of it when he wanted a fight to be fixed.

In his youth Parton had been a light-heavyweight boxer of some standing. When he was through with the business of battering an opponent in the ring, however, he became a small-time promoter, but one who wagered abnormally large bets on contests he arranged. Rumour had it that Pig Jack had found it profitable to drug the mouth-rinsing water provided for the opponents of his own fighters. Pig Jack Parton had also been known to use the drug for other scams as well. He had once held a publican's licence, but it had been taken from him after complaints that he had drugged customers' drinks. Those unfortunates had later been found sleeping in an alley, their pockets empty.

Pig Jack was now too old and feeble to be considered a suspect. He could not have been the "younger man" the cabby described. But Jack's son was a different matter.

Charlie Parton was a younger and slimmer edition of his father and it was quite likely that he had learned the old man's tricks and dubious wiles. But there was a problem. When Caminada saw him, Charlie was not sporting the watch-chain that had left a trail across Manchester, and he bore little resemblance to any known description of the wanted man. Charlie Parton was several inches taller than 5 foot 3 and he also had a moustache. But Caminada reasoned that, since the cabby had been seated, looking down on his fare, he might easily have seemed shorter than his real height. And the moustache? It was clearly a new addition to his features, barely a week old.

Caminada went to his chief. "I'm ready to make an

arrest," he announced. "But I'll need help."

He explained what he knew of the Partons and their circle and said that he expected violence. Caminada was thus given a couple of other detectives to help make the arrest. When he took them to the house where the Partons had lived for years, however, they were confronted by blank and curtainless windows. No one came to answer the door. The house was deserted.

It was a neighbour who called out to them. "You want Pig Jack?" he shouted.

"Is he about?" Caminada asked.

"He's gone. They've all gone, those Partons, and good riddance. But don't ask me where. I don't know."

It turned out that the Parton family had been gone for two days. But it did not take long for Caminada to find their new abode.

Caminada and his assistants then set a trap for Charlie Parton. They had no desire to give his father a chance to intervene with his fists. Thus, the first Pig Jack knew of his son's arrest was the word he received from the police station. The old man was furious. He smashed an entire room of furniture. But it was too late to do anything for Charlie. The boy was already being interrogated.

Charlie Parton, however, was a chip off the old block. He certainly didn't lose his nerve when he found himself in the hands of the police. Even the serious nature of the charge against him brought no reaction. Charlie still kept his cool and he had a story all very pat. He was in Liverpool on February 27th, the day the elderly man in the hackney carriage died.

"I was at a coursing meeting," he declared, vigorously denying he was anywhere near Manchester.

Then the driver of the cab was brought in. Immediately he declared: "That's the young villain who bilked me of my fare." He was utterly certain of the fact.

Charlie Parton licked his dry lips, and decided for once that he should keep his mouth shut.

But he had to open it later when it became necessary to

prove his claim of being in Liverpool on the day of the murder. Only then, realising he had been over-confident, did he make mention of being in a certain Liverpool street at a particular time, apparently believing that this would be good enough as an alibi and put him in the clear. In fact, however, it did the exact opposite.

The police throughout Liverpool had been trying to find a man of about 20 who had entered a chemist's shop and stolen a bottle of chloral hydrate. This theft had occurred a few days before the J.P. died in the hackney carriage. But the illuminating feature about the incident was that the chemist's shop was in the street named by Charlie Parton as the one he was in on February 27th, the day of the killing. Parton's thin alibi was suddenly threatening to provide a thick rope for his neck.

Caminada still needed more evidence, however, and this duly arrived. But it came from the most unlikely source. It came from Charlie's father. With his son in police hands, Pig Jack had changed drastically. After that first berserk outburst, the elder Parton had become subdued, as though realising that he was responsible for what Charlie had become: another Manchester thug.

That abrupt change set the scene for others. Men who had never been his friends were now prepared to talk. They seemed almost happy to pass on information. Caminada learned of pubs where customers drinking with the young Charlie had been taken ill – usually when Charlie was low in funds.

The case came before the Manchester magistrates, who decided that the prisoner had a capital charge to answer. Caminada had presented a tidy case. Charlie had made up to the J.P. in a bar and slipped some of the stolen chloral hydrate in his drink. The drug had left the old man more or less stupefied. Another similarly treated drink had proved fatal. In the cab, driving towards an address Charlie had given on the spur of the moment, he had watched the victim collapse. Yet somehow the old man had not merely become unconscious, like others before him.

A suddenly terrified Charlie had not known that the action of an ageing heart had been impaired, that a safe knock-out dose for a man in his 30s could prove fatal for a man of twice those years.

The trial opened during the Liverpool Assizes and was held at St George's Hall. The publicity had enormous crowds fighting to gain entry on the first day, and relays of police were sent to keep the overflow in the streets around the court from becoming disorderly.

The defence had only one recourse – mistaken identity. For Charlie Parton was clearly not the man described in the earlier statement by the bilked cabman.

However, the case was not decided by that cabby's statement, but by Jerome Caminada's clearly stated evidence. When he told of the stolen chloral hydrate, the case was turned around. And when the Liverpool chemist identified Charlie, it was virtually over.

The jury retired to consider their verdict two days after the trial commenced. When they returned to their seats not one of them looked at the prisoner – a certain sign that they had come back to deliver an adverse verdict. Sure enough, the foreman rose to intone: "We find the prisoner guilty."

Charlie Parton suddenly looked up. He was stunned, as though the full realisation of what it all meant had only just penetrated his fuddled mind. It is possible that he did not even hear himself sentenced to death by the judge.

However, his youth together with his eventual admission that he had indeed used the chloral on the elderly J.P., though only with the intention of drugging him, saved the lad from the gallows. On appeal the Home Secretary decided that penal servitude for life might be enough to ask of a young man still on the threshold of his manhood.

25

THE MANCHESTER CAB MYSTERY
PART II – The villain speaks

All the other stories in this collection are based on the facts of the case. This one, however, is different. Here it is the criminal who acts as narrator. Charles Parton, the man convicted of the murder of John Fletcher, gives his own account of the crime.

The Manchester Cab Mystery was a notorious and mysterious affair, but the truth about it has never been properly made public. Now, for the first time, I intend to disclose the real facts of the tragedy. No one is more qualified to do so than myself. I was in the cab with the "murdered" man, and I was afterwards sentenced to death as his murderer.

The curtain rises upon the drama in a street in Manchester late at night. A cab was rattling along the otherwise silent and almost deserted thoroughfare when a stray passer-by noticed in the flickering light from a gas-light, that the door of the vehicle was open and was swinging backwards and forwards.

"Hey!" he called to the driver, "your cab door's open."

Pulling up, the driver dismounted and made to close the door. He was just about to do so when he noticed his fare was lying in the seat with a deathly pallor upon him. He called to him, then shook him, but there was no response. The man was dead. The driver immediately got in touch with the police.

Jerome Caminada, the celebrated Manchester detective, took up the threads of the case, which was to bring him greater fame and glory than ever – at the expense of an innocent man.

The first suspicion of foul play arose when the cab-man

related that there had been another passenger in the cab, a youth of eighteen, but there had been no sign of him when the driver stopped. The police then made the discovery that the dead man, who was soon identified as a rich paper manufacturer named John Fletcher, Justice of the Peace and Town Councillor, had been robbed of money and a watch and chain valued at a hundred guineas. Further, a post-mortem showed that some sort of drug had been administered to him.

At this time cases of drugging for the purposes of robbery were frequent in Manchester and they were causing considerable alarm in the public's mind. Murder as well would have increased their concern still further. Jerome Caminada thus made up his mind that he would find the killer at all costs. The detective arrested hundreds of suspected criminals, and when, nine days after the discovery of the mystery, I was arrested and taken to the Town Hall, where the suspects were quartered, I found the place packed to the doors. I myself recognised at least fifty crooks with whom I had associated. Had it not been so tragic, it would have been laughable when, upon my arrival, there was a chorus of, "What, got you too, have they?" from scores of notorious characters.

But, give credit where credit is due. This time they had got hold of the right man.

I admit I robbed John Fletcher, not of five pounds and a watch, as the police suggested at the time, but of £500 in addition to the timepiece. But I did not murder him. I know that most criminals protest their innocence, just as I am doing, even after they have been convicted by damning evidence. But in my case, my innocence was proved. Medical testimony was eventually forthcoming to show that the man I robbed had died, not of poison but of heart failure. It took eleven years to establish that fact to the satisfaction of the authorities, and for most of those years I was languishing in solitary confinement to pay for the crime.

Eleven years of torture! No one knows the agony, the

unutterable anguish I endured, first in the shadow of the gallows, then wearing out the years behind those cold grey walls. They say condemned men get anything they want to eat while waiting to be hanged. It is not true. I was half-starved as I lay under sentence. Even after the reprieve, it was three years before I was granted the privilege and luxury of a cup of tea. And I shall have a tale to tell of other sufferings.

But before dealing, among other things, with my emotions as I waited for the day when I should be led from my cell and hanged, let me detail the inner history of the cab mystery. As I have indicated, I was only eighteen years of age at the time.

Like my father, I was something of a boxer, and my enthusiasm for sport led me to horse-racing, which was the beginning of my downfall. I became associated in Manchester with a racing gang in which were a number of known thieves, some of whom had already done penal servitude.

One day, I was walking along Deansgate when I met some of those "boys." With them was Mr John Fletcher, and the members of the clique signalled me to join them, one of them whispering that the old man had a lot of money on him. We went to a public house, where glasses of beer were ordered. While Fletcher's attention was diverted, one of the gang placed some chloral hydrate in his drink. This drug is a sedative, and was used then as extensively as aspirin is now to relieve nerve pains. The amount put in the glass was afterwards found to be thirty grains.

The drink was passed over to Fletcher and he took a sip of it. That was all he had, for the glass was later upset. But it was enough.

He began to get restless, and I suggested he should leave with me. He agreed, and I gave my confederates the wink that I would finish the business. Outside we hailed a cab, and I told the driver to go to the first address in Oxford Road that came to my mind. Fletcher himself did not know where he wanted to go, as by now the drink and the drug had thoroughly muddled his wits. We got in, and the cab had not proceeded far before I was searching through my companion's pockets. He tried to push me off, but his resistance was too feeble to do any good. I secured the notes, removed his watch and got out of the cab while it was still in motion. The next moment the darkness had swallowed me up.

When I jumped from the cab Fletcher was alive and unhurt. I used no violence whatever and had no doubt that the man would be fine and well by the following day. Little could I have known that, a few moments later, he would be dead.

Having placed me under lock and key, Caminada sought to get me to incriminate myself. To do this he induced a friend of my father's to carry out a bit of treachery. This man, who was also acquainted with the dead man's family, came to me and talked through the cell grating, imploring me to say where the watch was, as it was a family heirloom. Foolishly I told him what he wanted to hear.

Those words were my death warrant. Caminada had been standing behind my "friend" and had heard the fateful admission of my guilt. I was charged and, soon enough, I appeared at trial.

The evidence against me was purely circumstantial. I had not, of course, revealed the names of the accomplices with whom I had shared the proceeds of the robbery, so they were safe. But every word I told the court was the truth. The judge, addressing the jury before they retired to consider whether they should grant me life or death, said: "I am convinced in my own mind, and I think you will agree with me, that the prisoner at the bar had no intention of taking the deceased's life. His intentions were to stupefy for the purpose of robbery. But if you bring this mere boy in guilty of this charge, I have no alternative but to sentence him to death – the most painful duty I will have ever experienced in my whole career."

The judge then went on to stress what he described as

a scandal in the law of England. If I had been tried in Scotland or America, he said, I should have been tried for manslaughter on the evidence. But English law lays it down that where a man kills another, unintentionally or otherwise, and the crime is accompanied by robbery, he must be charged with murder. That law, glaring in its injustice is still on the Statute Book.

There was an awesome hush in the court when the jury retired. During the trial I had maintained my composure, even smiling sometimes, although the ordeal was such a terrible one. No one can imagine what ghastly horror fills the mind of the man who stands in the dock with his life at stake. Grave of face, the jurymen returned. The foreman rose to his feet. My heart seemed to stop beating.

"We find the prisoner guilty," he said, in a low voice, "but strongly recommend him to mercy."

The judge passed sentence of death upon me, and said he would see that the recommendation reached the proper quarters, and that it would be endorsed and supported by himself. I swayed and my brain reeled. For a minute or so it seemed that I must be dreaming. Two warders took me by the arms and I was led down the steps and out into a waiting cab. The trial had taken place at the Liverpool Assizes, and I was conveyed to Kirkdale Prison and placed in the condemned cell.

Night and day there was a warder with me, three of them taking it in turns to watch me until I should be handed over to the executioner. They seemed to me to be inhuman ghouls as they watched my every move. Now, when I look back and think of the conditions and circumstances in which they were going to send me to my doom, my blood boils.

For breakfast I had 8 oz of bread and a pint of porridge, and the same in the evening, and usually bully beef, bad potatoes, and bread at midday. We had pudding and soup three times a week. That wouldn't have been so bad if there had been enough, but being a healthy lad I had a big appetite, and was almost starving with the meagre fare.

Most of all I longed for a cup of tea. One day an official from the Home Office called to ask if I had any last request. "Yes," I replied, "give me a cup of tea!" After a lot of trouble and fuss my request was granted.

I broke down only once in the condemned cell. My mother and father, brothers and sister, came to say good-bye. The parting took place in a room divided into two by iron bars. I was on one side of the room, my loved ones on the other. In the middle and between us was a passage-way with iron bars on both sides, and up and down this a warder walked to make sure we did not try to shake hands. Two other warders were there to make sure no signs were passed.

I was not even allowed a farewell kiss from my mother. All I could do was to stand in my blue prison clothes and read the pain and misery in the eyes of my dear ones. When the interview, which lasted only a few minutes, was over and I was led away, my tiny sister called out, "This way, Charlie," and pointed to the door they had come in by. She thought I was at liberty to go with them, not knowing my life was forfeit.

The warders who watched over me night and day in the condemned cell tried to cheer me up as best they could, but what alleviation could there be from the thought ever in my mind that each day brought me nearer to the scaffold?

Time seemed to move incredibly swiftly. The day fixed for my death was about three weeks from the date of sentence. They still kept me on the fourth-class diet allowed under prison regulations. This was to me, a strong healthy youth of eighteen, practically starvation rations. I was hungry all the time.

The fourth day from the date fixed for my execution I was sitting talking to the warder on guard when the Chief Warder appeared. In his hand he held a sheet of official looking paper.

"Well, Parton," he said, "they've let you off."

My first emotion was of such intense relief that I almost broke down, but on top of that came the thought – I had been spared from the gallows, but the rest of my life would be spent within these grim walls. With the awful possibilities that this conjured up, my feelings changed.

I told myself I would prefer the momentary pang of the hangman's noose to the life-long misery of penal servitude. I had heard more than sufficient from my old associates to decide that death was preferable.

They took me from the condemned cell and exchanged the blue suit for the drab garb of the ordinary convict. For three weeks I was detained in Kirkdale Prison at Liverpool then I was removed to Stafford Jail. Here began another phase of the living martyrdom to which I was subjected. For nine months I was the victim of the "Silent System". This was the name given to solitary confinement regulations for penal servitude men. I was placed in a cell from which I was allowed out only one hour in twenty-four. During the other twenty-three hours I was alone, deprived even of the solace of books with which to keep my mind from becoming unhinged. The only break was when the warders came with my food. During the day I was kept at work making slippers.

For the first six months I was not allowed to have letters. Nor was I permitted to receive visitors. In due course I was removed to Portland. With 22 other convicts all chained together, I was placed in the luggage-van of the train and taken to Portland, where I was set to work in the quarries.

At the beginning conditions here were somewhat easy. But the time came when this comparative leniency gave way to a veritable reign of terror. Convicts who were insufficiently fed were given almost superhuman tasks to accomplish, such as filling so many trucks a day. Men were driven to such desperate straits that some put their arms under the truck wheels so that they were amputated and the victims could do no more manual labour. The system, however, was equal to them. For such men was introduced the mule-gang; halters were placed round their necks and they had to draw loaded trucks as if they were animals.

Within three months even those prisoners who had been notable for good conduct over periods of years were undergoing some punishment or other.

The prison governor died shortly after I arrived. On his death-bed he requested both the chaplains – Catholic and Protestant – to tell the prisoners that he had tried to do his duty, and if he had harmed any of us he had done so unintentionally, and he asked for our pardon and prayers. The following Sunday those old lags, whose hearts one would have imagined to have become long since hardened and unresponsive to sentiment, prayed for the dead governor with unashamed earnestness.

Another source of torture at Portland was the chain-gang. Convicts reported for bad conduct were submitted to this harshness. Round each ankle an iron clamp was riveted by the prison blacksmith, and to these clamps chains were attached which extended up the legs to the waist, where they were fixed to a body-belt. Night and day for six months, working, eating, or sleeping, the prisoner had to wear these chains, which all the while rasped the skin.

I was never sentenced to the chain-gang, but my plight was bad enough. The cell in which I was placed, and where I remained for nine years, provided sufficient torture in itself. It was seven feet high, six feet long and three feet wide. A man over six feet in height was thus unable to lie down in it. There was no window. The only illumination, which feebly flickered through the cell-door grating, came from a door at the end of the corridor. Certainly cells on the outside had windows, but one had to wait one's turn for them. In nine years my turn never came.

During the winter I would be out at work in the quarries until darkness came on. We would then be returned to our cells, where everything was pitch-dark. There was not even a candle.

Some of the convicts went mad in the Portland nightmare. Others became quite irresponsible in their light-headedness. They would stare to their feet in chapel and begin mumbling to themselves. In chapel one was not even allowed to turn one's head, let alone speak.

I was in Portland at the same time as John Lee, "the man they could not hang." I considered him to be a much inferior individual to most of my other companions. Lee had been sentenced for the murder of an old lady who had befriended him and his sister. He was placed three times on the scaffold and each time the drop refused to act. When Lee got off the scaffold the second time, a bag of potatoes was placed in position and the trap gave way as it should have done with Lee. But when Lee returned, the trap stayed shut yet again. Following the third and final attempt to hang the condemned man, a warder stepped on to the drop holding a rope attached to the gallows. The drop immediately gave way beneath him. Most people, particularly superstitious folks, regarded Lee's escape as a sign from Providence of his innocence of the murder. This belief was strengthened when it was declared that on her death-bed Lee's sister had stated she and not her brother had killed their benefactress.

This information was conveyed to the Home Secretary, who then got in touch with the prison chaplain. In the course of the official investigation that followed, the chaplain was informed of the statement. "Oh," he replied, "this man has already confessed to me." The sister apparently had made up the confession to get her brother released. Lee remained in prison for 23 years.

Another of my prison acquaintances was that notorious swindler and robber of the poor, Jabez Balfour. I also associated with a Peer of the Realm who had been sentenced to five years' penal servitude for forging his aunt's name. He went back again later in connection with the theft of some jewellery.

After the terrors of Portland I was glad to be removed to Dartmoor. Before leaving the very sore question of my treatment at Portland, I should like to mention that, although I was a Catholic, never once during the whole of the nine years did a priest visit me.

Captain Johnson was governor at Dartmoor, and Captain

Sir Basil Thompson was his deputy. Sir Basil was well liked by all the men. He was very humane. If there had been only a few more prison governors like him there would never have been the same number of criminals turned out from the prisons, which for the most part were nothing but training grounds for malefactors.

I remained in Dartmoor for two years, which made 11 years' imprisonment in all. During all this time my mother had been working hard organising a petition. She employed people to go round the country – she spent all her small fortune in this way – to get people's signatures. By this same time too, the medical aspects of the case had been thoroughly thrashed out in the columns of the medical journals. The Public Analyst of Leicester stated that the amount of drug placed in the dead man's drink – 30 grains – was insufficient to kill a baby. The dead man, too, had taken only a small sip. The analyst added his complete belief that the deceased's heart was in such a condition that he would have died that night in any case, even if I had never met him and taken him upon that fateful ride in the cab.

My mother's petition, combined with this revelation, resulted in my release. I had served eleven years for a murder I had not committed. In spite of that, however, I was not pardoned. I was released on ticket of leave, the only life sentence man ever discharged under 12 years. The ticket of leave meant that at any time I could be taken away again for the term of my natural life. If I even led an "idle life" this was what would happen to me.

Next I shall expose the evils of this iniquitous system which deprived me even of the right to choose my own religion. Since my release I have been "sent back" to terms totalling nearly ten years, and all for trivial offences.

On the ticket-of-leave card given to me when I passed through the gates of Dartmoor Prison there are some astonishing conditions under which I enjoy my so-called freedom. It is laid down that I must not "lead an idle and dissolute life, without visible means of obtaining an honest livelihood". Once every month I must report to the police, and if I stir beyond the district in which I reside I must give the authorities a reason for my movements. I am prohibited from being found in or upon any dwelling-house, or any building, yard, or premises being parcel of or attached to such dwelling house, or in or upon any shop, warehouse, counting-house, or other place of business, or in any garden or orchard, pleasure ground, and so on, without being able to account to the satisfaction of the court for my being there.

These are only a few of the regulations under which I am allowed to exist. If I do not observe them I am liable to undergo penal servitude for life. Imagine it! If I am found sitting in a public park and I am unable to prove that quiet enjoyment is my sole reason for being there, I can be sent to prison again, to remain there until death gives me release. The ticket-of-leave man is thus no better than a hounded dog. I have said that my soul is not my own, and I mean it.

I was only eighteen years of age when I was sentenced. Eleven years afterwards I was free again. Surrounded on all sides by the fetters under which I received my licence, I decided it would be better for me if I left the country and tried to start again. Without notifying the authorities I went to Canada. That to begin with, was an offence which could have made my liberty forfeit. But what other chance did I have? What other way could I have lived a life?

After wanderings in Canada, South Africa and New Zealand, I eventually settled down in the Argentine, where I set up in business. I tried to live down the past. My business – a café – prospered, and everything was going splendidly. But then the war broke out.

I returned to enlist – and once more brought myself within the reach of the law. Under the name of Charles Mack I joined the 10th Devons, and for training we went to Bath where I met the woman who is now my wife and the mother of my children. She herself had had a tragic life. I told her my story and we agreed to get married. We have never regretted it, although we have since often been separated by prison walls.

To cut a long story short, the time came when I once more found myself pursued by the police. A Manchester man in my regiment recognised me and, fearing arrest for failing to notify my movements, I fled. I had no intention of deserting for I still wanted to serve my country. But how could I have served it from behind prison bars? I resolved to join another regiment and this is exactly what I did.

Three days later I joined the 4th East Surreys. I gave a different name, as a result of which my wife could draw the allowance. It had already been stopped by my first regiment.

My family was soon in want, and in desperation I stole a bag at Euston Station. I was arrested. I do not complain about that, nor about my sentence of six months. What I do protest against is that, as I offended as a ticket-of-leave man, I was sent back, after completing the six months, to an "indefinite period" in Portland. Can you imagine the mental agony of that? I did not know whether I was in for a year or until I died! Outside, my wife and children were left to starve.

After three years I was slowly dying. The prison doctor could find nothing wrong with me and another medical man was called in. "Have you anything on your mind?" this doctor asked, when he also discovered no physical ailment. Anything on my mind!

They heard my story and passed it on to the authorities. As a result they took compassion on me. They allowed me out. Finally, nearly four years after I stole that bag, I was free once again.

In Scotland they are more humane. There, a life-sentence man is released after twenty years. He is out on ticket, but after seven years the licence expires and the man is really free. Why can we not do the same in England and not hound a man on licence until he dies? "You must not lead an idle life," my ticket says. How could I lead an honest one? If I approached an employer I had to produce my licence and tell him I was a ticket-of-leave man. Otherwise the police could arrest me again. With thousands of honest men available to get work, what hope is there for a man who has been convicted of murder?

A local magistrate, before whom I was brought for hawking balloons, asked me, "Why don't you get some regular employment?"

"Are you prepared to give me regular employment?" I asked him. "Would you be willing to have me behind your counter, handling your money, knowing the stigma attached to my name?"

I am lucky now in having solved the problem of employment. I earn an honest living by going round the country selling printed copies of the very licence which brought all this misery upon me.

This system reminds me of medieval torture. Hugo wrote of the martyrdom of Jean Valjean in the penitentiaries of France. There are Jean Valjeans alive in this country today in the persons of ticket-of-leave men who after years of living death, are set "free" from prison. With every hand against them, is it surprising that in time many of them come to be haters of the world and enemies of society?

It seems there is no one in this civilised land who has either the power, or the sympathy to put a stop to this distorted conception of justice.